T0294097

THE SHUDRAS

RETHINKING INDIA
Series editors: Aakash Singh Rathore, Mridula Mukherjee, Pushparaj Deshpande
and Syeda Hameed

OTHER BOOKS IN THE SERIES
Vision for a Nation: Paths and Perspectives
(Aakash Singh Rathore and Ashis Nandy, eds)

The Minority Conundrum: Living in Majoritarian Times
(Tanweer Fazal, ed.)

Reviving Jobs: An Agenda for Growth
(Santosh Mehrotra, ed.)

We the People: Establishing Rights and Deepening Democracy
(Nikhil Dey, Aruna Roy and Rakshita Swamy, eds)

RETHINKING INDIA 5

THE SHUDRAS
VISION FOR A
NEW PATH

EDITED BY

KANCHA ILAIAH SHEPHERD
KARTHIK RAJA KARUPPUSAMY

VINTAGE

An imprint of Penguin Random House

VINTAGE

USA | Canada | UK | Ireland | Australia
New Zealand | India | South Africa | China

Vintage is part of the Penguin Random House group of companies
whose addresses can be found at global.penguinrandomhouse.com

Published by Penguin Random House India Pvt. Ltd
7th Floor, Infinity Tower C, DLF Cyber City,
Gurgaon 122 002, Haryana, India

Penguin
Random House
India

First published in Vintage by Penguin Random House India 2021

Copyright © Samruddha Bharat Foundation 2021
The copyright for the individual pieces vests with the respective contributors

All rights reserved

10 9 8 7 6 5 4 3 2 1

This anthology of essays is a work of non-fiction. The views and opinions
expressed in the essays are those of the respective authors only and do not reflect
or represent the views and opinions held by any other person.
The essays in the book are based on a variety of sources, including published
materials and interviews and interactions conducted by the respective authors with
the persons mentioned in the essays. They reflect each author's own understanding
and conception of such materials and/or can be verified by research and the facts
are as reported by them which have been verified to the extent possible, and the
publishers are not in any way liable for the same.
The objective of this book or any of its essays is not to hurt any sentiments or be
biased in favor of or against any particular person, region, caste, society, gender,
creed, nation or religion.

ISBN 9780670092987

Typeset in Bembo Std by Manipal Technologies Limited, Manipal
Printed at Replika Press Pvt. Ltd, India

This book is sold subject to the condition that it shall not, by way of trade
or otherwise, be lent, resold, hired out, or otherwise circulated without the
publisher's prior consent in any form of binding or cover other than that in
which it is published and without a similar condition including this condition
being imposed on the subsequent purchaser.

www.penguin.co.in

MIX
Paper from
responsible sources
FSC® C016779

To

The great Phules, Mahatma Jyotirao and Savitribai, who initiated the
Shudra revolutionary movement of 'Read, Write and Fight' for the first time
in Indian history

Contents

Series Editors' Note   ix

Introduction   xv

The Nation and Its Shudras
  Arvind Kumar   1

The Socio-spiritual Slavery of Shudras:
A National Agenda for Their Liberation
  Sunil Sardar   17

Shudras and Democratic India
  Kancha Ilaiah Shepherd   36

The Importance of Shudra Politics in India
  Sharad Yadav and Omprakash Mahato   64

The Question of Bahujan Women
  Prachi Patil   86

A New Beginning for Shudras Still a Possibility
  Urmilesh   97

Production and Protection as Spirituality among Shudras
  Ram Shepherd Bheenaveni   115

Sociocultural Identity Formation among Shudras
   Bindu N. Doddahatti   136

Shudra Consciousness and the Future of the Nation
   Pallikonda Manikanta   150

The India of My Dreams
   Dr P. Vinay Kumar   167

Caste and Political Economy
   A Shudra Team   176

Notes   197
About the Contributors   225
About Samruddha Bharat Foundation   231

Series Editors' Note

Psychologists tell us that the only *true* enemies we have are the faces looking back at us in the mirror. Today, we in India need to take a long, hard look at ourselves in the mirror. With either actual or looming crises in every branch of government, at every level, be it central, state or local; with nearly every institution failing; with unemployment at historically high rates; with an ecosystem ready to implode; with a healthcare system in a shambles; with an education system on the brink of collapse; with gender, caste and class inequities unabating; with civil society increasingly characterized by exclusion, intolerance and violence; with our own minorities living in fear; our hundreds of millions of fellow citizens in penury; and with few prospects for the innumerable youth of this nation in the face of all these increasingly intractable problems, the reflection is not sightly. Our true enemies are not external to us, not Pakistani terrorists or Bangladeshi migrants, but our own selves: our own lack of imagination, communication, cooperation and dedication towards achieving the India of our destiny and dreams.

Our Constitution, as the preamble so eloquently attests, was founded upon the fundamental values of the dignity of the individual and the unity of the nation, envisioned in relation to a radically egalitarian justice. These bedrock ideas, though perhaps especially pioneered by the likes of Jawaharlal Nehru, B.R. Ambedkar, M.K. Gandhi, Maulana Azad, Sardar Patel, Sarojini Naidu, Jagjivan Ram, R. Amrit Kaur, Ram Manohar Lohia and others, had emerged as a broad consensus among the many founders of this nation, cutting across divergent social and political ideologies. Giving shape to that vision, the architects of modern India strived to ensure that each one of us is accorded equal opportunities to live with dignity and security, has equitable access to a better life, and is an equal partner in this nation's growth.

Yet, today we find these most basic constitutional principles under attack. Nearly all the public institutions that were originally created in order to fight against dominance and subservience are in the process of subversion, creating new hierarchies instead of dismantling them, generating inequities instead of ameliorating them. Government policy merely pays lip service to egalitarian considerations, while the actual administration of 'justice' and implementation of laws are in fact perpetuating precisely the opposite: illegality, criminality, corruption, bias, nepotism and injustice of every conceivable stripe. And the rapid rise of social intolerance and manifold exclusions (along the lines of gender, caste, religion, etc.) effectively whittle down and even sabotage an inclusive conception of citizenship, polity and nation.

In spite of these and all the other unmentioned but equally serious challenges posed at this moment, there are in fact new sites for sociopolitical assertion re-emerging. There are new calls arising for the reinstatement of the letter and spirit of our Constitution, not just *normatively* (where we battle things out ideologically) but also *practically* (the battle at the level of policy articulation and implementation). These calls are not simply partisan, nor are they exclusionary or zero-sum. They witness the wide participation of youth, women, the historically disadvantaged in the process of finding a new voice, minorities, members of majority communities, and progressive individuals all joining hands in solidarity.

We at the Samruddha Bharat Foundation proudly count ourselves among them. The Foundation's very raison d'être has been to take serious cognizance of India's present and future challenges, and to rise to them. Over the past two years, we have constituted numerous working groups to critically rethink social, economic and political paradigms to encourage a transformative spirit in India's polity. Over 400 of India's foremost academics, activists, professionals and policymakers across party lines have constructively engaged in this process. We have organized and assembled inputs from *jan sunwai*s (public hearings) and *jan manch*s (public platforms) that we conducted across several states, and discussed and debated these ideas with leaders of fourteen progressive political parties, in an effort to set benchmarks for a future common minimum programme. The overarching idea has been to try to breathe new life and spirit into the cold and self-serving logic of political and administrative processes, linking them to and informing them by grass-roots realities, fact-based research and social experience, and actionable social-scientific knowledge. And to do all of this with harmony and heart, with sincere emotion and national feeling.

In order to further disseminate these ideas, both to kick-start a national dialogue and to further build a consensus on them, we are bringing out this set of fourteen volumes highlighting innovative ideas that seek to deepen and further the promise of India. This is not an academic exercise; we do not merely spotlight structural problems, but also propose disruptive solutions to each of the pressing challenges that we collectively face. All the essays, though authored by top academics, technocrats, activists, intellectuals and so on, have been written purposively to be accessible to a general audience, whose creative imagination we aim to spark and whose critical feedback we intend to harness, leveraging it to further our common goals.

The inaugural volume has been specifically dedicated to our norms, to serve as a fresh reminder of our shared and shareable overlapping values and principles, collective heritage and resources. Titled *Vision for a Nation: Paths and Perspectives*, it champions a plural, inclusive, just, equitable and prosperous India, and is committed to individual dignity, which is the foundation of the unity and vibrancy of the nation.

The thirteen volumes that follow turn from the normative to the concrete. From addressing the problems faced by diverse communities—Adivasis, Dalit Bahujans, Other Backward Classes (OBCs)—as well as women and minorities, to articulating the challenges that we face with respect to jobs and unemployment, urbanization, healthcare and a rigged economy, to scrutinizing our higher education system or institutions more broadly, each volume details some ten specific policy solutions promising to systemically treat the issue(s), transforming the problem at a lasting *structural* level, not just a superficial one. These innovative and disruptive policy solutions flow from the authors' research, knowledge and experience, but they are especially characterized by their unflinching commitment to our collective normative understanding of who we can and ought to be.

The volumes that look at the concerns, needs and aspirations of Shudras, Dalits, Adivasis and women particularly look at how casteism has played havoc with India's development and stalled the possibility of the progressive transformation of Indian society. They first analyse how these sections of society have faced historical and structural discrimination against full participation in Indian spiritual, educational, social and political institutions for centuries. They also explore how the reforms that some of our epoch-making sociopolitical thinkers like Gautama Buddha, M.K. Gandhi, Jawaharlal Nehru and B.R. Ambedkar foregrounded are being systematically reversed by regressive forces and the ruling elite because of their ideological proclivities. These volumes therefore strive to address some of the most glaring social questions that India faces from a modernist perspective and propose a progressive blueprint that will secure spiritual, civil and political liberties for one and all.

What the individual volumes aim to offer, then, are navigable road maps for how we may begin to overcome the many specific challenges that we face, guiding us towards new ways of working cooperatively to rise above our differences, heal the wounds in our communities, recalibrate our modes of governance, and revitalize our institutions. Cumulatively, however, they achieve something of even greater synergy, greater import: they reconstruct that India of our imagination, of our aspirations, the India reflected in the constitutional preamble that we all surely want to be a part of.

Let us put aside that depiction of a mirror with an enemy staring back at us. Instead, together, we help to construct a whole new set of images. One where you may look at your nation and see your individual identity and dignity reflected in it, and when you look within your individual self, you may find the pride of your nation residing there.

Aakash Singh Rathore, Mridula Mukherjee, Pushparaj Deshpande
and Syeda Hameed

Introduction

Kancha Ilaiah Shepherd and Karthik Raja Karuppusamy

Shudras and the Brahminical Order

A careful, or even a casual, study of ancient Brahminical literature reveals how debilitating disabilities and servitudes were imposed on the Shudra community from the earliest of times. *Manusmriti,* a very influential legal text dated between second century BC and second century AD, stands as a fine specimen of the Brahminical tradition that systematically degrades manual labour and the productive process, while sanctifying the so-called spiritual–intellectual discourse of the Dwijas (those considered twice-born, with the right to wear the *janeu* or sacred thread), especially Brahmins.

Shudras—the catch-all Brahminical categorization for the working masses, including the erstwhile Untouchables—were 'destined' to do all the productive labour, because of which the ancient civilization survived. But the fruits of these productivities were appropriated by the Dwija castes. While there is some speculation that Vaishyas might have been involved in the supervision of agriculture, Brahmins and Kshatriyas have no recorded history of investing themselves in productive labour.[1] The Kautilyan state apparatus, as worked out in *Arthashastra*, provided the earliest systematic exposition for this exploitative system. *Arthashastra* laid the theoretical foundation for Dwijas to be out of productive labour and further insisted that the state must drive the economy to provide Dwijas a good life at the expense of Shudras.

Manu was categorical in denying Shudras and women the right to learn Sanskrit; listen to, read or recite the Vedas; bear arms; or trade. These were exclusively reserved for men from the Brahmin, Kshatriya and Vaishya varnas. Manu craftily ordained that to serve and obey the twice-born Dwija varnas by performing all laborious tasks was the sole spiritual agenda for Shudras. This injustice was glorified, then and now, as the ideal of *varnadharma*.

It appears that the whole spiritual and intellectual discourse of Brahminism and its attendant teleology revolves around the singular aim of successfully appropriating the productive labour of the Shudra masses by deploying varnadharma ideology reinforced by religious–text-based mythology. The numerous smritis, sutras, shastras and epics such as the Mahabharata, Ramayana, etc., can all be incriminated as creative myths that explicitly or implicitly, yet unwaveringly, uphold the crucial tenets of varnadharma ideology. This system reserves privilege and power for Dwijas, while parcelling out penalties and pain for Shudras, who are denied the right to wear a janeu on their body.

It is naive to ask why a denial of access to the Vedas matters in the twenty-first century. It matters not because it holds the eternal truth, as Brahmins have been deceptively claiming. Rather, it matters because it was the most elaborately constructed 'regime of truth' through which Shudras were violently discriminated against and excluded. Shockingly, the fact of Brahminical hegemony and its regimes of truth continue to haunt 'modern' life in every aspect, albeit through mutations and reproductions.

It matters even more because it runs parallel to the oppressive and exclusionary processes taking place in modern India. While still holding on to the glory of Sanskrit and the Vedas, Dwijas have also been building 'regimes of truth' in English-language discourse.[2] Even upper Shudras who are labelled as 'dominant castes'—Jats, Gujjars, Patels, Yadavs, Marathas, Nairs, Reddys, Kammas, Gounders, Lingayats and so on—are yet to come to terms with this double-edged sword in contemporary times.

Two Centuries of Shudra Politics

Savitribai and Jyotiba Phule, the Shudra social reformer couple of the nineteenth century, initiated the Bahujan revolution in the domains of education, inter-caste marriage, employment in government jobs, and also in the spiritual–religious structures of the colonial Bombay province. Jyotiba deployed his philosophically charged polemic against closely interwoven Brahminism based on the religious, sociopolitical and intellectual discourse that acted as the opium of the Shudra masses.

While cooperating with genuine reformers such as Justice Ranade, Phule had no hesitation in attacking and exposing the patent hypocrisy of those who called themselves nationalists. Later studies have indisputably established the duplicity of their nationalist claims and shown how they were simultaneously attached to the traditional caste-cultural order on the one hand, while monopolizing power in the newly emerging modern political order on the other.[3]

While the post-Peshwa era initiated by the British rulers brought relief and an opening for the mobility of Untouchables and Shudras in western India, even more so, it provided opportunities for the further entrenchment and re-valorization of region-bound Brahminical traditions into a pan-Indian phenomenon. Phule, educated in a Christian missionary English-medium school, was the first organic intellectual who could successfully critique the Shetji–Bhatji (Banias–Brahmins) for their economic and spiritual hegemony over the Shudra–Ati-Shudra (Shudra/ OBC/Dalit) productive masses. Phule located the primary basis of exploitation and the hold of Brahminic mythological tradition over the Shudra–Ati-Shudra community and predicted that the future would be as manipulative if revolutionary reforms were not achieved. This goal remains elusive.

If one carefully studies the modus operandi of Phule, both his writing and deeds, he demonstrated his nuanced understanding of the inextricable link between knowledge and power.[4] Phule understood that Brahminical power is underwritten by a network of mythical knowledge systems which were instrumental in giving rise to 'new regimes of truth'. Savitribai proved to be a pioneer in educating women of all castes, an act in itself anathema to Brahminical wisdom. Although the Phules initiated actual Satyashodhak social reform, even now they are made invisible in scholarly discussions of postcolonial modernity. For this, we cannot blame only the Hindutva school; all bhadralok intellectuals must be held responsible.

In the southern Madras Presidency, Iyothee Thass (1845– 1914), a Parayar Dalit intellectual of the nineteenth century, laid the ground for the politics and identity of casteless Tamizhan. Further, he pioneered and deployed the Dravidian ideology against the hegemonic discourse of Brahminical nationalism of his day.[5] Taking forward the legacy of Dravidian identity, Periyar E.V. Ramasamy Naicker worked wonders for the non-Brahmin constituency in the colonial province of Madras. Periyar, a staunch rationalist and atheist, engaged in a polemic against everything religious and mythical to unsettle orthodox beliefs and infuse anti-caste egalitarian consciousness. Like Santram B.A. in Punjab, Periyar has the distinction of translating and publishing Babasaheb Ambedkar's *Annihilation of Caste* in Tamil.[6] He also prophetically penned the tract *Sachchi Ramayana*[7] (The True Ramayana), a translated version of which still continues to be used by Hindi-speaking anti-caste activists to deconstruct and challenge the Aryan supremacist narrative of the Ramayana. The native genius and grounded discourse of Periyar, even half a century later, proves to be a foolproof wall against the Hindutva wave that is sweeping the nation.

However, the Periyar movement's weakness lies in the fact that its lasting influence got restricted to Tamil-speaking areas. Besides, frequent caste atrocities in the Dravidian land exposes the fact that anti-caste consciousness spawned and nurtured by Dravidian movements has severe limitations when it comes to Dalit emancipation. This happens because Shudra society still remains caste oppressive while suffering inequality from Dwijas above them.

While the western and southern parts of the subcontinent have witnessed a sustained movement against the hegemony of Brahminism since before Independence, the northern Hindi-speaking belt and eastern India have lagged behind. Until the rise of the Bahujan Samaj Party (BSP), the Samajwadi Party (SP), the Rashtriya Janata Dal (RJD) and the Janata Dal (United), Dwija dominance was largely undisturbed. In West Bengal and Odisha, it still remains so. But one crucial distinction is, while the south produced movements and leaders who could, to a considerable extent, conceptualize and operationalize an emancipatory vision outside, and often in opposition to that of the Brahminical order, the northern and eastern social movements tended to move within the normative contours of the Brahminical caste order. Even the emancipatory Shudra political movements in the Hindi belt were largely invested in the positional mobility of the backward castes rather than thinking and institutionalizing a foundational challenge to Brahminical Hinduism.[8]

The past century of Shudra struggle and emancipation was imagined in terms of education, employment and representation. While the state governments (especially the southern ones) were much more proactive in implementing affirmative action for the backward castes, the central government was less willing to offer them reservation. This was witnessed in the regimes of both the Congress and the Bharatiya Janata Party (BJP) in their evasions, silences and lack of tangible action.

Even the minimum safeguard aimed at ameliorating the 'backwardness' of the majority of castes in terms of education came to be challenged immediately after the Constitution came into being. In the infamous *The State of Madras v. Champakam Dorairajan*[9] case, the Madras High Court and the Supreme Court struck out the provisions of communal power-sharing politically gained through non-Brahmin movements and struggles during the first half of the twentieth century.[10] In its ruling, the Supreme Court upheld the Madras High Court judgment and struck down the government order (GO) regarding reservation rights passed in 1927 in the Madras Presidency. The GO had provided caste-based reservation in government jobs and college seats. The Supreme Court's verdict held that providing such reservation was in violation of Article 16 (2) of the Indian Constitution.

Yet, the momentum for a continued struggle for social justice was maintained in the south. The reservation rights of Shudras from the Madras Presidency was reinitiated through the First Amendment to the Constitution of India after energetic protests led by Periyar. Though it set the non-negotiability of social justice measures like reservation, Shudras across the subcontinent had to wait forty more years to get their due.

Mandal Commission and Its Aftermath

The facile facade of modernity and self-professed 'castelessness' of the Dwija citizens of India was put under severe strain on the eve of the declaration of the Mandal Commission.[11] Unlike the much cherished and celebrated 'stable' governments, it was the minority coalition governments that planted the seed of Mandal in 1979–80 and later gave life to it in 1990. While the right-wing Rashtriya Swayamsevak Sangh (RSS) and the BJP combine took to targeting Muslims (in this case, Babri Masjid) to weather the onward march of Dalits and Shudras, the 'left-liberal' academic scholars were busy finding ways to thwart the implementation of ameliorative measures for the backward Shudras whose exclusion was a known historical reality. Even forty years after capturing the ivory towers of elite higher educational institutions, Dwija social scientists claimed that there was inadequate data to ascertain the Shudra population or to evaluate whether or not they were marginalized.[12] At the same time, they opposed the caste census being enumerated. Brahminical cleverness and opportunism were deployed as systemic processes towards scuttling affirmative action for Shudras.

While the 1990s witnessed the implementation of OBC reservation in government employment, it took another two decades to bring reservation into higher education. Dwija-dominated public discourse is still able to vitiate the struggle for social justice and egalitarian society in the name of efficiency and merit. This cannot be checked unless Shudras gain anti-caste consciousness.

Shudras in a Hindu Rashtra

The present form of India as a nation state took shape after Partition in 1947. While being resolutely Brahminical in its core, it did manage to bring in an era of formal equality and electoral democracy with suffrage rights for all. However, even this is in great crisis now. The RSS and its political wing, the BJP, are gradually moving towards establishing their ultimate theocratic state called the Hindu Rashtra. Many thinkers and political pundits believe that the dangers of a Hindu Rashtra being formalized would be confined only to those professing minority religions. But the Shudras, Dalits and Adivasis of India will equally be victimized once a full-scale Hindu Rashtra is established, as their theoretical formulations and political practices indicate.

Though Dalits and Adivasis intellectually understand the impending danger, most Shudras, including Shudra regional party leaders and cadres who are outside the fold of reservation, do not. They have not studied the RSS–BJP's history and agenda seriously with the help of modern research tools. They generally assume that the RSS–BJP work for Hindus, which Shudras/OBCs are a part of.

Sidestepping the dynamics of caste relationships while studying Indian social reality has been a systemic feature amongst the Dwija intelligentsia during the last century. The binary of communal and secular has blocked any genuine discussion on caste from happening. Urban English-speaking Dwija intellectuals have put themselves 'above caste' by claiming a secular identity while completely ignoring their roots—of Dwija position and privilege.[13] The same secular intellectuals are now critiquing so-called majoritarianism, with an assumption that Shudras are as Hindu as Dwijas, and also taking for granted that Shudras have a role in formulating the RSS–BJP ideology and directing its day-to-day operations. This is neither so, nor will they be equal partners in the Hindu Rashtra power structure.

When compared to the communal question, caste issues have been given less significance by social scientists.[14] A major concern is that at times, the minority, particularly Muslim intellectuals, write and speak in the same tone as secular Dwija intellectuals. Quite tragically, all through modern Indian history, even upper-caste (caste is very much part of Indian Islam) Muslim intellectuals hardly ever wrote about caste and the spiritual and social slavery that Shudras and Dalits were subjected to by Dwijas. The intellectual disconnect between Ambedkar and Abul Kalam Azad, who represented Indian Muslims, during the Partition debate and in post-Partition governance, shows such intellectual caste-blindness. Shudra and Dalit intellectuals cannot buy unreformed minority religious discourse as an automatic unifier of Shudra/OBC/Dalit/Adivasi and minority forces. The Phule–Ambedkarite ideology also demands a commitment to democratic and constitutional forms of struggles, shunning all forms of organized violence.

Dalit intellectuals are often seen to valiantly shoulder and balance the ideological task of Bahujan unity—which in essence means de-casteized Shudra–Dalit unity—while at the same time having to deal with ongoing atrocities against Dalits in the rural sector committed by Shudras/OBCs. Since Dwijas in modern India work through spiritual authoritarianism, monopoly capitalism and state machinery, they do not form a significant part of agrarian production now. Thus, they cease to figure in these conflicts in a physical sense. New grounds need to be explored by Shudras on how to reconcile and transcend the conflicts arising in the rural caste economy. Only Shudra self-consciousness of the caste system and its negative role in their own lives will change the situation. If this responsibility of building Bahujan unity is not taken seriously by Shudras/OBCs, their dire situation will worsen in the Hindu Rashtra.

Some essays in this volume focus on showing where Shudras are placed in present RSS–BJP ideology and organizational structures, while evaluating the future of our democracy if the

RSS–BJP combine pushes its agenda of establishing a Hindu Rashtra in the near future.

The Present Constitution vs Hindu Rashtra

Not many could assess what a modern Hindu Rashtra would be in tandem with the Constitution that promises a secular, democratic and socialist republic and with an electoral system for various law-making and governing institutions to function in a time-bound manner. How would it be established? What instruments would the RSS–BJP under Brahmin–Bania leadership use within the present nation while constantly constructing the Muslim 'other' image? Only very sophisticated Shudra intellectual engagement with the RSS–BJP intellectual discourse, perspectives and practices could shed some light on what is in store for Shudras/OBCs along with minorities.

If the RSS-led BJP continues to be in power, the fate of the Constitution and the democratic system that emanated from it should be a major concern for Shudras/OBCs. Whether the RSS–BJP would radically change or even dismantle formal structures of secular, socialist, democratic institutions to create a full-fledged, modernized varnadharma order is a hard question that has to be dealt with.

If that happens, what will happen to Shudras, even though they have some regional parties under their control and the reservation tools at the disposal of OBCs? What damage would the division among them around the issue of reservation cause? One section is being pitted against the other within Shudra society. Though the outward division sought to be created by the RSS–BJP Dwija forces appears to be on religious lines, they are calculatedly ambiguous about existing hierarchical caste divisions. They derive support for legitimizing caste divisions from the same Hindu texts they profess to revere. For instance, on 30 November 1949, M.S. Golwalkar wrote in the RSS mouthpiece *Organiser*:

> . . . in our constitution there is no mention of the unique constitutional developments in ancient Bharat. Manu's laws were written long before Lycurgus of Sparta or Solon of Persia. To this day laws as enunciated in the *Manusmriti* excite the admiration of the world and elicit spontaneous obedience and conformity. But to our constitutional pundits that means nothing.[15]

In 2017, RSS head Mohan Bhagwat, in his address to the Akhil Bharatiya Adhivakta (Advocates) Parishad in Hyderabad, said that the Constitution was written 'based on foreign sources', which is 'something we must address'. He wanted the Constitution to be changed 'in line with the value systems of the country'. There seems to be an evident discomfort with the norms and values enshrined in our present Constitution.[16]

What If the Election System Is Dismantled?

In the last seventy years, the Indian masses have got used to being governed by elected agencies with the knowledge that they can change the ruling force once every five years if their aspirations are not fulfilled. The voting power of Shudras/OBCs plays a key role in changing governments as they form the largest social unit.

The Hindu Rashtra that the RSS–BJP want to establish may possibly resemble the organizational structure of the RSS. For Shudras/OBCs, leave alone Scheduled Castes and Scheduled Tribes (SC/STs), such a centralized organization poses a caste-cultural threat. Since Shudras were historically denied education, they depended on Brahminic guidance. Even seventy years of constitutional democracy has not given them the required confidence to do things on their own. The main reason for this lack of confidence lies in the Shudra's spiritual subordination.

RSS Structure and Shudras

According to one account, RSS donations, whose sources are hidden, are deposited in rich Bania houses.[17] Extrapolating from this, we can infer that not all financial transactions of the RSS are done through the legally functioning banking system. The tax returns of this largest Indian non-governmental organization (NGO) are not publicly shared.

The RSS believes in worshipping arms and openly uses lathis in parades. Non-violence is not its ideological principle. Going by their history and ideology, we know that establishment of the Hindu Rashtra is their definite direction. This will create a major crisis for Shudras, Dalits and Adivasis, along with religious minorities and secular Dwijas. Though there are many who say that they do not believe in caste, this volume does not take those claims at face value, as caste is an existential reality of every individual in India.

Historically, in India, caste has a longer and more concrete history than religion. Though the RSS projects its Hindu Rashtra ideology in religious terms, an open secret is that its structures are governed by caste ideology. A casteless religion with spiritual and social equality for all its members is impossible within the strictures of Hinduism. Shudra intellectuals, who are few and far between, have barely examined this idea of spiritual citizenship which was denied to their brethren on the basis of caste hierarchy.

Though the Hindu Rashtra is to be established by presenting the Muslim 'other' image, the real power in that Rashtra would not devolve to Shudras/OBCs or Dalit/Adivasis.[18] Dalit/Adivasis are constitutionally described as SC and ST and they got many constitutional guarantees only because of the secular democratic set-up. In a 2014 internal RSS meeting in Kerala, current RSS *sarsanghchalak* Mohan Bhagwat said:

> The Sangh should not get into eradicating or opposing caste. Caste is a system (though now perverted) that exists in the society. It would remain until the society believes in it.[19]

In such a scenario, if their utopian Hindu Rashtra is forced into existence, Shudras/Dalits/Adivasis, as historically oppressed communities and as structural unequals, may continue to suffer. Dwija progressives may face ideological attacks, but Dwijas as communities would continue to be safe and prosperous. In other words, the families of secular Dwijas, as part of Dwija socio-spiritual Brahminism, would get all the benefits that communal Dwija families get. The culture of caste does not disappear from a person's life simply because somebody claims to be secular or even communist.

Though there are a number of secular forces from a Dwija social background who are opposed to the Hindu Rashtra, they cannot stop it if Shudras do not work to stop it. Even if you take non-reserved (as per the Mandal report) Shudras like Jats, Gujjars, Patels, Kurmis, Marathas, Reddys, Kammas, Lingayats, Vokkaligas, Nairs, Vellalas and Naickers and so on together, they far outnumber Dwija castes. But what their status is in the RSS is a critical question that they have never examined or adequately understood.

Bhanwar Meghwanshi, who worked in the RSS and recently published the book *I Could Not Be Hindu*,[20] writes that the real policy decision-making body of the RSS, called the Akhil Bharatiya Pratinidhi Sabha (ABPS), consists of thirty-six members, of which there were twenty-six Brahmins, five Banias, three Kshatriyas and two Shudras (the latter comprise nearly 52 per cent of the population that includes all agrarian and artisanal communities). Though the caste composition of the ABPS is from 2003, it is quite likely that not much has changed.

The real power centre controlling the RSS is the office of the sarsanghchalak, who is supposed to be the unquestionable supremo. Of the six sarsanghchalaks who headed the RSS, five (K.B. Hedgewar, M.S. Golwalkar, M.D. Deoras, K.S. Sudarshan and Mohan Bhagwat) are Brahmins and one a Kshatriya (Rajendra Singh). No Dalit or Shudra ever became the sarsanghchalak of the RSS even though they are claimed as Hindus.

The RSS is structurally and philosophically controlled by Brahmins, while Banias control Sangh finances. The money collected in the form of donations, according to Meghwanshi, is kept in Bania homes. The Kshatriyas adore its structures as part of the varnadharma *parampara*, though they do not command much power.[21] Yogi Adityanath and Rajnath Singh are seen as part of the Dwija structure. To make Kshatriyas believe that it belongs to them too, one Kshatriya was made sarsanghchalak. What does that indicate? The organization operates on the basis of the classical varnadharma principle but not according to the constitutional secular principle.

Once the Hindu Rashtra Is Established

If a full-scale Hindu Rashtra is established, the very nature of the present constitutional governance may possibly change. The law- and policymaking bodies of the nation would resemble the structure and leadership of the RSS. They could easily exclude and ignore Shudras/OBCs as they did in the case of the Ram Janmabhoomi Teertha Kshetra Nirman Trust, which was formed very recently. Shudras/OBCs have not yet acquired spiritual, social, economic and philosophical power to understand the function of Dwija forces in spiritual and social domains. There is no notion of God creating all Hindus equal in Hinduism, and the RSS also does not say anything new about such a critical philosophical issue. We know that its silence is approval.

The RSS is a much older organization than the Indian Constitution and democracy. It is ninety-five years old, and the Constitution is seventy years old. In its ninety-five years of existence, the RSS did not give Shudras any leadership status or allow any transformation within its ranks to take place. The Indian Constitution and the present form of democracy allowed Shudras to emerge as regional powers in many states, and at the national level, a few leaders like Sardar Vallabhbhai Patel, Kamaraj Nadar, S. Nijalingappa, Neelam Sanjiva Reddy, V.K. Krishna Menon, Y.B. Chavan and so on occupied some top national positions though they could not become prime ministers from the ranks of the Congress. As a result of the secular, republican Constitution, Chaudhary Charan Singh and H.D. Deve Gowda became prime ministers, though they could survive only for a short time. Though the RSS claims Narendra Modi as an OBC prime minister, he did not come from an agrarian Shudra background.

Shudra Division a Self-Goal

Since Shudras were divided into two categories, reserved and non-reserved, after the 1990 Mandal reservation was implemented, there appeared divisions among them. While the relative socio-economic factors are different, their historical agrarian roots are common. Some Shudra families across the country emerged as landed gentry and feudal estate owners, yet their spiritual and social status in the Dwija system did not change. Based on their regional landownership and numerical strength, some sociologists and political scientists described them as 'dominant castes', but this dominance proved to be a deceptive concept in a pan-Indian socio-economic and spiritual scenario. Now, many Shudra regional parties in north India have been rendered powerless, and what controls them is the RSS–BJP hierarchical varnadharma order. A critical task of this volume is to show the paradoxical status of Shudras under RSS–BJP rule and highlight a new path for the protection of the present Constitution with its secular fabric, and to build larger coalitions with Dalits, Adivasis, Muslims and other minorities like Sikhs and Christians. Whatever be the religion, any communal religious agenda will go against the interests of Shudras/OBCs/Dalits/Adivasis.

We have established that the RSS is regulated and guided by varna/caste-based ideology. Stating this fact does not exonerate the Communist Party of India (CPI) and the Communist Party of India (Marxist) (CPI[M]) or the Congress party of subtle discriminatory practices of not allowing Dalits/Adivasis/Shudras upward mobility in party structures. However, the Indian National Congress steered the drafting of this Constitution under the leadership of Dr B.R. Ambedkar, a legal luminary whose contribution is the saving grace for non-Dwija communities. Jawaharlal Nehru and Sardar Vallabhbhai Patel also played key roles in the Constituent Assembly, while not always being in consonance with Dr Ambedkar.

The RSS and the communists did not believe in this Constitution—from two different points of view—when it was in the process of being made and adopted in 1950. The RSS was critical of it from the very beginning, stating that it did not take into account traditional Indian lineage and fell short of the standards set by the *Manusmriti*.[22] The communists opposed it from the point of view of a proletariat dictatorship. We call varnadharma rule a dictatorship as well because it is rule through the caste hierarchical authoritarian position without allowing any scope for democratic change. Proletariat dictatorship was the stated objective of the Communist Party of India by 1950. But the RSS never clearly stated its objective so clearly. It hides everything under the garb of *sanskriti* and parampara. Yet, both these forms of government would result in dictatorship for Shudras/OBCs/Dalits/Adivasis.

Shudra Interests Now

Shudra interests and transformation lie in opposing both these dictatorships. Shudras should work for the abolition of caste and untouchability and for women's equality. Any other form should not be acceptable to Shudra/Dalit/Adivasi forces. Any dictatorship in India is bound to reinforce Brahminic varnadharmic ideology because of India's socio-historical background. For other non-Brahminic religious minorities also, this Constitution is the safest guiding philosophy and systemic structure. Shudras/OBCs/Dalits/Adivasis must fight for common English-medium national school education, with due space for learning regional languages, with a secular, progressive and democratic curriculum.

As of now, the Shudra presence in intellectual discourse is minimal. This became clear when we embarked upon mobilizing intellectual resources for this volume. Scholars from the Shudra/ OBC community who can write about social and philosophical concerns in English are few, though in regional languages there is significant intellectual strength. A reliable indicator of this intellectual impoverishment would be the negligent percentage of well-educated Shudras working as professors in central universities and institutions across India.[23]

Shudras lack resources to learn and write with great facility in English, partly due to the historical disadvantage and partly due to inadequate implementation of the Mandal Commission's recommendations in higher education. Those Shudras who were capable of writing did not want to identify themselves as Shudra, an identity that makes their lives vulnerable and career opportunities scarce in the present atmosphere.

This vulnerability amongst Shudras strengthens RSS confidence because this organization has used Shudra/OBC muscle power in all its movements, without allowing any among them to occupy the highest positions. The caste configuration of the list of sarsanghchalaks so far tells that truth quite clearly. Yet, the fear of freedom among Shudras is very strong. This volume aims at shaking off that fear. Meanwhile, Dalits have overcome such an identity crisis primarily by deploying Ambedkarite ideology in their sociocultural and intellectual practices.

Who Are the 'Shudras'?

The Shudra category denotes the numerous productive castes which have historically built the material basis of our civilization, yet have been marginalized in terms of the power- and knowledge-sharing arrangement in the Brahminical order. They are currently known by multiple labels such as agrarian dominant castes, Backward Castes, Other Backward Classes (OBC), Most Backward Classes (MBC) or Extremely Backward Castes. The so-called dominant castes which were busy advancing claims for neo-Kshatriya status within the Brahminical varna ideal falls under the Shudra category.[24] While these distinctions and the history that produced these distinctions have political significance, for our purposes we will treat the Shudras as this vast mass of castes which generally earn their livelihood in production-oriented activities and have been disparaged and discriminated against from the days of the Rig Veda.

Prominent scholars have argued that one need not and should not see OBCs or Shudras forming a monolithic unit for all purposes and at all times. G. Aloysius, in his intervention on the OBC discourse, has flagged it as a state-driven discourse and not necessarily a progressive one.[25] Further, the complex and tortured history of how the OBC as a category came into modern existence and what implication it has for OBC women was discussed by Asha Singh and Nidhin Donald in their insightful article, exploring the issues and possibilities that spring from such terminology.[26] However, for the purpose of this volume, we are concerned with the Shudra community— which consists of thousands of sub-castes—for revitalization of a new national debate.

The essays give the reader an understanding of diverse issues that are plaguing the nation at this juncture, and put the Shudra question before the nation with a modernist approach. We hope that this volume of eleven essays exploring various aspects of national Shudra social forces will be successful in kindling the interest of intellectuals and the public alike in discussing the Shudra conundrum at this juncture.

Arvind Kumar's 'The Nation and Its Shudras' interrogates the hegemonic national imagination that claims to include every citizen on the one hand, while brazenly marginalizing Shudras as a whole on the other. Apart from reviewing the philosophical and ideological resources bestowed by Phule and Ambedkar, Kumar raises fresh questions about the material aspects of Shudra deprivation in the post-Independence era, and its incompatibility with the promise of an egalitarian, modern Indian nation.

Sunil Sardar's 'The Socio-spiritual Slavery of Shudras' takes up the spiritual dimension of the Shudra question. Holding Brahminical traditions as antithetical to dignity of the Shudra populace, Sardar captures sociopolitical movements across two millennia. He takes us on a panoramic historical journey of counter-traditions such as Ashoka's patronage of Buddhist dhamma, Basavanna's Bhakti movement, Guru Nanak's revolt against Brahminical traditions, Phule's Truth Seekers movement, and Ambedkar and his Buddhist revolution. Sardar, in line with Phule, posits the egalitarian Balirajya as the ultimate alternative to the hierarchical Ramrajya so that Shudras win their spiritual freedom.

Kancha Ilaiah Shepherd in 'Shudras and Democratic India' discusses the political fortunes of the Shudra category in the post-Independence scenario. Tracing fault lines in the Congress's approach towards Shudra communities across the nation, Ilaiah maps how they were alienated due to various economic and sociopolitical considerations. He reads the increasing appeal of the right-wing RSS–BJP's agenda of Hinduizing Shudras as a product of their systemic exclusion from all domains of national importance. In addition, the essay urges Shudras to value their production-oriented lives and strive for spiritual egalitarianism, which will forge a path towards their liberation from the refurbished Brahminical order fostered by the RSS and the BJP.

Sharad Yadav and Omprakash Mahato's essay brings home the anti-caste import of Lohiaite socialist ideology along with the struggles and complex political process that accompanied the implementation of the Mandal Commission report under the V.P. Singh government. Arguing for building up a broad lower-caste movement, he pleads with the current crop of Bahujan leaders to eschew from basing their political practice on a single caste. Omprakash Mahato has enriched this article by integrating seamlessly the subject matters that came up during the personal interview of Sharad Yadav.

Prachi Patil's intervention on 'The Question of Bahujan Women' addresses a series of issues. Firstly, it locates Bahujan women within the traditional matrix of the caste system. Secondly, it documents and rereads a few instances of Bahujan women's rebellion against the patriarchal caste system. Lastly, it engages with the Bahujan feminist standpoint that locates itself differentially from the Dalit feminist standpoint and the *savarna* feminist discourse. This essay aims to flesh out the intricacies of the graded location of Bahujan women on the axis of gender and caste, and map how these intricacies translate into questions of representation, resources and rights of Bahujan women in various domains in current times.

Urmilesh's essay presents a vivid account of political movements in Uttar Pradesh and Bihar. He takes stock of Bahujan leaders such as Karpoori Thakur, Lalu Yadav and Nitish Kumar from Bihar, and Kanshiram, Mulayam Singh Yadav and Mayawati from Uttar Pradesh in terms of their contribution to backward caste mobility. Simultaneously, he does not shy away from blaming the current leadership of the Bahujan parties for their ineffective fight against the BJP's capture of power.

Ram Shepherd Bheenaveni's essay explores the nature of the God and deity construction amongst Vedic Aryans and the pre-Vedic populace found in the Harappan civilization. Through an eclectic reading of ancient Vedic and religious practices from the non-Vedic populace, he sets out to establish a different genealogy for manipulative Dwija spirituality and the production- and protection-oriented Shudra spirituality. This essay is an effort to disentangle, and to some extent dismantle, the all-subsuming narratives of monolith Hinduism to bring out the complex nuances inherent in indigenous spiritual traditions of the subcontinent.

Bindu N. Doddahatti focuses on the sociocultural identities of upper Shudras like the Vokkaligas and Lingayats in Karnataka. Observing that Brahminical philosophical imagination has full control over Shudra ways of thinking and existing, she argues that despite the claims of Lingayats to a separate religion, their trajectory resembles that of the neo-Brahmin aspiring castes. She's equally critical of the Vokkaligas' neo-Kshatriya aspirations. The questions of violence against Dalits and women's status are also discussed.

Pallikonda Manikanta takes up the daunting task of mapping Shudra consciousness to track its complex trajectories. An engagement with philosophy shows that Shudras were excluded from text-based philosophical discourse, which has resulted in stagnation in terms of their philosophizing capacity. Shudra existence was viewed as an act of 'self-negation' in which the communities were alienated due to devaluation of their work culture, absence of historical memory and degradation of their food culture. Another strand of his inquiry takes us to how the 'enemy image' is constructed against Dalits, Muslims and Christians through the discourse propounded by the Brahminical RSS, extending his insights to the recent protests against the Citizenship Amendment Act (CAA) and the National Register of Citizens (NRC).

Dr P. Vinay Kumar's essay, 'The India of My Dreams', offers a personalized narrative of how his privileged OBC background makes it unfair for other backward-caste people hailing from modest means to compete against him or his children. His piece makes a plea for a nuanced understanding and framing of reservation policies that do justice for the weakest.

The Shudra Team's essay, 'Caste and Political Economy', looks at the centralization of capitalist wealth in the hands of the national bhadralok—particularly Banias and Brahmins, leaving agrarian Shudras—including the old feudal Shudras—far behind. It looks at the available data on caste-capital ownership and examines the caste monopoly capital and how this enabled the RSS–BJP to come to power in 2014. It forecasts how the anti-secular capital and the newly formed RSS–BJP nexus would pose a threat to the nation's constitutional secular democracy and capitalist modernity itself.

The Nation and Its Shudras[1]

Arvind Kumar

'. . . without education wisdom was lost; without wisdom morals were lost; without morals development was lost; without development wealth was lost; without wealth the Shudras were ruined; so much has happened through lack of education.'[2]

—Jyotiba Phule

Mahatma Jyotiba Phule had rightly foreseen the symptoms of the disease the Shudras had historically been suffering from for a century and a half. He also very wisely attempted to diagnose what could be understood as the 'Shudra problem' both through his writings and the Satyashodhak movement in solidarity with his comrade and wife, Savitribai Phule. The biggest tragedy for both the Shudra women and men of the Indian nation however, was that they failed to adopt Phule as their cultural and philosophical mentor to eradicate this problem. Nonetheless, B.R. Ambedkar, by recognizing Gautama Buddha and Jyotiba Phule as his philosophical guides or gurus, led millions of Dalits (who were placed even lower than Shudras in the varna/jati hierarchy) towards the idea of Prabuddha Bharat, enlightened India. Contrary to the Dalit community's progress towards emancipation, the Shudras of contemporary India remained as per the Hindu caste order, giving Brahminism enough scope to control them.

This essay does not attempt to give a detailed historical account of Shudras as a social category or their identity formation in India. Rather, the purpose is to establish through various sources how this social category remained segregated and excluded through different epochs of time. There has been a deliberate neglect of academic deliberation on the social and cultural aspects of Shudras, who at all points of time have constituted the majority (Bahujan) of Indian society. A 'nation' is made by numerous efforts of its subjects or citizenry. However, it is appalling that the huge mass of Shudras who have been crucial to nation-making have miserably failed in claiming or reclaiming their legitimate credit in this process. This essay, instead of suggesting any solutions, seeks to yet again establish the Shudra problem, and put it in perspective.

The Nation

A phrase that has gained some popularity in recent times, supported by votaries of self-styled nationalists, more specifically from many right-wing organizations in India, is 'nation first'. For a theoretical scrutiny of the subject, one is obligated to ask what 'nation' means to a layman. And further, what it owes its own subjects, who ultimately constitute the nation which is so sacrosanct in people's beliefs. A popular theorist, Benedict Anderson, has painstakingly deliberated on this subject. A rudimentary definition of 'nation', drawing from his scholarship, would be as follows:

A nation is to a great extent an 'imagined' community, held together by the collective beliefs, aspirations and imaginations of its members. It is based on certain assumptions which people make about the collective whole with which they identify . . . a nation is constituted by belief . . . a nation exists when its members believe that they belong together.[3]

According to noted historian Romila Thapar, the idea of nation and nationalism in the Indian context, too, is a Western import and a relatively recent phenomenon. Therefore, to presuppose the idea of the 'Indian nation' during the ancient and medieval periods is fraught with conceptual quandary. The nation becomes a reality and derives its legitimacy from various groups which come together and encourage a secular identity to ensure inclusive unity, which remains a characteristic feature of all modern nationalisms.[4] At the same time, she cautions that it has to be an account of a shared past which binds people together. Therefore, in the context of a nation, its history should function as a bond. History cannot be dominated by any single identity, and so nationalism does not exist for any particular identity. The evolution of the nationalist idea and an imaginary nation emanating from this idea in India is strongly linked to colonialism.[5] The varied subjects assembled on a common platform to imagine themselves as a single nation based on the premise of egalitarianism. As Thapar recently remarked:

Anti-colonial nationalism saw India as a nation of citizens, who, irrespective of origins, and with a substantially similar identity, were all of equal status and were coming together in the demand for independence.[6]

But the promise of independence did not result in the desired goal of dignity in terms of either labour, equality or justice as envisioned in the basic philosophy of constitutional democracy. It is in this very context that Gopal Guru offers fresh insight for a nuanced understanding of the idea of a nation. Guru takes the bull by the horns when he flips the popular phrase, 'Do not think what the nation does for you but think what you can do for the nation' to 'What can the nation do for you?' In doing so, he categorically underlines that the nation has a moral duty towards a large section of the tormented humanity or citizenry which ultimately constitutes the body of a nation.[7] Guru adds further that in order to have a holistic understanding of the nation and the complex relationship that exists between the nation and its nationals, one needs to ask:

> . . . if we separate the nation from the theory question or the moral question and send the discussion on holiday as the right-wing supporters of nationalism seem to be doing, what implications does it have for the social groups that exist on the margins and even outside the margins of the Indian nation . . . nation offers us the analytical opportunity to decide its normative stamina of the state. It offers us an opportunity to decide its normative stamina in terms of equality, justice, freedom and dignity. The dignity of the individual is coextensive with the dignity of the nation.[8]

The marginalized sections of the nation are numerous. And the story of the Shudras as a social group obviously has its own set of problems. Like any other social group, they are not homogeneous, and therefore, do not share any single definitive servility or disability. Various ruptures during anti-colonial struggles were clear evidence of such dichotomies and contradictions. The dominant theoretical constructions built around the idea of the nation found serious challenges from various kinds of academic writings.[9] But the big question about Shudras as the subject of the nation has been most profoundly posed by none other than Phule himself in his writings, where he unequivocally declared:

> There cannot be a 'nation' worth the name until and unless all the people of the land of King Bali, such as the Shudras and Ati-Shudras, Bhils and fishermen etc. become truly educated and are able to think independently for themselves and are uniformly unified and emotionally integrated.[10]

How inclusive was the Indian national movement? This is a pertinent question that remained untouched by mainstream academia until, to an extent, the Marxist and later the subaltern school raised the underlying problems related to class, with skewed attention towards other marginalities such as caste and gender. The dominant narrative and discourse on nation and nationalism were unambiguously Brahminical and patriarchal in nature. But scholars like Gail Omvedt unearthed the hidden treasures of history by highlighting the pressing concerns of anti-caste movements under the leadership of Phule, Periyar, Ambedkar, etc., and brought the importance of various identities to the fore. She writes:

> The question of identity and existence of the nation was precisely the point taken up by Phule in the nineteenth century in opposing the elite led nationalist project at its very beginning. His argument was that a society divided by caste could not constitute a genuine nation and that those claiming to represent the nation were in fact its destroyers since they not only ignored these hierarchical divisions but actually sought to maintain them as a basis for their power.[11]

The Shudras

The historicity of the word 'Shudra' can be traced back to the time of the Indo-Aryan social system of the Indian subcontinent. There are contentious debates around its origin and most importantly about its Kshatriya origin.[12] Both Shudras and Ati-Shudras, that is, the fourth varna of the Indo-Aryan society since later Vedic times and the ex-Untouchables, respectively, continued to face violence despite being the productive class. During colonial times, Phule was the first to champion the cause of Shudras under the banner of the Non-Brahmin movement. Ambedkar iterated that the Non-Brahmin movement was a political movement of Shudras, and it was well known that he himself was connected with it.[13] Ambedkar wrote a year before the Indian nation was declared independent:

> Under the system of *chaturvarnya*, Shudra is not only placed at the bottom of the gradation but he is subjected to innumerable ignominies and disabilities so as to prevent him from rising above the condition fixed for him by law. Indeed, until the fifth varna of the Untouchables came into being, the Shudras were in the eyes of the Hindus, the lowest of the low. This shows the nature of what might be called the problem of the Shudras. If people have no idea of the magnitude of problem, it is because they have not cared to know what the population of the Shudras is. Unfortunately, the census does not show their population separately. But there is no doubt that excluding the Untouchables the Shudras form about 75 to 80 per cent of Hindus. A treatise which deals with so vast a population cannot be considered to be dealing with a trivial problem.[14]

There is no denying the fact that modern-day Shudras are not exactly the same community as they were in ancient times and that they are no more governed by ancient *dharmashastras*. It is a huge, heterogeneous category of communities, most of whom are engaged in peasantry, animal farming, shepherding, fishing, carpentry, pottery, smith work and an innumerable list of artisanal and craft works. A major chunk of these people have been categorized as Other Backward Classes (OBCs) in contemporary parlance, signifying an administrative category. It is interesting to note that this class of people, along with Dalits and Adivasis, represents the subaltern working class and producing class of the nation. Sharad Patil has very dexterously established this cause:

> Dasas and Sudras were the first ever creators of wealth, in the sense of surplus product in ancient India. The great Indian civilization, which, their ceaseless, back-breaking toil spread over nearly three millennia has raised and nourished, has, in return, fashioned and perpetuated the shackles of their slavery and servitude. State power has terrorized them into smoldering submission, religion has preached to them the preordained birthright of servitude, and philosophy has revealed to them the evanescence and unreality of 'this' world of travail and the eternity and reality of 'that' world of bliss.[15]

An important aspect which has mostly been ignored in the academic discussion on and around the caste question is the etymology of the very term 'Shudra'. If one attempts to unravel the semantics of the word or explore how the fourth varna of the then Vedic society came to be called Shudras, R.S. Sharma has the most plausible explanation. He states even etymologically, 'It appears that just as the common European word "slave" and Sanskrit "dasa" were derived from the names of conquered peoples, so also the word "Shudra" was derived from a conquered tribe of that name.'[16] On close scrutiny, it is evident that there has been a consistent textual tradition of degrading and stigmatizing this particular varna/jati order. Sharma further provides us with an apt illustration to substantiate this fact:

> A recent writer derives the term Sudra from the root *svi* 'swell'+the root *dra* 'run' and suggests that this term means 'one who runs after gross life'; therefore, according to him the sudra is 'an unintelligent fellow meant for manual labour. It is extraordinary that he should have derived the term sudra from two roots, and that too hardly without any old etymological basis. The meaning which labours to ascribe to this term only betrays the traditional attitude towards the sudra, but does not throw any light on its origin.[17]

It is Brahminism as an ideology which brings Shudras at loggerheads with their own nation, which they have built so laboriously. Even the nationalist movement operated with the strong support of Brahminical idioms which were deeply patriarchal, casteist and supremacist. Despite progressive pretensions, the idea of modernity had sluggish penetration in the Indian social system. The notion of secularism was at a nascent stage under colonial rulers as they themselves were guided by Gentoo code laws.[18] The subjects of the nation, that is, the citizenry, were to be equal in the eyes of the nation, irrespective of their social, cultural, economic, linguistic or any other diversity. But the social reality remained aloof from these utopian constitutional promises. Braj Ranjan Mani makes rightful claim of such veracity:

> The Shudra was given the name *padaja*—born from the feet—implying thereby that the God created the Shudra to be the eternal slave. On the one hand, thousands of words were invented to uphold Brahmanical supremacy and glorify the

Brahmans: *brahmajnani, vedagya, acharya, upadhyay, devavani, shshtragya, pandit, manushydeva, bhudeva,* etc. On the other hand scores of words were coined to abuse the shudras: *danav, daitya, rakshas, pishacha, chandala, maleccha, kshudra, nikrihta, dwijdasa,* etc.[19]

The picture has always been quite complex and paradoxical. There came a stage where many sub-castes of those belonging to Shudras as a social group started to be called dominant castes[20] and thus were termed one of the biggest beneficiaries of the Brahminical caste order and hierarchies. Many of these caste groups are also accused of being the tormentor in cases of caste atrocities against Dalits.[21] It is argued that even while their ritual and social positions are inferior to the savarna castes, they are economically and politically superior to them. It is further argued that major Shudra castes are dominant castes in different pockets of the country, like Jats, Marathas, Vokkaligas, Yadavs, Koeris, Kurmis, etc. But one wonders why they are negligent or near absent from power positions at the national level.[22] Omvedt unravels another complex conundrum as she explains how certain landowning communities belonging to Shudra castes, including Patils among Kunbis or Gaudas among Vokkaligas, Reddys among Kapus or Chaudharis among Kammas, belonged to what can be best understood as 'peasant cultivators', at best claiming precedence over *balutedars* (caste-based village hereditary workers) and Dalits of their villages, but still classified as Shudras and treated as rustic 'village idiots' in their popular proverbs and stories.[23]

Omvedt provides one such vivid illustration:

> The Kunbi caste is crooked as a sickle but by beating it becomes straight.
> Kunbis and flour improve by pounding.

A Kunbi has no sense; he forgets whatever he learns.

The Kunbi died of seeing a ghost, the Brahman from the wind in the stomach, and the goldsmith from the bile.

The Kunbi is always planting, whether his crop lives or dies.[24]

Such indecent and humiliating remarks have been common for even those Shudras who have carved out their considerable position in public life. Karpoori Thakur, who rose to the position of chief minister of Bihar, was often subject to casteist slurs, one of many such being: '*Karpoori kar poora, kursi chod dhar astura.*'[25] A similar casteist taunt was faced by Sharad Yadav—who rose to the position of Union minister and has been conferred with the Best Parliamentarian Award—while contesting the parliamentary by-election from Amethi against Rajiv Gandhi in 1981. The casteist Congress party workers had then remarked: '*Sharad Yadav wapas jao, laathi pakdo bhains charaao.*'[26]

One important reason for the current state of affairs of the Shudra castes is rooted in their failure to develop a connection with any universal language. It is needless to reiterate that language plays one of the most crucial roles in creating hegemony in the Gramscian sense of the term. Shudras have miserably failed in using this particular tool for raising their concerns and making their points of view heard to the world beyond their immediate realm. Strangely enough, there has been an emotive demand for education in the mother tongue, mostly from Shudra and Bahujan caste groups. But a noted Shudra intellectual, Kancha Ilaiah Shepherd, asks a pertinent question about why Shudras do not send their children to English-medium schools while Brahmin–Banias always prefer to do so. Is it not true that English is the singular language which still connects the entire nation, even if one ignores the role it played in unifying India during the nationalist movement? A majority of intellectuals belonging to Shudra caste groups, beginning from the Bhakti saints of the medieval period to those from contemporary times, could not communicate their ideas, knowledge and philosophies to the outside world only because they failed to master any dominant ruling language such as Sanskrit, Persian or English. Ambedkar is an exception. Ilaiah has rightly captured the historical crisis of Shudras when he writes:

> The Shudras, rather than embracing English-language education, let themselves be swayed by Brahmin nationalist propaganda. Bal Gangadhar Tilak, a Brahmin now considered a national icon, was emblematic. After Jotirao and Savitribai Phule, both Shudras, established their pioneering movement of education for women and oppressed castes in Maharashtra, Tilak marshalled Brahmin criticism against them. He opposed all calls for universal education, arguing that educating women and the oppressed castes would endanger the caste order, and so, in his view, the Indian nation. Brahmin nationalists also portrayed the missionary schools as an existential threat, and campaigned against them. The Shudras, by and large, rallied behind the nationalists.[27]

Nation for/against Its Unequal Citizens[28]

Coming back to the question posed by Gopal Guru about the normative stamina of a nation for its own subject or citizens, the following part of this essay will attempt an assessment of the efforts taken for the benefit of Shudras. In 1946, Ambedkar raised a pertinent question in his aptly titled work, *Who Were the Shudras? How They Came to Be the Fourth Varna in the Indo-Aryan Society.*[29] Jyotiba Phule, along with his wife, Savitribai Phule, did an unprecedented task of awakening the Shudra masses in the western part of colonial India. He laid the foundation of the Non-Brahmin movement, displaying robust and hard-hitting criticism to Brahminism when other parts of the colonial quarters were busy with either social reform movements by the likes of Raja Ram Mohan Roy or Ishwar Chandra Vidyasagar, or revivalist movements by the likes of Dayanand Saraswati or Swami Vivekananda. Having realized Phule's unparalleled contribution, Ambedkar dedicated his monograph to him.[30] But the tragedy of the Shudras on the eve of the nation's independence could not have been articulated better than was done by Ambedkar in the following words:

> The book is written for the ignorant and uninformed Shudras, who do not know how they came to be what they are. They do not care how artistically the theme is handled. All they desire is full harvest of the material the bigger the better . . . it is Shudras who have largely been instrumental in sustaining the infamous system of chaturvarna, though it has been the primary cause of their degradation and that only the shudras can destroy the chaturvarna . . .[31]

The Constituent Assembly assigned with the task of drafting the Indian Constitution held its first meeting on 9 December 1946. The Objective Resolution was moved by Jawaharlal Nehru on 13 December 1946 and adopted unanimously on 22 January 1947. The Assembly had categorically resolved one item on its agenda, '. . . wherein the minorities, backward and tribal areas, depressed and other backward classes shall be provided adequate safeguards'.[32] But nothing concrete happened for the large masses of Shudras who would eventually fall into the category of OBCs, except for the creation in 1953 of the First Backward Classes Commission headed by Kaka Kalelkar, a Brahmin parliamentarian belonging to the Congress party. The commission was biased since its creation and submitted a voluminous report which was lost in the stacks of files and reports gathering thick piles of dust. The net output was nil.

The social classes specified as OBCs in the Objective Resolution were nothing but a group of castes in the Indian context who were extremely backward both socially and educationally, even if some fraction of them were economically well-to-do, like Marathas in Maharashtra or Jats in Uttar Pradesh and Haryana. An important aspect which sociologists of modern India have missed is the question of spiritual superiority of savarnas, and what is even more tragic is the lack of self-actualization by Shudras themselves of their own inferiority, thereby providing legitimacy to what Ambedkar has succinctly explained as 'graded inequality'.

On the social and cultural front, however, there have been some attempts to overcome such inferiority by being organized into various social organizations. Many Shudra caste groups like Mahatos and Yadavs in Bihar and eastern Uttar Pradesh started asserting their right to wear the sacred thread in a bid to claim Kshatriya status, refused to work in the land of Bhumihars and Brahmins, tried promoting education and initiated internal social reform. Another Shudra caste called Noniya in parts of Bihar and Madhya Pradesh claimed the status of Chauhan Rajputs. All of this at the cost of facing atrocities from Dwija castes who felt their monopoly of power was gradually slipping away.[33] Aloysius, for instance, mentions the role played by such organizations:

Not much is known about the activities of the Tribeni Sangh, a federation of local Koeri, Kurmi and Yadav castes and the Raghav Samaj, an association between the Kurmis and Koeris except that these Shudra castes in the wake of rising political consciousness, organized themselves to challenge the Brahmanical order and came forward to join the new political community.[34]

Ambedkar identified yet another problem concerning Shudras. At around the time he finished writing *States and Minorities*,[35] he realized that since there was no educating or organizing of the Shudra worker-peasant, a majority of them identified themselves as Hindus, as against not just Muslims but even Dalits.[36] During the fieldwork for this essay, an informant belonging to one of the Shudra castes, who was in his early twenties during the turbulent 1990s, recollected that he along with his fellow caste brethren felt emotionally more connected to Kamandal rather than with the question of Mandal. He further revealed that during the euphoria of the Ram Janmabhoomi campaign, slogan chanting like '*bachcha bachcha Ram ka, janmabhoomi ke kaam ka*'[37] provided them with a sense of accomplishment.

The Congress party, which largely remained under the strong grip of Brahminism, gradually lost its sheen; the Socialist Party under leaders like Ram Manohar Lohia, J.B. Kripalani, Bhupendra Narayan Mandal, etc., gave a slogan of '*sansopa ne bandhi gaanth, pichhda pawe sau me saath*',[38] having realized the mammoth size of the vote bank consisting of Shudra caste groups. The Janata Party, after coming to power at the Centre in 1977, constituted the Second Backward Classes Commission under the chairmanship of B.P. Mandal, a Shudra parliamentarian from Bihar's Madhepura constituency. The commission submitted its report in 1980. It diligently identified the markers of backwardness, primary among them being social and educational backwardness. More than 3000 caste groups were enumerated to be officially called OBCs, which included more than 80 per cent of the nation's Muslim populace. The commission made various recommendations; only one was finally implemented, that is, 27 per cent reservation for OBCs in government services, a decade later in 1990 by the United Front government led by V.P. Singh.

The half-hearted efforts on behalf of the ruling regimes soon got exposed. Even after the Supreme Court's ruling in favour of the Mandal Commission recommendations in the Indra Sawhney judgment,[39] the implementation of reservation for Shudras/OBCs was deliberately delayed by the Brahminical executive. Nothing can explain how the nation has not been able to implement its own enacted law in some three decades. So much so, the Department of Personnel and Training brought out a Consolidated Instruction for SCs, STs and OBCs as late as June 2010.[40] Not that SC and ST reservation has fully been implemented as mandated, the representation of OBCs as on 1 January 2017 was 17 and 14 per cent respectively for Group A and B services in some twenty-four ministries of the central government since 8 September 1993, when the implementation of reservation began.[41] It took another decade and a half, as late as 2008, for the central government to announce the entry of Shudras into institutions of higher learning in what is popularly known as Mandal II. It is horrendous to note that their representation in academia is visibly abysmal. The number of professors and associate professors appointed under OBC reservation in some forty central universities is zero. On the contrary, the figures for the general caste category for these positions are 95.2 and 92.9 per cent respectively.[42] In such a lopsided demographic space of higher learning, the prevalent caste prejudices and discrimination does huge damage to the self-respect and self-confidence of the large Shudra and Ati-Shudra masses.[43]

Even recently, on 30 November 2019, while Dharmendra Parmar of Bhadwan village, Madhya Pradesh (belonging to the Shudra caste, now categorized as OBC) was in his wedding procession, he was pushed off his horse by Rajput men, his shirt was torn, his father thrashed, stones pelted on his guests, and car and motorcycles battered. According to the elected sarpanch of the village, Kailash Malviya, who belongs to the Dalit community, the procession was the first one to be taken out by the backward community after twenty years that did not consist of motorcycles and tractors as per the Rajput diktat.[44] The groom, too, testified, '. . . they are threatened by our assertion, and rise up the social ladder. Why should we consult them for every decision since we are educated . . . we refused to work their fields too, which riled them further.'[45]

Shudras might have wrested considerable political power in Parliament and state assemblies in the aftermath of the Mandal movement, which Christophe Jaffrelot named as 'India's Silent Revolution'.[46] But Michel Foucault's dictum, 'knowledge is power',[47] explains why a small minority of savarnas in Indian society are over-represented in almost all spheres of the nation's life. Alas! Shudras are bound to continue suffering until they smash the Brahminical contrivance which has pushed them deep into philosophical and ontological darkness. Only then will they be capable of building on intellectual capital with which they can reclaim their nation.

The Socio-spiritual Slavery of Shudras: A National Agenda for Their Liberation

Sunil Sardar

Origins and Facets of Shudra Slavery

India's Other Backward Classes (OBCs), who are historically known as Shudras, have existed in a state of social and spiritual slavery in India for over 3000 years. To understand this phenomenon, we need to clarify who the OBCs are. When the Indian Constitution came into effect on 26 January 1950, it instituted reservations for SCs and STs. These castes and tribes were listed in a Schedule of the Constitution, which is how they obtained their official name in independent India. Earlier, the masses belonging to Untouchable castes were officially known as Depressed Classes. Many other terms have been used to refer to them, such as Dalits, Harijans, etc. They were ideologically framed as existing in a perpetual state of pollution due to their birth outside of the traditional fourfold varna system.

While the Constitution secured reservations and protections for SCs and STs, it also required the government to work for the welfare of backward classes other than SCs and STs.

Therefore, India adopted the nomenclature of Other Backward Classes to refer to castes that existed separate from the SCs and STs yet did not belong to India's Dwija castes either. These middle castes were born into the bottom of the varna system and were called Shudras according to Brahminical texts. The earliest Brahminical scripture, the Rig Veda, contains the *Purusha Sukta*, a hymn declaring how mankind was created out of the sacrifice of the first man. From his mouth came Brahmins, from his arms came Kshatriyas, from his legs came Vaishyas, and from his feet came Shudras. This hierarchy of Brahmin, Kshatriya, Vaishya and Shudra constitutes the classical fourfold varna system of Hinduism. These castes are again identified in later Brahminical texts like the *Manusmriti*, *Arthashastra*, dharmashastras and the Bhagavad Gita. OBCs are Shudras, and their status as social and spiritual slaves started from the very beginning of Brahminical Hinduism.

The *Manusmriti* discusses laws and codes to govern Hindu society, and Manu required Shudras to exist as an abused, servile class. Some of the well-known rules of the *Manusmriti* are that Shudras may not take a name that denotes respect or dignity; Shudras exist to serve the other three castes; Shudras may not receive an education, learn the Vedas or learn Sanskrit; Shudras may not acquire wealth; and Shudras must speak only with great caution around Brahmins. Draconian punishments are prescribed for a Shudra who violates these commands. These include pouring hot oil into their mouth, poking them with a red-hot iron nail, cutting out the tongue or even castration. Other Hindu texts may not have such a cruel law and punishment system, but they do not seek to correct or overturn these harsh restrictions either. For example, the Bhagavad Gita says that Shudras are created to serve the other three varnas, thus agreeing with the *Manusmriti*'s basic assertion that Shudras are the servile caste, and providing tacit approval to Manu's harsher rules.

These texts show us the historical extent of the slavery of OBCs, and they also open the door to our understanding of the type of slavery experienced. The most common understanding of Shudras throughout the history of Hinduism is that they are servants of upper castes, as Brahminical scriptures unanimously agree. A human being born to serve others is a slave. Shudras are blacksmiths, goldsmiths, shepherds, farmers, cowherds, oil pressers, cultivators, gardeners, toddy tappers, carpenters, weavers, potters, cleaners, washermen, fishermen and bricklayers. Among Shudra castes, there are no priests, merchants, ministers, kings, accountants, scribes, authors, judges, advocates or executives. For thousands of years, they have existed in a degraded status, denied education, wealth and status, while being allowed to learn nothing more than their ancestral trades.

Even modern Hindu reformers like Mahatma Gandhi have agreed that this state is their proper status and that all Hindus should pursue their caste-based ancestral calling. In Gandhi's vision, '. . . the Shudra, who performs body-labour in a spirit of service and duty, who has nothing to call his own and who has no desire for ownership, is worthy of the world's homage; he is the lord of all because he is the greatest servant. The dutiful Shudra will, of course, repudiate any such claim, but the gods will shower their choicest blessings on him'.[1] When foreigners such as Herodotus, Megasthenes, Ptolemy, Pliny the Elder, Strabo and Marco Polo wrote about India, they mentioned their observations of these working and servile classes.

Not only were Shudras forced to serve, they were also kept in poverty. Even if a Shudra proved himself an able financier, the *Manusmriti* ruled that it is injurious to the Brahmin if the Shudra acquired wealth. The presence of an overpopulated class of slaves, coupled with an underpopulated class of rulers, ensured that the slaves never became wealthy. Manu seemed to believe that all the wealth in India was static and that money existed in a zero-sum game, whereby if someone gained wealth, it was necessarily taken from someone else, and thus if the Shudra acquired wealth, he necessarily took it from its rightful owner, the Brahmin. In those instances when Shudras were able to amass wealth, they risked riots and threats to their property and person. Even today, rioting and looting in India are frequently done by castes who feel threatened by the growth of wealth and status of castes beneath them in the hierarchy. If the possession of wealth by the Shudra is injurious to the Brahmin, the upper castes ensure that they injure the Shudra in turn.

Ashwini Deshpande is an Indian economist who has researched economic inequality in India, and her findings reveal the continued exploitative existence of caste in India today.

> In no state in India have the OBCs 'taken over' or surpassed the upper castes at the topmost end of the occupational spectrum . . . The main point that emerges from this is the continuing dominance of upper castes in prestigious, upper-rung occupations. It would be a reasonable assumption that these also would be better-paying occupations. Hence, we find no evidence of a substantial *reversal* of the traditional association between caste hierarchy and economic power.[2]

The social slavery of Shudras wasn't just in economic terms either. Upper-caste Hindus emphasized the depraved condition of Shudras by requiring them to take undignified names and to speak to Brahmins with respect, even if the Brahmin was a drunken deadbeat. An older Shudra was required to address a younger Brahmin with an honorific title and was punished if he didn't. When a Shudra is born, his mother is supposed to give the child to a Brahmin priest who calculates a name based on

his astrology, and it is always an abusive name. This practice is
continued to this day. Noted sociologist Kancha Ilaiah Shepherd,
himself a Shudra, has written about the abuse he suffered from
other students and teachers because of his surname, Ilaiah, and
his struggle with depression as a result.[3]

Spiritual Slavery: Past and Present

The social slavery of Shudras, seen by their forced servility,
poverty and self-image, coexisted with their spiritual slavery.
The spiritual slavery of Shudras has been so total that it has
robbed them of even being able to dream of and desire equality
with Brahmins. Shudras were not allowed to learn Sanskrit,
the language of Brahmins and the gods. This restriction forever
preserved the career of Brahmins against the competition of a
people that could have replaced them. By not learning Sanskrit,
Shudras were not allowed to learn mantras. Mantras are the
syllabic Sanskrit chants that make the gods dance. By chanting
a mantra, the chanter is able to secure a blessing or a curse from
the gods. The gods become little more than vending machines,
distributing anything the chanter asks for, so long as he has the
right mantra. The Brahmin secured the mantras for himself,
and by doing so, became even more powerful than the gods.
The Shudra was forced to do for the Brahmin anything he
demanded in order to receive the mantra he needed to heal
his sick wife, or bless his farm, or curse his neighbour. In fact,
the Brahmin came to be known as Bhudev, or god on earth,
because he held spiritual and religious authority, and no one
could oppose him.

Denying Sanskrit to Shudras didn't just protect Brahmins'
mantras, it also protected their scriptures. All Hindu texts were
written in Sanskrit. They claimed that the gods spoke Sanskrit,
and when the gods revealed their scriptures to mankind, they

revealed them in Sanskrit. The real reason all their scriptures were in Sanskrit is that Shudras didn't know Sanskrit, which would allow them to read and understand the scriptures for themselves, or worse, to write them. Scholars estimate that the Rig Veda existed orally for almost a thousand years before it was ever written down. This was not because of the lack of a recording medium, but because by writing it down it might fall into the wrong hands—Shudra hands—and its power would be undone. The knowledge of Sanskrit by Brahmins was key to their domination over India. For as long as Brahminism has existed in India, Shudras have lived in a state of ignorance of Hindu religion. They do not know the laws, codes or procedures. Instead of teaching Shudras about the Hindu religion and their relationship with the gods, they are taught nothing other than the need to come to them repeatedly for blessings and protection from evil spirits.

Shudras cannot be priests. They cannot administrate in temples in any way, especially India's fabulously wealthy temples. They cannot perform their own weddings and funerals. They cannot pray for a blessing if they move into a new home or get a new job. They cannot collect financial offerings for the gods, and can only give them. They have no control over their own lives. As Valmiki's Ramayana shows, they cannot perform penance, as Shambuka did, or they may be decapitated.[4]

With the authority of the Brahmin so complete over the Shudra, the Brahmin is able to force the Shudra to do anything ridiculous, and he'll have no choice but to do it. He may require the Shudra to walk a thousand kilometres just to acquire water from a place he thinks is holy, then send him to a temple another thousand kilometres away, and the Shudra will never question or doubt the Brahmin's wisdom. The Brahmin may abuse him, still the Shudra will pay him money. The Brahmin can tell the

Shudra that his birth chart or horoscope is bad, and the Shudra will sell his house to pay to fix the problem. The Brahmin can kick the Shudra, and the Shudra will press his feet.

Although the Brahminical scriptures of Hinduism give no scope for the advancement of Shudras, there are moments in history when they have been able to assert and prove themselves. Sometimes they do so within the Brahminical scheme, as was done by Dantidurga, founder of the Rashtrakuta empire. He fought so magnificently that he established himself as king, and the Brahmins performed a ritual known as *hiranyagarbha*, in which Dantidurga emerged from a golden womb reborn as a Kshatriya. However, most Shudras must rebel against the Brahminical schemes to find a place of equality within India. We will look at five such rebellions: Ashoka and Buddhism, Basavanna and the Lingayats, Guru Nanak and Sikhism, Phule and the Truthseekers, and Ambedkar and Buddhism.

Historical Waves of Spiritual Revolt against Brahminism

Ashoka and Buddhism

Chandragupta Maurya, founder of the Mauryan empire, has a disputed ancestry. According to Buddhist sources, he is a Kshatriya, but Brahminical sources consider him a Shudra.[5] Many believe he became a Jain during his lifetime and that he ended his life in Jain fashion by fasting on a hill later renamed Chandragiri in Karnataka. Scholars believe his son and successor, Bindusara, followed the Ajivika faith, which is a heterodox Indian faith opposed to Brahminism. Bindusara's son, Ashoka, was the most accomplished of the Mauryan kings, and perhaps the greatest king that ever ruled India, and his conversion to Buddhism is undisputed. He promoted Buddhist Dhamma, patronized the Buddhist Sangha, sent Buddhist missionaries, established social welfare schemes in Buddha's name, and enacted Buddhist principles like non-violence throughout his empire.

As Braj Ranjan Mani puts it:

> Ashoka's sterling contribution to Indian civilization is his magnanimous policy of *dhamma* which held together a vast and heterogeneous empire. His *dhamma*—founded on the broader principles of social responsibility, uniform laws, tolerance, and non-violence—was deeply influenced by his personal faith in Buddhism. Rock Edict 5 reports that people are increasingly abstaining from the sacrificial slaughter of living creatures, and behaving properly with their relatives and elders. The king and the commoner were cooperating, and there was something approaching what may be called public order and decency.[6]

There's no doubt this public order and decency would have been far preferable to the Shudras than the Vedic caste order that enslaved them before and after.

Whether Ashoka came from a Shudra background or not, his undermining of Brahminism and establishment of Buddhism provided Shudras with opportunities they had not had since Brahminism was introduced to India. The Brahmin general Pushyamitra Shunga betrayed and killed the final Mauryan king and established the Shunga dynasty, a far less illustrious dynasty than the one they usurped. The vehemence with which the Brahmins annihilated the Buddhists under the Shungas betrays their dread of the egalitarian and compassionate India forged by the Mauryas. Mani eloquently describes the zeal of Brahmins under Shunga rule:

> Led by Pushyamitra Shunga, the brahman commander of the last Mauryan king Brihadratha, brahmans hatched a conspiracy.

Pushyamitra beheaded his master during a military parade in 185 BC . . . the regicide . . . was the Brahmanical backlash against the egalitarian Buddhism . . . After burning scores of monasteries in and around Pataliputra he went to Sakala (Sialkot in West Punjab) and offered a reward of 100 *dinars* or gold pieces for the head of every Buddhist monk. That he unleashed a reign of terror against the Buddhist monks and adherents is corroborated by many sources including the Tibetan and Chinese records.[7]

The vehemence with which the Brahmins annihilated the Buddhists once their king, Pushyamitra Shunga, betrayed and killed the final Mauryan king proves the hatred they had towards the new-found India of Buddhist Dhamma and equality. Shudras were once again chained in Brahminism.

Basavanna and the Lingayats

Basavanna was a twelfth-century religious figure held responsible, variously, for either establishing or strengthening the Lingayat faith. Although a Brahmin, he was part of the Bhakti movement, a widespread movement with many Shudra leaders that sought alternatives to caste-based dharma by pursuing devotion to God and ignoring Vedic rituals and sacrifices long performed by Brahminical stalwarts like the Gupta emperors. Caste distinctions didn't exist in the Bhakti movement, and Basavanna learned to accept his new, humbled position as an equal with everyone else. The most dramatic symbol of this new-found equality was the distribution of the Linga. The Linga was a symbol of Shiva worship, found in many temples and houses throughout India. But Basavanna rejected temples and the idea that people could only approach God through a Brahmin mediator, so he distributed small, hand-held Lingas to every one of his followers without distinction. With a Linga in hand, any Lingayat was able to pray and communicate directly with God wherever they were at any time of day. Shudras converted to the Lingayat tradition en masse, thrilled with the freedom they found from Brahminism in the tiny Linga in their hands.

Guru Nanak and Sikhism

The Bhakti movement also contributed to the rise of Sikhism, an anti-Brahminical faith like the Lingayats founded by Guru Nanak in Punjab. Guru Nanak was a Hindu Khatri, whose origins are unknown but who had acquired a respected place in India. Guru Nanak followed the Bhakti tradition which, as we saw with Basavanna, opposed Brahminism. The significant difference between Guru Nanak and Basavanna was that the latter lived in an area mostly void of Muslims, while Guru Nanak lived in Punjab, an area with immense Islamic influence. Therefore, in addition to Bhakti, Guru Nanak was influenced by another no-caste, no-idol religion. He wrote many verses that established a new religion called Sikhism, which won over Shudra believers from both Muslim and Hindu backgrounds. It's also important to note that Guru Nanak's verses were included in the Guru Granth Sahib along with verses from Kabir, a low-caste Muslim weaver who followed the Bhakti tradition as well. The many influences combined to produce a completely new religion, Sikhism, which believed in one God, with no mediator and no idol, that was equally accessible to all Sikhs. Just like in Buddhism and Lingayatism, Shudras found freedom from caste restrictions in Sikhism.

Phule and the Truthseekers

The next movement to study is that of the Truthseekers of Mahatma Jyotiba Phule. Unlike Ashoka, Basavanna and Guru

Nanak, there is no doubt that Phule was a Satyashodhak (Truthseeker) in a Shudra family. He was educated in a Christian mission school, and he married Savitribai when he was thirteen. The two of them founded the Truthseekers Society in 1873 and published a book called *Slavery*.[8] Phule takes the myths of Hinduism and flips them so that the gods and heroes become devils and villains, and uses them to show how Brahmins captured and enslaved Indian Shudras. He presents Bali Raja—a mythical king of India in whose kingdom equality reigns—as the true and rightful king of India who will return and bring freedom for all the oppressed. He says that Jesus Christ is this Bali Raja. Members of the Truthseekers Society were required to pledge that they would promote equality of all, worship one God, and reject Brahminism as seen from the Vedas. Even today, Shudras acknowledge Phule as their leader and mahatma.

Phule's book *Slavery* was so called because it described the ways and means in which Hinduism had enslaved the Shudras. One example that was commonly employed by Christian missionaries against the Brahmins in nineteenth-century Maharashtra, and one that Phule agreed with, was that the Brahmins had their scriptures in the Vedas and the Gita, but the Shudras had none.

> The idea that Hinduism had failed its believers [that is, the Shudras] in not providing them with a consistent and intelligible religious text that would guide them in their everyday lives formed a persistent criticism. Radicals like Phule came to see in the traditional functioning of Hindu sacred texts a source of social control, the evidence of a Brahman conspiracy to defraud ordinary Hindus [Shudras].[9]

One acceptable means to escape this Brahminical order was conversion. One conversion that struck at the heart of Brahminical spiritual slavery was that of Pandita Ramabai. She was a Chitpavan

Brahmin scholar who rejected Hinduism after learning about its low view of women, and publicly converted to Christianity.

> She was attacked viciously by both orthodox and reformist brahmans. She also soon found herself in deep conflict with the colonial and racist attitude of the contemporary Anglican church. Phule defended her right to conversion. However, more than Christianity offering salvation, it represents for him an *escape* from oppressive Brahmanism.[10]

> The culmination was Phule's emphasis on Bali Raja, King Bali. This was in a sense his reply to the elite's use of Ram, Ganpati, or Kali; it was a symbol that united Maharashtrian peasants with the tales of Aryan invasion. Bali . . . was an ancient symbol for the peasant and at the same time represented a sort of golden age, represented in the Marathi saying, *ida pida javo, balica rajya yevo* (let troubles and sorrows go and the kingdom of Bali come).[11]

King Bali was the final liberator of the slaves, the king who sacrificed himself for his subjects (the Shudras) and would one day return to save them from Brahminical rule and establish his kingdom of love and justice forever. Phule wrote quite clearly about Bali Raja in *Slavery*:

> . . . one great champion of the downtrodden, the holiest of the holy, the great sage and lover of Truth, Baliraja, came into this world. He realized that the great Almighty God, our great Father and Creator, had given us the true and holy knowledge and had granted everyone an equal right to it. He fathomed the Divine Will—that this knowledge be shared by all alike. Therefore, he undertook the task of releasing his poor oppressed brethren from the bondage of slavery by

wicked, cunning and treacherous hunters like the brahmans
and strove to establish the kingdom of God on earth.[12]

In his usual provocative style, Phule compares Bali Raja to Jesus
Christ, claims that the Bhatjis had enslaved the Shudras–Ati-
Shudras and that Christian missionaries would bring the message
of Bali Raja to India and set the Shudras and Ati-Shudras free.
His utopia was that in the kingdom of Bali Raja alone, the
entirety of the spiritual slavery of all sections would be broken.[13]

Ambedkar and Buddhism

The final movement is Ambedkar and his Buddhism. Ambedkar
is the only Dalit to be examined in this essay. He considered
Kabir, Phule and Buddha to be his gurus, so there's no need to
reintroduce those influences. Ambedkar's views on caste are seen
most clearly in his undelivered speech 'Annihilation of Caste'. He
identifies Vedic Brahminism to be the root cause of the genesis
of the caste system in India, and proclaims that the annihilation
of the caste system cannot be done inside Hinduism but requires
another religion. In the speech, he announces his intention to
convert, which is why it wasn't allowed to be delivered. After
many years of searching for his new religion, Ambedkar opted to
mix Buddhism with his own teachings, creating a new strand of
Buddhism—Navayana Buddhism. He wrote *The Buddha and His
Dhamma*[14] to guide his followers, and on the day he converted,
half a million Dalits converted with him.

In all five of the movements we've examined, we can clearly
see that the freedom of OBCs from the social and spiritual
slavery of Brahminism requires religious reform even as far as
conversion. They all rejected the Vedas, temples, Hindu idols,
the caste system and Brahminical scriptures. One of the foremost
contemporary scholars of the spiritual slavery of Shudras/OBCs,

Kancha Ilaiah Shepherd, says, 'In my view, unless the battle is won in the spiritual realm as well as in the day-to-day processes, they [OBCs] cannot succeed.'[15] And again he says, 'What the Hindutva Brahminic forces are afraid of is that the Dalits have a definite agenda of their spiritual liberation (most of them are embracing either Christianity or Buddhism), and if the OBCs, too, who are the main source of their muscle power, work out a spiritual liberation agenda, Brahminism and Hinduism will collapse like a house of cards.'[16] Shepherd is saying that OBCs cannot be free until they find it in the spiritual realm as Dalits have done by converting to Christianity or Buddhism.

The Future of Shudra Spiritual Liberation

The nation is now at the crossroads. The present ruling dispensation, in the name of nationalism, has disempowered the entire Shudra community at the national and regional level. Within the Hindu spiritual and social context, they could at best become regional political rulers with strong roots in the agrarian economy. But spiritually, they are totally under the grip of Brahminism. Even politically, they could not emerge as national players as the national political domain, in Mahatma Phule's language, is under the control of Shetjis (Banias) and Bhatjis (Brahmins). Why is this so?

Mahatma Phule came from the Kumbhi-Mali community, which is considered to be outside the fold of the Other Backward Classes reservation category. Marathas, who recently fought for a place in the reservation category, got only state-level quotas, but they are not part of the central reservation list. Marathas claim that Phule belongs to their community. There is such a scope given Phule's discourses around Shudra slavery of his own time. Phule owned Chhatrapati Shivaji as his community hero. Now, Marathas own Shivaji as their community hero and celebrate his *jayanti* and *vardhanti*, or birth and death anniversaries.

Phule broadly divided the entire productive mass of India into two categories: Shudras and Ati-Shudras. He also characterized the ruling and non-productive communities into two categories: Bhatjis (Brahmins) and Shetjis (Banias). He came to a conclusion based on his assessment of contemporary Maharashtrian society that both Shudras and Ati-Shudras were in positions of semi-slavery (Shudras) and slavery (Ati-Shudras). Though Ambedkar wrote a full-length book called *Who Were the Shudras?*[17] as part of his larger nationalist canvas of writing about all the oppressed communities, Mahatma Jyotirao Phule was the first Shudra to write about Shudras as a community. He powerfully demonstrated how they were historically oppressed by Brahmin–Banias and were continuing to be oppressed in the nineteenth century all over the Indian subcontinent.

He located two main reasons for the semi-slave food-producing conditions of Shudras: (1) The Aryan varnadharma (which is now being described as Hinduism); (2) Complete lack of education among Shudras even in regional languages like Marathi. He was the first English- and Marathi-educated Shudra writer in the known history of India. Though Sri Krishna is said to have composed the Bhagavad Gita, as a Yadav, there is no historical evidence for his composition or writing as the Mahabharata as a text is known as mythology. Secondly, Mahatma Phule is the only known modern Indian writer who became aware of the system of slavery in the world. Hence, his famous book *Gulamgiri*[18] (written in Marathi) which later got translated into English as *Slavery*[19] was dedicated to American Negros, who are now known as African-Americans. In the mid-nineteenth century, Phule thought that the conditions of Indian Shudras and African-Americans were similar. He knew that the conditions of Ati-Shudras (in Bengal, Untouchables are still known as Namashudras) were worse because they were Untouchable slaves for all above them.

Phule realized that Shudras, like African-Americans, were 'touchables' for all Sanatan dharmic Shetjis and Bhatjis, but the way they were exploited and oppressed was exactly like the treatment meted out by white slave masters in America. Hence, Phule dedicated *Gulamgiri* to African-Americans. He noted in his dedication: 'In an earnest desire that my countrymen may take their (African-American) example as their guide in the emancipation of their Sudra Brethren from the trammels of Brahmin thralldom.'[20] What is the Brahmin thralldom that Phule was talking about in 1873? Phule wrote this just two years after the British rulers made a law declaring many Shudra communities as criminal tribes. The Criminal Tribes Act was passed in 1871. No Brahmin–Bania sect, though there are sects and *gotras* among them, was part of the criminal tribal group. The British government acted on the advice of Brahmin pandits to determine which occupational groups were criminal, and many Shudras were deemed such. Shudras were not seen as part of the Sanatan (Hindu) religion at that time.

In such times, Phule saw Bali Raja (the Balichakravarthy of the Kerala region) as the Shudra liberator. Unlike the Brahmin tradition that the RSS–BJP call *parampara,* Phule did not see Brahminic gods/goddesses as liberators of Shudra/Dalit slaves and semi-slaves. Phule's Bali Raja, who was crushed by Vamana, was a Shudra saviour as he was a martyr. Like Jesus, he was killed for seeking spiritual and social equality for Shudras. He himself was a Shudra and stood for their spiritual, social and political equality.

Post independence, as a result of Ambedkar's Constitution and Pandit Jawaharlal Nehru's secular early administration for sixteen years, the political liberation of Shudras has been achieved. They have the right to vote and the right to contest elections and hence could emerge as strong regional rulers. However, while Chaudhary Charan Singh and Deve Gowda (two Shudras who established their own parties and ruled their states as chief ministers) became prime ministers for a short time, they could not emerge as long-standing national leaders.

Phule's assessment was that without the spiritual liberation of Shudras, they could not acquire national stature. National political parties like the Congress and the BJP could never be headed by a Shudra with authority, as all other structures would not support such a person. It's the same as Shudras being Hindus without Shudra priests controlling the temple system and Hindu spiritual ideology. Though Narendra Modi has an OBC certificate, his caste community was never part of a Shudra agrarian or artisanal background. Only as late as 1994 did the Social Welfare Department of the Gujarat government pass a notification that included thirty-six castes as OBCs, including that of the Modh Ghanchi community to which Modi belongs.[21]

Phule himself wanted to establish a Sarvajanic Satyadharma religion for Shudras and Ati-Shudras, centralizing the philosophy of Bali Raja. But he died before he could do that. I am a Maharashtra Christian and was a grassroots worker from the days of the Shetkari Sanghatana of Sharad Joshi. I know how there are many similarities between Mahabali and Jesus, who wanted to bring the kingdom of god on to earth with spiritual, social and economic equality for all communities, individuals and groups.[22]

Supporters of the present regime want to portray any attempt of Shudra, Dalit and Adivasi communities or individuals to liberate themselves from spiritual slavery as conversion to Christianity. They have launched a Ghar Vapsi programme as well. The Satyashodhak movement started by Phule that I am a part of does not believe in conversion. It works for spreading the message of truth and peace that Bali Raja left behind. If the Asura king Mahabaliraja wanted to kill Vamana, he could have done so. But he chose to fulfil his promise, not kill. The Shudras of India belong to his dynasty. They produce food and feed those who hate them too. Shetjis and Bhatjis, according to Phule, hated Shudras and Ati-Shudras, but the latter never refused to part with foodgrains, vegetables, milk, ghee and so on that they produced with their hard labour. Sometimes they starved and fed the non-producers with the higher humanitarian values that Bali Raja espoused. This is the Shudra truth and we Truthseekers never believe in myths. Truthseekers, following the philosophy and teachings of Jyotiba Phule, believe in science and faith as two sides of God's creation. God for us is a Truthkeeper, but not a killer as in Hindu mythologies. A Satyashodhak believes in the creator and in nature as his 'book' of Truth. All other religious books have a limitation of words, cultures and translations, whereas nature is unlimited and undefiled. Mahatma Jyotirao Phule, as a Satyashodhak, wrote extensively about the worship of God in his poems. Satyashodhaks believe that science can't exist without faith because faith is the main source through which mankind becomes creative, while science provides the reason for our dreams and beliefs.

Identity politics has reached a peak in India during the BJP regime. Prime Minister Narendra Modi's own self-identification as an OBC gave a new boost to this. However, Shudras, even though a majority in the country, did not use Phule's methodology to construct a unified identity for themselves at the national level. Their identity remains regional with their specific regional caste names. If they look back to their roots and reinvent themselves, leaving the reservation issue aside, they could become a powerful social mass.

Many Shudras/Dalits, not only in Kerala, believe that Bali Raja comes back to deliver the Shudras, Ati-Shudras and Adivasis from all forms of slavery. Despite that, the Shudra heritage of Balirajya has not been fully explored so far in academic circles.

In future, more serious studies need to be devoted to Bali Raja and his kingdom. Bali Raja is seen by Shudras in the same way that Jews view the Messiah. The concept of Balirajya is like that of the kingdom of god where equality of all forms for all people of God's creation is guaranteed. In Balirajya, there will be no caste, creed, race and gender inequality. All forms of violence against all human beings by the state or by one human being against another would also be abolished.

Shudras and Democratic India

Kancha Ilaiah Shepherd

The social category 'Shudra' is a historical one. If the Rig Veda originated in around 1500 BC, the Shudra category is at least as old as that. It was as per the Rig Veda that Indian society was said to have been divided into four varnas: Shudra, Vaishya, Kshatriya and Brahmin. Of these, Shudras were considered the lowest.[1] In other words, they served as slaves for the other three varna/castes in ancient and medieval times. This category of people who were classified as the fourth varna continues to exist with the same pan-Indian name and the same status. Even in the twenty-first century, they are stuck in the same position as mentioned in the Rig Veda, particularly in the spiritual and cultural domains. In the political domain and in terms of property ownership, Shudras have advanced and acquired rights. Historically, they were not supposed to rule a state unless Brahmin priests gave them Kshatriya status. However, they can become rulers in democratic India without formally acquiring Kshatriya status. The most critical intervention in classical caste relationships has been made by constitutional democracy.

Shudras and Dalits in contemporary India perform production, artisanal and labour work. Meanwhile, those who belong to the other three varnas, even today, live without soiling their hands. The agrarian revolution that occurred in the pre-Rig Vedic or pre-Aryan period can be seen as a Shudra heritage.[2] Harappans, who practised agriculture, established the village economy and built cities like Harappa, Mohenjo-Daro, Dholavira and so on. After the destruction or collapse of the civilization, the people belonging to it were designated as Shudras. In the subsequently established pastoral economy, they were gradually turned into slaves. The character of the slavish mentality that they have internalized can be seen even today. Unless Shudras overcome their spiritual and social slavish mentality and fight for equality in all spheres of life, the caste system will never be abolished. Till then, Brahminism's hegemony over Shudras/OBCs and Dalits will not be dismantled. Till then, Ambedkar's dream of abolishing the caste system—the very cause of untouchability—will never be achieved. Until the system of castes and varnas is abolished, India as a nation will not be able to reach the socio-economic levels of China, Europe or the US. The issue, therefore, is centrally related to the principle of dignity of labour, of all Indian human hands working in all fields of life.

Shudras treat the anti-production, non-agrarian lifestyle of Brahmins, Kshatriyas and Vaishyas as God-given. Any challenge to this unproductive yet superior status is treated as blasphemous and fearsome. So far, Shudras have no understanding of the idea of God, religion and human equality in this life or the life hereafter. They have been living as beasts of burden without experiencing equality in temples or society, and without the notion of heavenly attainment after death. Hence, they fear and respect their oppressors, who do not produce food resources, but only practise consumption, sitting above them.

If this understanding does not change, India will not change. If Shudras do not change, Dalit lives will not change either. Hence, a serious study of Shudra history is essential to move in the direction of abolition or annihilation of the caste system and human untouchability in India.

Even in the twenty-first century, the categories Vaishya, Kshatriya and Brahmin remain as they were in Rig Vedic times—hegemonic and anti-Shudra. Meanwhile, the Shudras of Vedic times are now divided into several sub-castes. In this essay, we will examine how the RSS and the BJP are handling them, and the role of constitutional democracy in shaping them.

Vedic society was pastoral. When the agrarian economy of the Harappan civilization disappeared, a mere cattle economy took its place in the Rig Vedic period. It needs common sense to realize that without an advanced cattle and agrarian economy, Harappans could not have built such sprawling cities. In the Vedic period, there was no urban civilization. It was a pastoral economy coupled with the division of society into graded varnas.

Shudras were the main cattle-grazers, and Vaishyas, it appears, were the supervisors. Perhaps some kind of fieldwork culture was present amongst the latter at that time. But they too do not participate in agrarian production work any more. Brahmins and Kshatriyas, even then, stayed totally away from production and agrarian and cattle-rearing work. However, these three castes that are known as Dwija (twice-born) castes share many common rights in the Hindu religion. Shudras do not have basic rights in Hindu society, though they are said to belong to the same religion. In other words, they do not have spiritual citizenship and a place in its philosophical discourse.

There are no studies to tell us the condition of Shudras at different phases of history. Our concern in this essay, however, is their contemporary situation. More specifically, what the

Hindutva ideology has done so far and will probably do to them in future.

There have been some changes in the social categorization of Shudras today compared to Rig Vedic and medieval times. They were divided into various social categories based on their occupation in the agrarian sector. They have been handling tasks from tilling land to cattle-rearing and anything in between for thousands of years. They were classified into artisanal communities such as weavers, carpenters, smiths, potters, tappers, fisherfolk, fruit gatherers, brick-makers, barbers, washermen and so on. Below Shudras, the social category of Dalits was formed almost in every village. They were deemed untouchable for all caste communities and did labour like leather work, cleaning of the village and so on.

A section of Shudras, over time, emerged as village-level landowners and feudal estate owners along with Kshatriyas, Brahmins and some Muslims. Banias were confined to business both in rural and urban areas. By 1947, Shudras easily formed the largest constituency, accounting for about 52 per cent of the population, as per the 1931 Census, while Dalits formed 18 per cent. Perhaps Vaishyas, Kshatriyas and Brahmins together might have constituted about 7 per cent of the total population. The remaining were Muslims, Christians, Sikhs and Adivasis. Even today, the main agrarian economy is run by Shudras, with the support of Dalits.[3]

Today, in some states, top Shudra communities like Kammas, Reddys, Marathas, Jats, Yadavs, Kurmis, Lingayats, etc., have their own regional political parties. These include the Telugu Desam Party (TDP), YSR Congress, Telangana Rashtra Samithi (TRS), Janata Dal (Secular), SP, Dravida Munnetra Kazhagam (DMK), All-India Anna Dravida Munnetra Kazhagam (AIADMK), RJD, Nationalist Congress Party (NCP) and so on. Over time, these regional parties weakened the hold of national parties, especially the Congress. This slowly led to the rise of the BJP as an alternative national party in the 1990s.

During Jawaharlal Nehru's time, the Shudra landed gentry sided with the Congress. Capitalist accumulation was weak till the 1970s, so the feudal Shudras felt that they were the real power centres in villages. Until 1990, the economy was mainly agrarian. Shudra landlords dominated the economy from the village to the district level. Only in some pockets did Brahmin and Muslim landlords have control. The main contradiction till the 1990s in terms of class was between tenants, agrarian labour and landlords who, in many states, were upper-caste Shudras.

However, the change, slowly but surely, began from the early 1970s onward. Slowly, the Indian industrial economy, both private and government, began to overtake the agrarian economy. In the 1971 elections, Indira Gandhi directly reached out to the village electorate, undercutting the rural control of Shudra landlords. She found great support among the Dalits. The landlords showed their power by attacking and burning Dalit localities across India, in places like Belchi in Bihar and Karamchedu in Andhra Pradesh. Under the leadership of the feudal Shudra landlord Neelam Sanjiva Reddy, the landed gentry tried to weaken Indira Gandhi. The Shudra feudal syndicate made Reddy contest for the post of president of India, but Indira Gandhi, with the support of the growing industrial class, defeated these efforts by propping up an independent Brahmin candidate, V.V. Giri, who eventually won.

In this process, Indira Gandhi constituted a coalition of non-Shudra upper castes (Brahmins and a section of Bania industrialists), Dalits, Adivasis, Muslims and other minorities. Added to this, she had broad-based women support as she was perceived as a strong woman leader, often likened to Goddess Durga or Kali in villages. Shudra landlords began to be sidelined by the Congress. Hence, a large section of Shudras shifted to the

newly formed Janata Party under the leadership of Jayaprakash
Narayan and subsequently, after the 1977 victory, saw to it that
the Mandal Commission was constituted under the leadership of
a Shudra Yadav leader, B.P. Mandal.

During this period, the Jana Sangh, which had merged with
the Janata Party to make it the single largest party, expanded its
relations with Shudras. There was no OBC category in India
at that time. Having supported the constitution of the Mandal
Commission, though with the pressure of young OBC leaders
like Sharad Yadav, Mulayam Singh and Lalu Prasad Yadav, the
Jana Sangh, after breaking with the Janata Party, changed its
name to Bharatiya Janata Party and used every opportunity to
project itself as pro-Shudra. The anti-Muslim and anti-Dalit
feudal networks within the Shudras helped the BJP strengthen
the Hindu ideological bondage of Shudras during that time.
Dominated by Brahmin–Banias, the party now took a more
progressive posture than the Congress by slowly Hinduizing the
Shudra/OBC masses up to the village level. After the V.P. Singh
government implemented OBC reservation, both the Congress
and the BJP played the subtle trick of flip-flopping between
opposing and supporting the policy, but the BJP cleverly used the
Babri Masjid–Ram Temple issue to further Hinduize Shudras/
OBCs. However, the emergence of pro-feudal Shudra regional
parties not only weakened the Congress but also checkmated
the rise of the BJP till 1999.

Even after the Congress returned to power in 1980, it did
not include Shudras in its electoral coalition, and continued to
be a combine of non-Shudra upper castes, minorities, Dalits
and Adivasis. Both Indira Gandhi and Rajiv Gandhi refused
to implement the Mandal Commission's recommendations.
Under the V.P. Singh regime, Shudras got an upper hand and
got the Mandal Commission report implemented. Meanwhile,
the Shudra landed gentry also formed several regional parties in

the north. At this juncture, the RSS–BJP mobilized uneducated lower Shudra youth around the Ram Janmabhoomi issue, and the demolition of the Babri Masjid gave the required impetus to their aggressive campaign. The 'Jai Sri Ram' slogan and the tying of a saffron thread around the wrists of Shudras/OBCs, giving them a Hindu identity, were part of that package. They portrayed the Congress–Muslim relationship as appeasement targeted against Shudras/OBC interests. By 1999, things had shifted in their favour, and in 2014, the trend became more vibrant, as witnessed by the BJP's meteoric rise to power.

After the nationalization of banks in 1969, a change began to take place in the market economy of India. However, the parallel growth of the private sector with the support of the banking system meant that Indian capital started accumulating in the hands of a few Indian industrialists and businessmen. They subsequently started backing the Congress in electoral politics. The Indian Banias saw the Congress as the party of Mahatma Gandhi, who came from their community. Indira Gandhi's name linked her to Mahatma Gandhi as an added factor. Even the big industrial Banias supported the Congress more than the Jana Sangh with that sentiment. The Congress started financing elections with the support of newly accumulating Bania capital, neglecting the weakening Shudra landlords. The land reform programme weakened them further. At the same time, the Brahmin–Bania intellectual class, both educated abroad and in Indian universities, became more Congress-friendly, and even the left intellectuals became more pro-Congress.

A notable fact is that among these intellectuals, there were hardly any Shudras. As a result, by the beginning of the twenty-first century, the Shudra elite were in regional politics, whether as leaders of their own regional parties or with the Congress or the BJP. Not a single leader emerged with the required quality of English education and modern sophistication. Thus, the Congress, the BJP and even the communist parties were populated, at the central level, by Brahmin–Bania leadership. Though the communist parties have had Shudra leaders like Puchalapalli Sundarayya and Chandra Rajeswara Rao, they were never caste conscious. They also did not train and promote Shudra/OBC young leaders who could grapple with the problems of caste and class and lead a national campaign. Hence, the communist parties came under the grip of Brahminic forces. As the BJP began to grow, they began to weaken.

Quite tragically, Shudra/OBC communities failed to produce a sophisticated English-educated intellectual class that could enter the central universities, English media and the corridors of sophisticated writing. A small section of Shudras was confined to agrarian riches, which are of middle-class nature, with local power lying in its control of a state's regional language. The remaining were either lower middle class agrarian or urban labour. Even the Shudra/OBC regional rich did not aspire for a national power base. The real power base lay with the bureaucratic and intellectual class and, in those spheres too, Shudras/OBCs were unable to gain a foothold.

Spiritual intellectuals play a critical role in developing such a national-level intellectual force. Historically, there is no such spiritual intellectual force among Shudras. Amongst Brahmin and Bania castes, the spiritual intellectual force generated a national discourse around spiritual texts. A common thread of cultural codes was constructed across the country within Brahmin–Bania caste communities, even more than amongst Kshatriyas, due to the culture of reading Brahminic texts like the Ramayana, Mahabharata and particularly the Bhagavad Gita. They promoted the Gita, but not Sri Krishna, as he was a Shudra. Instead, they promoted Rama, a Kshatriya who was always under the control of a Brahmin guru.

Shudras did not even have a strategy like the Brahminic RSS to promote Krishna. Crucial textual knowledge was not allowed to spread among them. Nor did they understand the importance of spiritual textual engagement and philosophical growth as they were historically confined to tilling land and producing food and attaining satisfaction through these activities. They never understood that their heads were under the control of Brahmin priests, and their purse under the control of Bania business forces. Until India became a fully grown capitalist country after the liberalization of 1991, they naively thought they were the rulers of India. Now, Shudras are nowhere and there is no brain and money power among them to fight the all-round authority of Brahmin–Banias. In spiritual, social, business and political fields, Brahmin–Bania brain power controls the nerve centres of the nation.

Even in Europe and the Middle Eastern countries, social and political thinkers and political leaders emerged from families and communities that had long engaged with Biblical and Quranic spiritual intellectual discourse. Here, such spiritual intellectual discourse was confined to one community, Brahmins, and later extended to Banias and Kshatriyas. Yogi Adityanath, a Kshatriya, came into political leadership from spiritual leadership. Mahatma Gandhi, Ram Manohar Lohia and Narendra Modi came from a Bania background with familial engagement and a spiritual knowledge of Hinduism, and the childhood text-reading culture of the community. All Brahmin leaders have that spiritual and political capital. Shudras/OBCs do not have these resources even now.

Tamil and Bengali Brahmins, for example, entered national power structures in a systematic way, both through the political and bureaucratic power mechanism. They got into English media quite significantly, and have a strong sense of nationhood. Shudras/OBCs have no such sense as they possess only a very strong sense of region. This localism of Shudras/OBCs gave enormous scope to Brahmin–Bania communities to handle everything on a national scale—wealth and power.

Meanwhile, because of the reservation system, a small section of Dalits and reserved-category Shudras (OBCs) and English-educated Muslims also became somewhat visible in Delhi. Particularly after the BJP came to power by overthrowing the regional parties, the Shudra upper layer started feeling the pinch. The castes which ruled the states found themselves deprived of any share in bureaucratic, intellectual and political power at the national level, and started demanding to be included in the reservation system. Marathas, Patels, Jats and Gujjars managed some reservation space within their states because of their organized fight. The BJP government, just before the 2019 elections, enacted a law through the Constitution (103rd Amendment) Act, 2019, granting 10 per cent reservation in jobs and education for the economically weak among Dwijas, Shudra castes and minorities that were so far deprived of any reservation benefits. This step made the lower middle class and poor amongst the Shudra and non-Shudra upper castes vote for the BJP in the 2019 elections. The Hinduized Shudras also voted for the BJP.

However, historically, the Congress's loss of power and their inability to produce tall national leaders and intellectuals among the Shudras led them to frustration. The Shudra upper layer like Jats, Yadavs, Kammas, Reddys, Marathas, Lingayats and Vokkaligas, Patels and so on started regional parties, leaving the entire national political and economic space to Brahmins and Banias. The Congress slowly started concentrating on the Muslim minority, Brahmin–Banias and Dalits at the village level and national level. As a result, its village-level membership shrunk sharply. The regional parties started coming to power with a hope of forming a Shudra regional party coalition at the Centre till 1999. They played a key role in coalition governments till 2004. But gradually, the country returned to national parties. The BJP slowly gained the upper hand by weakening the regional parties and also the Congress.

From the 1970s to the mid-1990s, the BJP worked its way up. It started Hinduizing Shudras and gradually taking a section of them into its fold. During the same period, the RSS–BJP also worked among Adivasis to bring them under the Hindu fold by Brahminizing their native deities. In south India, more Dalits became Christians, and in north India, particularly in Maharashtra, educated Dalit sections became Buddhists, a path Ambedkar had shown them in 1956. Kanshiram's BSP gave Dalits their political identity in the north and state power in Uttar Pradesh for some time. This weakened the Congress further in the north.

The RSS–BJP were reluctant to have Untouchables move into new religions like Buddhism and Christianity and start their own political parties. Within their fold, they started a Dalit Morcha, and to show their inclusiveness, made Bangaru Laxman, a Dalit, the president of the party (2000–01), though his political life came to an end with a corruption trap, jail and unsung death. Since the Congress had no religious agenda, it kept Dalits in good spirits, except in a few north Indian states. It made Damodaram Sanjivayya the president of the party in the 1960s, and the first Dalit chief minister of Andhra Pradesh (1960–62). From the Congress fold, K.R. Narayanan became the first Dalit president of India, and from the RSS–BJP fold, Ram Nath Kovind the second Dalit president.

However, Sangh Parivar forces put pressure on Congress-ruled states to legislate anti-conversion laws. The Congress had no non-party mechanism to mobilize social forces against the BJP. The Brahminic forces within the Congress, by and large, sided with the RSS–BJP agenda on the issues of religion, reservation and restoring the classical varna-based social order. The Congress never believed in organizing Shudras/OBCs as historically marginalized people. It was using caste as an election tool. Later, the BJP started using the same technique in a different way, with the claim of establishing a Hindu Rashtra as its ultimate goal. Unless Shudras/OBCs get spiritual power and emerge as a spiritual philosophical force, taking over every role, including Hindu priesthood, they will slip to the classical Hindu varna-based position. Politics in India will become more spiritualized, and Brahmins, Banias and Kshatriyas will continue to control the system in modernist–capitalist authoritarian Hindu mode. Shudras/OBCs will remain second-grade citizenry. There is no other path. In a system of spiritual untouchability and hierarchy, the entire varnadharmic system will come back. Already, the backward mobility in the socio-spiritual relations of Shudras have been prevalent ever since the BJP came to power in 1999. From 2014 onwards, that backward movement's pace has increased.

If the RSS–BJP defederalize the present federal nation state, power will be concentrated in the hands of Brahmin–Banias and Kshatriyas. The Hindu social system, even before the BJP came to power, did not get out of the varnadharma sentiment. The largest community—Shudras—did not dare to break that negative sentiment of varnadharma-based spiritual nationalism. Without the required philosophical energy and assertion of spiritual authority, they cannot become equal to Brahmins, Banias and Kshatriyas. They will have to take that spiritual power within Hinduism into their hands, or they must move out of the fold of Hinduism and acquire that strength elsewhere.

Historically, once Shudras became the regional power and started opposing the Congress, they came to power in many states, and as a result, the Congress further weakened. During the P.V. Narasimha Rao regime, the Congress was more Brahminized, and after the BJP came to power with Atal Bihari

Vajpayee as the prime minister, Brahminism with a Hindu nationalist cultural agenda got stronger. Shudras, even with their regional rule, played only a secondary role without producing even a single pan-Indian national leader who could address all communities and rally voters from the Delhi base. Shudras as a pan-Indian category never tried to create an identity for themselves. Brahmins, Banias, Khatris and Kshatriyas always retained their identity and remained connected at an all-India level. Shudras were divided into hundreds of castes and became region-specific, and hence never developed a national identity of their own. Banias as a community have historical business roots, and a section of them transformed into modern capitalists. With their pan-Indian community name and culture and business networks, they became a powerful organized force across the country. Mahatma Gandhi and Ram Manohar Lohia laid a political and philosophical foundation for their power and legitimacy. In the post-Mandal sociopolitical environment, they preferred the BJP for national rule, and now Narendra Modi and Amit Shah have become their political representatives.

The ten-year rule of the Manmohan Singh regime provided the RSS–BJP the scope to convince the Shudras/OBC masses that non-Hindu minorities—Manmohan Singh from a Sikh background and Sonia Gandhi from a Christian background—were ruling over Hindus. The RSS–BJP attack on Sonia Gandhi as an Italian *beti*, leaving out her Indian *bahuness*, is well known. By the 2014 general elections, a favourable atmosphere for Hindutva nationalists to sweep the polls had been systematically created. Apart from corruption issues, they harped on the fact that the then Congress president, Sonia Gandhi, was a Christian with an Italian family background, Prime Minister Manmohan Singh a Sikh with a Khatri community background, and Mohammad Hamid Ansari a Muslim vice president. Neither Singh nor Ansari were vote-pullers from their communities.

None of the three, Gandhi, Singh or Ansari, were counter-campaigners and vote mobilizers as Modi proved to be. The first woman president, for one term, was Pratibha Patil while Pranab Mukherjee was president for another term. Nobody looked at Patil's presence in Rashtrapati Bhavan as that of a Shudra woman. They deliberately played down the social background of India's first woman president. On the other hand, Pranab Mukherjee, a Bengali Brahmin, was owned by both the Congress and the BJP and was given the Bharat Ratna by the Modi government. Quite surprisingly, the Congress, while in power, did not appoint vocal Mandal supporters as vice chancellors of central universities. Thus, it gave enough scope to the RSS–BJP to mobilize OBCs across the country against it by the 2014 elections.

Neither the Congress nor Shudra regional parties produced sophisticated intellectuals who could negate RSS–BJP propaganda by opposing Brahminic ideology and Bania control of the economy. Within the Congress, many Brahminic forces existed. English-educated Congress intellectuals have been hooked to the secularism propaganda which is not found persuasive by Shudra/OBC communities. They thought that the BJP–RSS was giving them a pan-Indian identity by describing them as Hindu. This gradually pushed forward their Hinduization process, of course, without them getting the essential spiritual powers. Conferring a Hindu identity on Shudras was necessary for the RSS–BJP, because Muslims have an international identity, and Christians an even larger one. For Shudras/OBCs who were literate and educated, a national-level religious identity became a modernist necessity. However, they hardly understood the design of the Brahmin–Bania combine.

Between the Ram Janmabhoomi movement in 1992 and 1999, the year in which the BJP came to power in Delhi, the Sangh Parivar network spread Hindu symbols in almost every village. The sight of educated young men tying saffron threads to their wrists spread all over India. This activity did not leave out that part of the population which spoke only regional languages, particularly Shudras/OBCs. They were desecularized on a day-to-day basis by being taken to Hindu pilgrimages and political programmes. This process proved adequate to bring the BJP to power at an all-India level, which happened in 1999 and 2014. For Shudras/OBCs who were living without an identity, a higher level of spiritual consciousness was required, and in the absence of such consciousness, their thirst for identity was harvested by the RSS–BJP. The Congress and left parties kept harping on the principle of secularism, which did not appeal to Shudras/OBCs.

The regional parties depended on Brahmin–Bania intellectuals to defend them in national-level ideological discourse; hence, many such parties sent them to the Rajya Sabha. Satish Mishra of the BSP, Pavan Varma of the JD(U) and Gaurav Bhatia of the SP are good examples. Under Mishra's intellectual guidance, Mayawati lost her independent thinking and leadership capacity. Shudras/OBCs/Dalits/Adivasis have not yet developed a confident ruling class from their own fold. The Congress helped Muslims and Dalits train some leaders to run the administration in a modern democracy, but it did not have any scope for OBCs. When Narendra Modi declared himself an OBC prime ministerial candidate in 2014, after twelve years of chief ministerial experience in Gujarat, OBCs across the nation, more so in north India, identified with him as he was seen as 'our man'. Caste engenders sentiment and ownership. The RSS–BJP did a lot of ground-level campaigning about his OBC background without mentioning that his community has a Bania sub-caste character, not that of a Shudra agrarian OBC. Brahmins and Banias have interconnectivity in whichever party they work with. OBCs also developed some kind of pan-Indian identity of neglect, and hence immediately identified with Modi. Congress intellectuals remained an alienated intellectual force as they mostly hailed from Dwija communities. They never understood the social psychology of Shudras. There is no cultural connectivity between the OBC masses and Brahminic intellectuals. The expressions of Mani Shankar Aiyar, Shashi Tharoor (though he is Shudra, he always behaves as if he does not know what caste is), Manish Tewari and Janardan Dwivedi have definitely alienated Shudras/OBCs and driven them to support Modi.

The higher Shudra regional rulers served their own caste interests and never organized the whole Shudra mass into social cohesion. They developed antipathy against each other. This antagonism was used by the BJP in the 2014 and 2019 elections. The neglect of the Congress and communist intellectuals in studying caste identity and aspirations, and the organizational and ideological weakness created by this was used by the RSS–BJP to its full advantage.

Quite ironically, the upper-caste Shudras first accepted Gandhian Hinduism, though Gandhi said the varna social order should not be disturbed. That means Shudras could not claim equal spiritual rights under the Hindu religion. When equal spiritual rights are denied in a religion, particularly when it is organized as a national religion with centralized organizations like the RSS–BJP and the Vishwa Hindu Parishad (VHP), unequal Shudras cannot even get national-level economic power. They cannot enter national-level business. They cannot run national political parties, because religious organizational structure plays a key role in projecting national leadership. When Shudras do not have priesthood rights in Hinduism, they do not have networks that build leadership. To overcome this problem of religious acceptance, Rahul Gandhi declared himself a Brahmin. Once he did that, OBCs supported Modi with more vigour, finding affinity towards their caste identity.

The Modi kind of identity politics played a critical role, but that did not mean Shudras/OBCs became aware of their spiritual rights. Though Modi comes from Gujarati Bania roots, he has been successfully projected as an OBC leader. So, how much he furthers OBC interests is a critical thing in Indian history. Shudra regional leaders like Chaudhary Charan Singh and H.D. Deve Gowda became prime ministers, but the state power did not allow any leader to push spiritual and social reform, nor were they conscious about it. They were also not leaders who came to power on their own strength. Perhaps they were the weakest prime ministers of India.

Shudras/OBCs did not become conscious of the fact that they could not become priests in Hindu temples. They had no right to interpret Hindu spiritual books. Yet, they were willing to be led by either Brahmin or Bania leadership. In every village and town, Shudras were being guided by Brahmin priests. That very guidance slowly extended to politics.[4] Thus, the Brahmin priestly grip on Shudras/OBCs in the spiritual domain was systematically deployed in the political domain by the RSS–BJP.

After Mahatma Gandhi emerged as a political spiritual leader, Shudras came under the spell of Bania leadership as well. It was in this atmosphere that Ram Manohar Lohia emerged as a socialist leader in Bihar and Uttar Pradesh. His influence extended to several states in north India and some pockets of south India. Not a single leader similar to the stature of Gandhi or Lohia emerged from amongst Shudras. From amongst Brahmins, Jawaharlal Nehru emerged as the most popular leader and he became the first prime minister. But gradually, the RSS–BJP also projected Atal Bihari Vajpayee as a national leader. Vajpayee's image is being projected further after his death as he was the first RSS–BJP prime minister, that too with a Brahmin lineage, as Nehru was for the Congress. Currently, Modi, as the second RSS–BJP prime minister and mass leader, is being successfully projected as the tallest national leader by the BJP–RSS. The Shudra landlord class could not produce a single leader of that stature. Without the approval of the Hindu spiritual system, such standing could not be accorded to any Shudra leader.

By forming regional parties, Shudras tried to get away from Brahmin–Bania control in terms of politics, but in terms of the spiritual system, even at the regional level, they were guided by Brahmin priests. The RSS–BJP used this priestly power to take a lot of people into their fold. The VHP brought temple priests into BJP control and created a strong anti-Congress network amongst them. Thus, the temple system was completely politicized by the RSS–BJP by the mid-1990s. They nurtured strong anti-Muslim feelings. These campaigns attracted numerous Shudras towards the BJP–RSS. Though they did not have equal spiritual rights, including the right to priesthood, which is critical in a religious system even to attain moksha, they were willing to be with the RSS–BJP. Despite being told by priests that they were just Shudras because of their *poorva janma phala* (sins in an earlier life) and that they could not attain liberation in the next life, Shudras still went with them. If they do not suspect the intention of caste-centred priestly forces, they can never be liberated. Their complete integration into the religion is only possible with the transformation of Hinduism into a spiritual democratic system. That seems to be an unrealizable dream for now.

The RSS is a Hindu organization established by the Chitpavan Brahmins of Maharashtra, and shaped under their philosophical guidance. This process continues even to this day. It presents an image of Muslims and Christians as others. According to the RSS, Hinduism includes all castes, but they have no agenda for institutionalizing the equality of all castes. Actually, it was more disturbed with the dislocation of the varnadharma order than the problem of Muslims and Christians.

Bania capitalism fulfilled the RSS dream of coming to power more than the earlier form of feudalism, because under feudal relations, Shudras had village-level power through which Brahmins were kept under their control, at least in social and political spheres. That was an era where Brahmins were not anglicized. But now, Brahmins are urbanized and anglicized while Shudras remained within agrarian rural settings. Even the former Shudra feudal forces did not acquire English-medium education to match the Brahmin–Bania intellectual class.

In the feudal era, Bania *shahukars* in the village were under Shudra control. After Brahmin–Banias got English education and organized themselves in spheres such as politics, bureaucracy, universities, media and the software industry, they increased their control on all Shudra/OBC social forces. Banias got a complete grip over national capital. They established a nexus between a well-connected market economy, from remote villages to cities like Mumbai. The control of Narendra Modi and Mohan Bhagwat after the 1999 and 2014 elections on national capital, social and political forces became possible in this background. Their gain in the system is the loss of Shudras/OBCs. In this entire process, spiritual politics played a critical role. If only the RSS–BJP did not claim Hindu heritage, they would not have achieved this grip over Shudra/OBC forces. During the ten years of the Sonia Gandhi–Manmohan Singh regime, the contradiction between minorities and Shudras/OBCs increased. That was fully taken advantage of by the RSS–BJP.

But Shudras/OBCs may suffer their spiritual and social inequality for a long time yet. This may prolong their absence in the Delhi-level national leadership. Not only that, even their right to religious and spiritual moksha would not be realized. If a community does not have the right to priesthood, how does that community have the right to moksha? Not that every individual in a religion becomes a priest or wishes to become one, but once you believe in religion and religious destiny, the right to priesthood becomes critical. Shudra leaders like Venkaiah Naidu played a critical role in drawing Shudra leaders and cadres into the Hindutva fold. But even he never realized the importance of equal spiritual rights in his own life.

Hindutva forces draw a link between Hinduism and nationalism. Actually, God and religion are universal. The nation state can have many religions or one religion, or else it can have a large number of people who do not believe in any religion or faith. However, the critical role of religious discourse and emotions in the Indian electoral system is well established. When that religious power is combined with control on the monopoly capital of a nation, capturing political power becomes easy. Weakened feudalism cannot stop those in control from centralizing everything. In that situation, the state authority and religious authority operate on a similar centralized model. Indian Brahmin–Bania forces are operating with this formula now. It will take a long time to break that control.

Since the Congress emphasized on secularism to keep the support of Muslims, it alienated several Shudras because the latter did not agree with the secularism discourse. Thus, what remained was mainly Brahmin intellectual discourse from the Congress and communist platforms—which have generally come to be known as containing left-liberal intellectuals. But they were mainly a Western and Indian university-educated lot. The Shudra class, which failed to produce a highly educated English-speaking intellectual class, went by the Hindi/regional-language discourse concocted by the RSS–BJP. They were more comfortable with the BJP, which was talking about religious nationalism, mainly in non-English languages. But at the same time, the RSS–BJP also had a huge English-educated Brahmin–Bania intellectual force which subscribed to the Hindutva ideology in the background. Shudra/OBC regional parties do not have a matching intellectual force ready now. If they do not realize it, it will not emerge in the near future.

Shudras/OBCs had yet another problem in hand. In central and regional universities, left-liberal intellectuals were not enthusiastic about implementing OBC reservation. Though they were by and large bilingual, they were mostly English-educated. Speaking good English has been part of their meritocracy. This academic-cum-intellectual force treated Shudra, Dalit and Adivasis, who hardly had any English-medium education, as unworthy. At the same time, they never talked about English becoming the language of teaching in all government rural schools. Having realized this alienation of Shudras from left-liberalism, the RSS–BJP started supporting OBC reservation, which they were opposed to in the beginning. Gradually, this led to the promotion of Narendra Modi, whose community managed to include itself in the OBC list despite being from a business-caste background—Modh Ghanchi.[5] This was a trump card played by the RSS–BJP in the 2014 elections. Till the Congress faced a crushing defeat, neither the party nor the Brahminic liberal intellectuals supporting it realized what was in store in that election.

What the Congress leadership failed to understand was that those communities which felt alienated would look for a political platform where they would get recognition. For castes that had lost their identity, getting one was of prime importance. The communist parties, both the CPI and the CPI(M), also failed to understand this aspiration of Shudra/OBC communities; hence their class movement slowly lost its relevance in India.

Shudras found a demagogue in Modi, as they could not understand the intellectual discourse imported from foreign universities. As Indian feudalism kept weakening, capital accumulation got concentrated in the hands of very Hinduized Bania families. Most of the capitalists who accrued wealth after liberalization of the economy slowly moved away from the Congress and towards the RSS-BJP. Around this time, in the 1990s, the RSS-BJP were increasingly organizing masses around issues such as Ram Temple in Ayodhya. Hindu festival mobilization also became the market purchasing power in cities and small towns. The Hindu sentiment of Brahminic industry and business along with the market mobility of the masses worked in favour of the BJP. The majority of the market forces in India are Shudras, Dalits and Adivasis. They were said to be siding with Hindutva by the 2014 elections.

After Sonia Gandhi became president of the Congress, Western-educated Brahmins rallied round her, but the RSS–BJP went on telling Shudras/OBCs that they had neither power nor support in the Congress camp. Shudras/OBCs started believing this narrative. After Manmohan Singh became prime minister, the campaign was that Christians and Sikh minorities were ruling the Hindu majority. Shudras/OBCs started believing this because under Manmohan Singh, no OBC was given any visible position. The president, vice president, chairman of the Planning Commission and the University Grants Commission chairman were all either Muslim, Dalit or Sikh. Though Pratibha Patil, a Shudra woman, was made president for one term, she had no mass contact with Shudras/OBCs. She came from a business family with a Maratha background and she was also seen as anti-reservationist.

Regional parties had no power to control the central higher educational institutions, which were seen as Brahmin–Bania strongholds. We must not forget the fact that the most powerful and quality knowledge production universities, teaching and research institutes like Jawaharlal Nehru University (JNU), IITs, Indian Institutes of Management (IIMs) and well-established medical universities are under the control of the Centre. Regional universities and sub-standard research institutes are under the state governments. Shudras were in control of state institutions and they implemented reservation, but they could not produce intellectuals and leaders who challenged those educated in the best institutes who happened to be mostly Brahmin–Banias. The CPI(M) is a classic example. Two of its top leaders are from JNU, Prakash Karat and Sitaram Yechury, and they never gave a chance to even a single SC/ST leader to get into the politburo. The CPI(M)'s apex bodies conduct their business in English, but neither in West Bengal nor in Tripura was a single good English-speaking Shudra/Adivasi/Dalit leader allowed to grow. Hence, neither Shudras/OBCs nor SC/STs could get into the top intellectual leadership ranks of the CPI(M).[6] From the south in particular, some Shudra leaders emerged because of better English teaching. Shudras/OBC activists were kept only at the mass mobilization level. The Congress has a better representation of SC/STs than the communist parties, but not Shudras/OBCs.

The RSS has been an anti-reservation organization, and Mohan Bhagwat himself has, on record, opposed reservation, most recently in a statement on 19 August 2019 that the question of reservation must be debated. The RSS chief said that 'there should be open-hearted debate pertaining to reservation given to SC/ST/OBCs'.[7] He has made such statements earlier as well. The BJP government at the Centre and in states has implemented, one after another, the RSS's long-term agendas. State governments have made cow protections laws, destabilizing the economy of Shudra farmers who graze cattle, and the food economy of Dalits, Adivasis and Muslims. The central government has brought in the triple talaq law and the abrogation of Article 370. The other major issues of its long-term resolve are building the Ram temple and abrogation of reservation. The same Narendra Modi who galvanized OBC votes may be forced to enact a reservation abrogation legislation. Brahmin intellectuals working from Congress platforms may fully support such a legislation. Mohan Bhagwat's claims about 'debating' reservations cannot be lightly dismissed as he is one of the heavyweights in RSS–BJP networks.

The former feudal Shudras and OBCs have not understood the game plan of the RSS–BJP. If the Congress dismantled Shudra feudal political power at the village level and some Shudra-led parties came to power in states, now the RSS–BJP continue to dismantle their power structures in almost all states using the OBC card and MBC (Most Backward Castes) card, thus not allowing any national leadership to emerge from amongst Shudras. The Hindu spiritual system would not accept that. Now, since the RSS is defining Shudras, OBCs, Dalits and Adivasis as Hindus, these groups should ask for priesthood rights in that religion. They should become interpreters of religious texts. They must take the philosophical leading position in Hinduism. Their priests must guide them to their ultimate authority. Even in a modern democracy, spiritual power is the ultimate controlling authority. Shudras do not have that.

Some Shudras/OBCs, meanwhile, became middle-level leaders in the RSS–BJP and slowly forced the Sangh to come to terms with the reservation issue, but that seems to be a short-term survival situation. By promising 10 per cent reservation for economically weaker sections (EWS), the BJP neutralized the issue of caste-based reservation and led the Congress into its trap.[8] Post-Mandal, the BJP tried to project Sardar Patel as a better leader than Jawaharlal Nehru. The strategy was first used by L.K. Advani, who was later compared with Patel. Advani is a Sindhi Marwari. The BJP needed a national icon to be pitted against Nehru because they do not have one in the pantheon of their own ideological fold.[9]

Sardar Patel, a Gujarati Shudra who contested Nehru on many fronts, is very well known. Maybe Advani, and later Modi and Shah, owned Patel because he also came from Gujarat and was a pro-RSS Shudra leader. This helped Modi more than anybody else as he himself claimed to be a Gujarati OBC.

By deploying Modi at the forefront in the battle against the Congress, the BJP has taken away all OBCs from the fold of regional Shudra leaders. In Uttar Pradesh, Bihar, Maharashtra, Haryana and to some extent in Karnataka, Shudra leadership has been weakened. It still remains somewhat stable in Tamil Nadu, Andhra Pradesh and Telangana. In West Bengal and Odisha, power continues to be in the hands of Brahmins.

The regional Shudra forces responsible for the weakening of the Congress in many states helped the BJP in turn. The revival of the Congress is impossible without this support group coming back into its fold. The only way it can do this is by inviting all regional parties with Shudra leadership to associate with it. But it needs a leader like Mahatma Gandhi to convince all these leaders to come together. Nevertheless, Rahul Gandhi can at least try. The Congress needs to work out two modes of functioning if it wants to gain its pre-Independence status. After Mahatma Gandhi's death, it has not evolved a moral leader who can remain outside the formal power structure of the party and government and play a leadership role. It has to find one now. Secondly, its formal power-handling leadership should emerge from amongst Shudras/OBCs/Dalits. To start with, it must work on Shudras, whatever the caste background within that broad category, and prop up someone capable of handling national and international issues. Without roping in existing regional leaders and giving them national platforms that give them the necessary national stature, it cannot defeat the BJP and come to power. The regional party leaders must also understand that without emerging as national leaders from the platform of a national party, they will not be able to change the power structures of the nation, which as of now is working against them.

Democracy has given something to Shudras. For the first time, they have got the right to vote and the right to contest with any non-Shudra person in elections. They can go to schools where their children can compete with non-Shudra upper-caste children. They can compete with Brahmins in the political domain. These competing rights were not there in the Hindu–Brahminic religious sphere. They could not go to Hindu theological gurukuls; they could not compete for spiritual power with Brahmin priests; they could not become rulers without ritual elevation as Kshatriyas by consent of the Brahmin priests. They could not do business with Banias without Brahmins giving them Bania status with *upanayana* and so on. Democracy has bestowed political rights on Shudras in many spheres because of the Indian Constitution, but the Rig Veda and Manu dharma still bind them in the spiritual realm as they did in pre-medieval times. Shudras exercised all these rights in Harappan times. They were spiritual, social and economic leaders. They built villages and cities and worshipped their gods and goddesses. They travelled across the seas for business. They ruled themselves in a communitarian democratic consciousness. They lost all those rights, freedoms and egalitarian spiritual ideas once the Rig Vedic pastoral economy began with Aryan Brahminism and the varna order in place.

If Shudras had fought for their spiritual equal rights at that time, the Sanatan dharma would have been transformed into Hinduism on the lines of Christianity, and their status in democracy at the national level would be different. A number of great thinkers, scholars, intellectuals and political leaders would have emerged from amongst them. They remained second-grade citizens in the spiritual realm and consented to keep Dalits as third-grade citizens. Shudra thinkers or philosophers did not spring up to tell them that spiritual democracy is the fountainhead of social democracy and political democracy. There can be no autonomous political democracy divorced from the spiritual democratic system. They never engaged in the discourse of ideas and transformative thinking. They hung around raw muscle power, regional political power, small, regional land and financial power. Hence, Shudra top leaders did not emerge from Congress or RSS–BJP platforms. There is no scope for this in the near future either, unless they get a share in spiritual capital.

There is a need for a Shudra movement of enlightenment linked to the mobilization of forces in spiritual, social and political spheres. The nationalist enlightenment movement has only produced Brahmin–Bania intellectuals and spiritual and social leaders. Shudras remained their followers. One of the main reasons for this was that not many Shudra youths acquired modern education in English. When Babasaheb Ambedkar, Mahatma Gandhi and Jawaharlal Nehru emerged as eminent intellectual leaders by constantly writing and leading the masses, Shudras remained only a part of the mass, that too only around Gandhi and Nehru.

If the Shudra enlightenment movement does not start now, they will be led by Brahmin–Bania political, spiritual and social forces operating from RSS–BJP platforms for a long time to come. The RSS platform will not be allowed to slip from the hands of Brahmins so long as the Hindu spiritual system—encompassing temples, peethas, Hindu civil societal organizations—is under the control of Brahmins as conductors of its philosophical domain. Shudras will not be allowed to lead Delhi power structures either. With the Hindutva system running political and social systems, the Indian Constitution will be made to serve the interests of the Hindu spiritual system—which in essence means the interests of Brahmins and Banias. The only course left for Shudras is to wage a spiritual revolutionary battle for total equality.

The Importance of Shudra Politics in India[1]

Sharad Yadav and Omprakash Mahato

A long with Dr B.R. Ambedkar, Dr Ram Manohar Lohia devoted his life to combat caste-based injustice and inequality through a distinctly Indian version of socialism, which gave centrality to individual welfare and development. However, unlike other contemporary socialist leaders, it was not class that formed the basis of Dr Lohia's understanding of inequality, but caste and gender. For him, 'Caste restricts opportunity, restricted opportunity constricts ability, constricted ability further restricts opportunity, where caste prevails; opportunity and ability are restricted to ever-narrowing circles of the people.'[2]

That is why Dr Lohia argued:

> The fight for equality will necessarily have to mean a struggle against the entrenched ruling class and all that it stands for viz. caste (*savarna*), English education and wealth. Over 90 per cent of the ruling class in India belong to the upper castes and most of them possess both the other characteristics of

wealth and English education. However, it is the element of caste that makes the whole situation almost hopelessly irredeemable.[3]

But Lohia's anti-English stand proved to be anti-Dalit Bahujan in later times as the Dwija castes educated their children in private English-medium schools, denying the benefit of that Indian and global language to Dalit Bahujans, in fact, to all Shudras including Jats, Yadavs, Gujjars, Patels and so on.

However, we must see his arguments in the context of Nehruvian politics and their opposition to each other. The Nehruvian socialist model in which 'each Five Year plan seems to be providing a fresh stream of five lakhs to a million people to the country's ruling classes . . . Perhaps the most disastrous feature of the whole situation is the uplift of a limited section of backward and low castes into the ruling classes of the country'.[4] This model of socialism has only given an illusion of class conflict between the bureaucratic class and the industrial or trading class. In contrast, both these classes belong to the upper castes. Their superficial conflict deceived the people, but in fact, at the ground level, it created more inequality in society. Lohia's 'Hindi–Hindustani' campaign is now used by the RSS as 'Hindu, Hindi and Hindustani', while allowing English-medium education to proliferate in the private sector. The Hindi pride campaign forced the majority of north Indian Shudra/OBC/Dalit forces to remain immobile and underdeveloped.

To eradicate inequality, Dr Lohia proposed first, the principle of legal equality where all men are equal before the law; second, the principle of political equality that called for, much like Ambedkar did, 'one man, one vote'; and third, the principle of economic equality which raises everyone's living standards. He also consistently persuaded political parties to work for the removal of 'the disinterestedness of the low caste people' and for 'breaking the hegemony of the savarnas'. Since the Dwija castes led most political parties, they could not be expected to usher in real equality. Of course, while he was sympathetic towards the lower castes, he was not an abolitionist. Lohia, having come from a Bania caste himself, stood between Ambedkar and Gandhi on the caste issue, while Nehru, being a secular Brahmin, refused to recognize the fault lines emerging out of the contradictions of the caste system.

Lohia urged the ruling powers to 'openly and frankly adopt a scheme of preferential opportunities to the mass of the people and to fight for the removal of distinctions based not only on wealth but also on cultural and social elements'.[5] That is precisely why Lohia consistently argued that 'equality is not a mere levelling-down process but also implies levelling up'. As an immediate measure, he suggested giving constitutional sanction to the scheme of preferential opportunities to the extent of 60 to 70 per cent of leadership posts in 'politics, government services, the military, trade and industry to women and Sudras, Dalits, Adivasis and the backward castes and religious minorities'.[6]

But unfortunately, he did not visualize an education system with one common national language such as English as the medium of instruction for all communities, without which the oppressed castes could not become rulers. Lohia knew that historically Shudras were denied Sanskrit education. In the mid-nineteenth century itself, Mahatma Phule had stressed on the need for equal medium and content education. Lohia could be hailed as a progressive philosopher for his time. But he never recognized the great role of Ambedkar, who was his contemporary, and of Mahatma Phule and Periyar Ramasamy, who led the nation in different directions. This put him at a severe disadvantage when trying to make sense of and mount an effective fight against the well-entrenched caste system.

Lohia argued that people must reject the 'old caste policy' which created 'vertical solidarity of the castes', and instead adopt a 'new caste policy' of his 'socialist model' that sought to bring 'horizontal solidarity' of the backward classes, Dalits, Adivasis, minorities, women, peasants and the working class.[7] This idea of horizontal solidarity shaped Mandal–Other Backward Classes (OBC) politics, which not only questioned caste inequalities but also advocated intersectional caste-based affirmative action. To this extent, though he came from a Bania background, Lohia was working within the anti-caste tradition. The notion of 'horizontal solidarity' (Bahujan identity) has become even more relevant given the unprecedented social, cultural, economic and political realities of India in these past few years. Because of Lohia, many Bania castes of north India enlisted themselves in the OBC list once the Mandal movement began to gain victories. Narendra Modi, a Gujarati from a lower-ranking Modh Ghanchi business community, benefited from the OBC categorization and became prime minister of the nation with that identity. But he proved to be the opposite of Lohia in his political career, working as a member of the RSS which never openly fought for the causes of OBC communities during the Mandal movement or later. Lohia had a consistent stand on the negative role of the Indian caste system. Even now, pro-reservation political parties like the Samajwadi Party, the JD(U) and the RJD treat Lohia as their ideological guru. So far, Modi has not gone on record ideologically opposing the caste system.

Means to the Socialist Goal

Lohia advocated constructive programmes, ideological training and civil disobedience or satyagraha to attain the socialist goal.

He firmly believed that socialism must be radical, cannot always comply with the sluggish process of constitutionalism, and this method of persuasion and law-making are not suitable for developing nations. Under his leadership, the Socialist Party attempted to unfold a whole range of constructive activities centred around the agricultural sector, and to move the people to dig for canals, wells, tanks, roads and other projects. The Hindu Kisan Panchayat, an organ of the Socialist Party, fought against injustice and attempted to change people's habits with regard to food, raising of crops and making of manure, and assisted them in storing and marketing of produce and in finding good tools.

Lohia also extended support to the Bhoodan and Sarvodaya movements, which carried forward the Gandhian vision of societal reconstruction. He advocated 'propaganda meetings' and 'study circles' in every village to equip politicians as much with regional knowledge as with 'theory' for political indoctrination. And, Lohia was aware that the law may not always deliver the goods, and people can become impatient and disillusioned with constitutional processes. Therefore, he advocated the Gandhian idea of civil disobedience, popularly known as satyagraha, as a singularly effective tool to fulfil the socialist goal. However, these things were addressed in the historical context of Brahminism and its concept of non-dignity of labour. Having had a foreign education background like many other Brahminic leaders, he realized that his ideology should transcend casteism. But over a period of time, the RSS–BJP forces weakened the influence of the Lohiawadi socialists by deploying the deeply religious, polarizing ideology around the Ram Mandir and Babri Masjid issue. Still, it cannot be denied that the Shudras/OBCs emerged as regional power managers in north India because of Lohia's anti-caste socialist ideology.

The Constitutional Idea and Ambedkar's One Individual, One Vote, One Value

Lohia was influenced by Dr Ambedkar's idea of one individual, one vote and one value to empower the historically marginalized sections of Indian society. Ambedkar put forward apprehensions and possibilities about the transition from colonial rule to democracy from his Buddhist perspective. To maintain democracy not only in form but also in substance, he emphasized constitutional methods to accomplish social and economic objectives. He believed that the Grammar of Anarchy that Gandhi left behind needed to be abandoned sooner than later in order to sustain the constitutional proceduralism and democracy that relies on it.[8] The most important thing, Ambedkar said, was that Indians must not be merely content with political democracy and instead, as a collective society, must transform the nation into a social and economic democracy. On 26 January 1950, he said:

> We are going to enter into a life of contradictions. In politics, we will have equality, and in social and economic life, we will have inequality. In politics, we will recognise the principle of one man, one vote, one value. In our social and economic life, we shall, by reason of our social and economic structure, continue to deny the principle of one man, one value. How long shall we continue to live this life of contradictions? How long shall we continue to deny equality in our social and economic life? If we continue to deny for long, we will do so only by putting our political democracy in peril. We must remove this contradiction at the earliest possible moment or else those who suffer from inequality will blow up the structure of political democracy which the assembly has laboriously built up.[9]

The north Indian Shudras who followed Lohia could never properly negotiate with Ambedkarite Dalits. This gradually gave rise to the Lohiaite Samajwadi Party under the leadership of Mulayam Singh Yadav, and the Ambedkarite Dalit BSP under the leadership of Kanshiram in Uttar Pradesh. In the process, after the implementation of the Mandal Commission report, agrarian Shudras like Jats were separated from both these forces. These developments weakened the Brahmin-centred Congress in that state by 1994. Subsequently, these developments brought the Hindutvawadi Kshatriya Yogi Adityanath to power in Uttar Pradesh.

Shudra Caste Associations in North India

Since ancient times, several travellers from across the world have visited India and mentioned the regressive caste system in their writings and travelogues. The caste system, according to ancient texts, originated from the mythology of Brahma (a divine figure) who is believed to have given birth to men and women from his head, arms, thighs and feet. Brahmins, born from his head, controlled knowledge and the education system. Kshatriyas, born from his arms, became mighty warriors and rulers. Vaishyas, born from his thighs, became traders. Amongst other things, two things always confused me. First, how did Brahma give birth to people (Shudras) from his feet to do menial jobs? And second, why did he only reproduce from four body parts and not use his neck, chest, stomach, calves, etc.? I hope someone who still believes in the caste system and is its ardent supporter will be able to rationally and scientifically answer these questions.

Shudras, the 'lowest' in the social hierarchy along with Dalits, are the people who were—and unfortunately still are—marginalized and kept away from opportunities for thousands of years. They have been pushed to the bottom of the society—culturally, socially, economically and politically—by the Hindu caste system. This system that creates a hierarchy among people defines their work based on their birth and governs our society in the worst possible way.

India, on independence and the adoption of the Constitution drafted by Ambedkar, became a land of its people, by the people and for the people. Our founding fathers, after a prolonged struggle for independence from colonial rule, constituted India into a sovereign, socialist, secular, democratic republic and ensured social, economic and political justice to all the people, and promised liberty of thought, expression, belief, faith and worship; equality of status and opportunities to promote this; and fraternity assuring the dignity of every individual and the unity and integrity of our nation. Ambedkar gave all Indian citizens a promising Constitution that assures social justice along with political and economic justice to all those who had been left behind. This document ensures his vision of one man, one vote, one value. It is our responsibility to work towards the social and economic empowerment of Shudras and all other marginalized communities.

Unlike Dalits, Shudras were not directly excluded from society. Neither did they live in isolation, nor were they subjected to rampant discrimination. They formed a large section of the spiritually 'untouchable' community, while socially they were treated as 'touchable' by the Dwijas. Post-Mandal, if we revisit Shudra politics in the Indian state, it is interesting to note that the politicization of Shudras in southern India and northern India was shaped on different lines. While southern and western India politicized Shudras through ethnicization, northern India followed a different trajectory. Since the upper castes, mostly Brahmins, constituted a lower proportion of the population in the south and west Indian provinces, it helped Shudras to form a caste federation and thereby attack the social hierarchy, as put by Jaffrelot in *India's Silent Revolution*.[10] In north Indian politics, caste association operated within the fold of Sanskritization. Therefore, instead of questioning and revolting against Sanskritized rituals, the Shudras in the north adopted it to climb onto the upper fold of 'graded inequality'. As a dominant caste among the Shudra communities, Yadavs started associating themselves with the lineage of Krishna, and the Kurmis and the Koiris claimed they were Kshatriyas. The caste association did get formed, but it did not lead to the formation of a caste federation like in the southern states. The resilience of Sanskritization has impacted Shudras by preventing them from forming non-Brahmin groups or the caste federation. As a result, the status of Shudras in the south is slightly better than in the north. But overall, there is limited growth and representation of these communities in government services. For instance, there is not a single OBC professor in all the forty central universities, including prestigious and self-proclaimed progressive institutions and universities such as the IITs, JNU and Delhi University.[11]

Revisiting Mandal Politics

In the year 1917, the term 'backward class' was first used by the Madras administration to generate a policy favouring the uneducated. Jawaharlal Nehru used the term in his speech before the Constituent Assembly in 1946, in his Objective Resolution.[12] He announced a special measure for tribal areas, backward classes, minorities, depressed classes and OBCs. An administrative category was created by the state, which it then had to fill. Ambedkar clarified that 'backward class' was nothing but an amalgamation of certain castes.

Since Independence, the historically marginalized and backward castes started mobilizing for their rights. On 29 January 1953, Nehru, the first prime minister of India, constituted the

Backward Classes Commission under the chairmanship of Kaka Saheb Kelkar, adhering to Article 340 of the Constitution of India. It was popularly known as the Kelkar Commission. The major work undertaken by this commission was to identify backward classes and castes, investigate the condition of all such socially and educationally backward classes and make recommendations for their upliftment. The majority of the members who were part of the commission selected four criteria for defining OBCs: low social position in the caste hierarchy within Hindu society, lack of general education among major sections of a caste or community, inadequate or no representation in government services, and inadequate representation in the field of trade, commerce and industry. Caste was not a criterion, but it was a key element in defining OBCs.

The Kelkar Commission submitted its report in 1955.[13] It recommended reservation of 70 per cent seats in all technical and professional institutions for qualified students of backward classes, and quotas in state and central administration: 25 per cent of vacancies in Class I, 33.3 per cent in Class II, 40 per cent in Class III and IV. It advised the government to undertake caste-wise enumeration of the population in the Census of 1961 and special economic measures to uplift OBCs such as extensive land reforms, reorganization of the village economy, Bhoodan movement, development of livestock and dairy farming, development of rural housing, public health and rural water supply, adult literacy programmes, etc. After its comprehensive recommendations, differences in opinion emerged on whether the reservation should be given to the 2399 backward castes or communities identified. The commitment of socialist movements compelled the Indian political class to believe in social change and support reservation for backward castes. Unfortunately, no concrete action was taken, and the historic opportunity was lost.

During the Emergency (1975–77), all socialist leaders came together on one platform and formed the Janata Party government in 1977. In its manifesto, the Janata Party promised to undertake measures for social and educational upliftment of people belonging to backward castes and communities. The social upliftment of backward castes once again became the subject of mainstream discourse in Indian polity and society. To fulfil its promise of social and educational empowerment of the backward castes, the Janata Party government formed a six-member committee under the chairmanship of B.P. Mandal, former chief minister of Bihar, on 1 January 1979. This commission was popularly known as the Mandal Commission.

The Janata Party government was committed to the cause of social and educational empowerment of farmers, workers and people belonging to backward castes. Rather than striving to undo the historical injustice done to these communities, what they were ensuring was the delivery of social justice. After the formation of the Mandal Commission, I met then Prime Minister Morarji Desai, Jagjivan Ram and Chaudhary Charan Singh and congratulated them on the much-needed initiative. Unfortunately, due to internal conspiracies and politics, the Janata Party government fell in 1979. In January 1980, the Congress party won the election with a majority and formed the government.

Based on the 1931 Census data,[14] using eleven social, educational and economic indicators, the commission identified 3743 different castes and communities as members of Other Backward Classes. The OBC category, it estimated, comprised 52 per cent of the Indian population. I arranged many meetings between B.P. Mandal and Chaudhary Charan Singh in 1979. The affluent Jat community of Uttar Pradesh and Haryana were naively against the idea of being listed as a backward class. A convoy of local Jat leaders from Bharatpur met Chaudhary Charan Singh to request him to make sure Jats were not listed as a backward class in the Mandal Commission report. Mandal had not included them in the list in the first place. The commission submitted its report to the president of India, Giani Zail Singh, in December 1980.[15] One of the major recommendations of the Mandal Commission was to provide 27 per cent reservation to 'socially and educationally backward classes' for jobs in central services and public undertakings.

After submitting the report to the president, Mandal met Prime Minister Indira Gandhi. She made him wait for a long time, but still, the meeting went as expected. After meeting her, Mandal was distressed and frustrated. He came straight to my house and described the meeting, saying, '*Main apni report Ganga mein visarjit kar aaya hun.*' (I have immersed my report in the Ganga.) He was confident that the government would not proceed with it. The report was tabled in Parliament, but regrettably, I was not a member of Parliament in the seventh Lok Sabha. Nevertheless, I tried my best to mobilize parliamentarians of the Lok Dal and the Janata Party to encourage a meaningful discussion on the Mandal Commission report. But his instinct was right. The report was elbowed into cold storage.

On 11 October 1988, the Janata Dal was formed by the merger of the Jan Morcha, the Janata Party, the Lok Dal and the Congress (S), and Vishwanath Pratap Singh was elected as party president. In the 1989 general election, a federation of the Janata Dal with various regional parties, including the Dravida Munnetra Kazhagam, the Telugu Desam Party and the Asom Gana Parishad, came into being, called the National Front (India), with V.P. Singh as convener and N.T. Rama Rao as president. I always believed that the Mandal Commission was a remarkably unique initiative that exposed social inequalities in Indian society and ascertained the historical injustices to the backward castes with facts and statistics. However, for ten years, governments had dodged its recommendations. The Mandal Commission report had included the backward classes of the Hindu, Muslim, Sikh and Christian communities. The Janata Party and the Lok Dal started a movement to ensure justice to all these backward classes.

Their manifesto promised to implement the Mandal Commission recommendations. The people belonging to the backward classes became extremely hopeful and voted for the Janata Dal in the 1989 election. The National Front, with its allies, won the elections, earned a simple majority in the Lok Sabha, and V.P. Singh became the seventh prime minister of India in December 1989. Soon after the formation of the government, the hopes of the backward classes started diminishing as people in the government who previously belonged to the Indian National Congress did not wish for the Mandal Commission's recommendations to be implemented. Their Bahujan politics was limited to gaining votes from backward classes and keeping them in the dark. Therefore, the backward classes were exasperated and dismayed by this attitude of the Janata Dal government.

Socialist leaders were worried because of this crisis. The Lok Dal, with more than seventy parliamentarians, had supported the Janata Dal government but received a disproportionate share in the cabinet. Not only the prime ministership but even other important ministries like home affairs, external affairs, defence, etc., were given to parliamentarians of the Janata Dal. In this testing situation, it became troublesome to keep everyone together. Besides, the resentment among the backward classes was growing. We, therefore, started mobilizing all socialist leaders and putting pressure on the Janata Dal government to fulfil its manifesto promise of implementing the recommendations of the Mandal Commission. We strongly believed that without this, no true justice would be served to Shudras.

V.P. Singh's entourage vehemently opposed the recommendations of the Mandal Commission. To overcome this, he established a committee under the chairmanship of Chaudhary Devi Lal, the deputy prime minister and a prominent Jat leader. He knew it was due to Chaudhary Charan Singh's intervention that Mandal did not include Jats in the list of backward classes. However, many local Jat leaders and groups were putting pressure on their political leaders to be included in the reservation category. Taking advantage of the situation, V.P. Singh played a master stroke. He was sure that being the most prominent Jat leader, Devi Lal would not implement the Mandal recommendations without including Jats, despite the fact that he was against it. Chaudhary Ajit Singh, general secretary of the Janata Dal and minister of industry, also started campaigning for the rights of backward classes and asserted that Jats be included in the OBC list. Devi Lal was caught in a political dilemma: On the one hand, he did not want Ajit Singh to take credit for the inclusion of Jats as a backward class, and on the other, he could not risk the ire of his own Jat community by not including them. Therefore, V.P. Singh thought this would be the end of the discussion on the Mandal Commission.

During this time, Devi Lal had received some documents and complaints against two cabinet ministers, which he sent to the Prime Minister's Office for inspection.[16] This incident resulted in another ruckus in the government. Meanwhile, I was keeping a close eye on the implications of a political row related to Devi Lal's son Om Prakash Chautala's chief ministership in Haryana, at the Centre. These games were being played to disorient V.P. Singh and not let him implement the recommendations of the Mandal Commission. As Devi Lal was a Jat leader who came up from the grassroots, his popularity was increasing. In this context, Singh, instead of asking for a clarification from the accused cabinet ministers, called Devi Lal and dropped him from his cabinet. In response, Devi Lal announced a massive rally of farmers and backward classes in Delhi to show his clout. On 3 August 1990, Singh called me in the morning and said, 'Brother Sharad, I can't tolerate Chaudhary Devi Lal any more.' I assured him that I would speak to Devi Lal and close this chapter once and for all. But I requested him not to drop Devi Lal from the cabinet. To this, Singh replied that he had already sent the order to the president. This made me discontinue the conversation. The next morning at 7 a.m., the prime minister sent one of his close aides to my residence to request me to come over to his office. For three long hours, we discussed Devi Lal and his political stand. He wanted to take me into confidence so that I did not jump ship with Devi Lal, which would have meant that he would not have remained prime minister any more.

Taking advantage of the situation, I urged him to announce the implementation of the Mandal Commission recommendations immediately. He first agreed to make an announcement on 15 August 1990 from Red Fort. I had to tell him clearly that if he wanted to implement the recommendations, he had to do it before 9 August 1990; otherwise I would have no choice but to join Devi Lal's rally in Delhi. As I saw it, the implementation of these recommendations would fulfil the dreams of Ambedkar, Karpoori Thakur, Lohia and Jayaprakash Narayan, who believed and dreamt of an equitable society. The Janata Dal government he was leading had emerged from socialist struggles. The backward classes who helped him get elected as prime minister, who were marginalized for more than thousands of years, were looking at him with just expectation to implement the recommendations submitted by the Mandal Commission.

To save his government, Singh, after discussing it with a few of his close political aides, agreed to do so. On 6 August

1990, he called a cabinet meeting at his house at 6 p.m. with the main agenda of discussing the implementation of the Mandal Commission recommendations. Despite a warning from his close aides, the very next day, on 7 August 1990, the government accepted the Mandal Commission's recommendations and announced that it would implement the reservation scheme under which 27 per cent jobs would be earmarked for OBCs. And finally, on 13 August 1990, it notified the implementation of OBC reservation. On 10 August 1990, the Dwija castes had started to protest against reservation. For about a month, students, bureaucrats and teachers participated in protests all over the country, public property was destroyed, and roads were blocked.

The Janata Dal emerged under the stalwart leadership of Jayaprakash Narayan, Karpoori Thakur, Chaudhary Charan Singh and V.P. Singh, dominant political figures with a commitment to social change, and shaped the political discourse in the second half of the twentieth century in India. Their party and its leadership always believed that all the major problems in India were a result of the caste system. The implementation of the Mandal Commission recommendations or 'Mandalization' of Indian politics ensured that all communities, be they backward castes, the upper class, farmers or Muslims, got an opportunity for not just economic but also social mobility and upliftment.

Justifying the Need for Reservation and Social Justice

Affirmative action, in simple terms, is all about representation and enabling access for people or communities who were/are historically unrepresented and to remedy the historical injustice inflicted by the dominant socio-economic and political castes on Dalits, Adivasis, women and backward communities. In post-

Independence India, the Constitution promises and guarantees reservation in public educational institutions under Articles 15 (4), (5) and (6), and in government services and jobs under Articles 16 (4) and (6), and in the legislatures (Parliament and state legislatures) under Article 334. Earlier, reservation was provided only on the basis of social and educational backwardness of community or (caste). However, after the 103rd Constitutional Amendment in 2019, reservation was extended to economically weaker sections. The major objectives of reservation for Dalits, Adivasis and OBCs are not only to reserve jobs in public services but also to empower them and ensure their participation in the decision-making processes of the state.

However, recent data shows that, despite the reservation policy, the quotas are not requisitely filled, leading to under-representation of already disadvantaged and marginalized social groups of SCs, STs and especially OBCs in the higher echelons of government services and most of its institutions. The Department of Personnel and Training in 2018 under the Right to Information Act revealed that in the forty central universities, OBC reservation is only applicable up to the level of assistant professor and its share is almost half (14.38 per cent) of their 27 per cent legal entitlement. Significantly, the number of professors and associate professors in central universities appointed under OBC reservation is 0 per cent.[17] In the IITs and IIMs, out of the total 9640 sanctioned faculty strength, the representation of SCs, STs and OBCs altogether make up just 9 per cent of the total faculty in IITs and 6 per cent of the total faculty in IIMs. As per data received from seventy-eight ministries and departments, including their attached and subordinate offices, the representation of SCs, STs and OBCs in posts and services of the central government as on 1 January 2016 was 17.49 per cent, 8.47 per cent and 21.57 per cent respectively.[18]

This grave violation of the reservation policy demands serious introspection as to why, despite constitutional guarantees, the representation of SCs, STs and OBCs is skewed in educational institutions and government jobs. This reflects not only caste prejudices, but also the unwillingness of dominant castes to give up their inherited privileges, often expressed through deceptive notions of merit and efficiency.

We need to find new modalities of implementing reservation and removing the institutional discrimination that includes the lack of support to weak students and ascribing insinuations to their capability, which has restricted their participation in public spaces. More so, what is needed is to ensure that reservation is only one part of the move towards an egalitarian society. However, we need to constantly keep asking the fundamental question about what needs to be done after reservation. We need to provide an institutional and societal support system so that the benefits of reservation are equally availed of by all who are entitled.

Affirmative action is important to uplift backward classes not only economically and socially, but also politically. Sadly, all dominant backward classes see the benefit of reservation but fail to understand its objective. They have land, resources and opportunities and are not looked down upon. Their economic affluence has provided them with respect in society, whereas the classes which have been kept away from resources should get the first claim over them and the opportunities ensured by the government.

Till recently, holding land meant economic and social hegemonic dominant castes did not ask for anything. But now, when education and jobs have become important, they have started demanding reservation. For instance, the Patidars of Gujarat demand that either they be given reservation or reservation should be scrapped entirely. This reflects an inadequate understanding of the mechanisms of social justice even within the upper Shudra community.

Lessons from the Legacy of Socialist Politics

The 2019 Lok Sabha election was a classic case of Mandal vs Kamandal politics fought in the most fertile grounds for 'backward class' consolidation in north India. The BJP, under the leadership of Narendra Modi, has precipitated an existential crisis for the socialist vision of Lohia. The SP, the BSP and the RJD were supposed to work with that vision but did not. The appeal of these parties for social justice to Dalits, OBCs and Muslims, fuelled by the twin engines of reservation and safeguards, failed in the face of the BJP's strong cultural, Hindu nationalistic and caste-centred politics. As the results in Uttar Pradesh and Bihar show, the RJD, SP and BSP failed to stitch together the basic social coalition of OBCs, Dalits and Muslims, which was considered their home constituency and which had powered their surge in the Hindi heartland under Lalu Prasad Yadav, Mulayam Singh Yadav as well as Kanshiram–Mayawati. Over time, the umbrella of OBC and Dalit outfits ceded chunks of their traditional vote banks to the BJP.

Secondly, Shudras/OBCs, even after forming the government in Bihar and Uttar Pradesh, could not challenge the tenets of Hinduism where their spiritual equality is not established. Caste association did take place in the early days, but they functioned around the logic of Sanskritization. They never challenged Brahminism and pure vegetarianism. The caste federation that could unify all Shudras was absent within the Shudras in Uttar Pradesh and Bihar. Moreover, the caste 'associations served as a vehicle for Sanskritisation', as argued by Jaffrelot.[19] The RJD in Bihar and the SP in Uttar Pradesh did appeal to the conscience of Dalits, Muslims, OBCs and Adivasis but the process was visible merely in the course of vote-bank politics. As a result, the battle that the former socialist leaders won was limited to the political sphere. The social sphere was kept Brahminic. The social structure played an important role in keeping caste alive and functional. Shudras, instead of challenging the social hierarchy, tried to achieve upward mobility by imitating Brahmins. The concept of purity was deeply embedded within Shudras in Uttar Pradesh and Bihar. Therefore, in these states, instead of tearing the janeu, Shudras asked for janeus to make themselves equivalent to Brahmins and Kshatriyas. This was visible in the janeu *andolan* or janeu movement in Bihar. But they could not become equals. The failure of socialist parties in questioning the social hierarchy created space for right-wing political parties to gain through faith and religion.

Thirdly, the politics of subcategorization within Shudras and the failure of the RJD and the SP to capture the political aspiration of the lower section within OBCs paved the way for mistrust within the community. It was mainly Brahmins, Rajputs, Kayasthas and Bhumihars who lost political power, and the Yadavs and Kurmis were the major beneficiaries among Shudras. The domination of Yadavs in Bihar politics was challenged by a different type of social engineering by the Nitish Kumar–led JD(U), by categorizing Shudras and OBCs into Extremely Backward Caste (EBC), Backward Caste (BC-I) and Backward Caste (BC-II). However, nobody addressed the unequal education system. The bureaucratic and intellectual power remained in the hands of Brahmins, Kayasthas and Bhoomihars.

Lastly, the Mandal Commission played the unifying factor for all OBC communities, as the aspiration of different castes among OBCs was nearly the same. But Dalits and OBCs were never united. Untouchability was not seriously addressed. Post-

Mandal politics abandoned all other egalitarian agendas. In regional parties, new cadres are neither being promoted nor are they given key responsibilities.

Strategizing for the Future

The caste federation within the lower castes is invisible at the current juncture in Indian politics. In north India, the first attempt to unite backward castes was in Bihar in 1930, during the Triveni Sangh, named after the rivers Ganga, Yamuna and Saraswati, between the Yadavs, Kurmis and Koeris. To counter these forces, the Congress formed the Backward Class Federation in 1935. Later on, not much discourse around caste took place. Since Shudras/OBCs did not produce sophisticated English-educated intellectuals, the discourse was only around political power and land. This has its limitations. The RSS–BJP used this Hindi–Sanskrit base in its favour.

But at the current juncture, it is disheartening to see that the RJD, SP, BSP and JD(U) have shown their serious limitations. These parties have moved away from the larger anti-RSS–BJP agenda and kept themselves engaged in a cockfight. Leaders like Lohia, Karpoori Thakur, Lalu Prasad Yadav, Mulayam Singh Yadav, Charan Singh, Kanshiram and others created their own spaces and had their own narratives. The context in which their politics operated is different from the one that exists today. Moreover, the past three decades of Shudra/Bahujan politics has been governed on the lines drawn during the Mandal agitation. Now they need a new strategy.

Despite the rule of regional parties in the post-Mandal era, the state machinery at the national and regional levels remained Brahminic. It constantly created and took advantage of rifts between minorities and Hindus. Also, the tensions between Dalits and Shudras were politically encashed by casteist forces. The only way out is for all secular parties and forces, including the Congress and regional parties headed by Shudras/OBCs/Dalits/Adivasis, to form a broad national coalition to defeat the RSS–BJP and save the secular Constitution and democracy.

The Question of Bahujan Women

Prachi Patil

Who Are Bahujan Women?

Shudra, OBC and Bahujan are categories that are often used to talk about various communities clubbed within the Shudra varna in the four-varna hierarchy. But I am using 'Bahujan' here in the way that the general media uses it, to refer to Shudras/OBCs, not including SCs and STs. This essay aims to engage with the women who belong to these various contested categories. Bahujan women, as I refer to them, have had a rich tradition of resistance against caste, patriarchy and Brahminism. Mainstream historical and even Dwija-led feminist narratives have expunged the revolutionary struggles of Bahujan women from the annals of social history. However, their revolutionary struggles have been kept alive through oral traditions and local booklets and pamphlets produced and reproduced during anti-caste movements. These are being revived by Bahujan scholars. The Bahujan feminist standpoint locates itself differentially from the Dalit feminist and Dwija feminist discourses. Bahujan women are uniquely located within the caste–gender matrix.

Above the Dalits and below the savarna Dwijas, they are the middle castes. Thus, while they are unquestionably subordinate to men of their own caste and savarna men, they also share a differential power relationship with female members of both the Dalit and savarna castes. With the former, they share a dominant power relation while they have a subordinate position in the power matrix vis-à-vis the latter.

The English word 'caste' encompasses two levels of an integrated system: varna, the four main categories or endogamous groups called jatis, and the multitudinous subdivisions within each varna. Varna is broadly organized as a four-tiered socio-economic system determined by the familial line, although not all four varnas are present in every region of India. The caste system outlined in the ancient Hindu scripture, the *Manusmriti*, prescribed social status along with occupation. The highest varna (caste) is the Brahmins, who traditionally worked as Hindu temple priests, followed by the Kshatriyas (the warrior caste), the Vaishyas (the merchant/trader caste) and the Shudras (the servant caste).[1] These castes are the main source constructing caste hierarchies and untouchability. The first three remain in the top order of society as it functions now. They impose restrictions on social intercourse with them. The Hindus believe that the Shudras were born out of the feet of Brahma, as is stated in the *Apastamba Dharma Sutra*.[2] The popular understanding among scholars and academicians about the origin of the Shudras is that they were the indigenous people of India who were captured and co-opted by the Aryans into the fold of Hindu religion.

According to Ram Sharan Sharma, 'large sections of people, Aryans and pre-Aryans, were reduced to that position, partly through external and partly through internal conflicts. Since the conflicts centred mainly around the possession of cattle, and perhaps latterly of land and its produce, those who were dispossessed of these and impoverished came to be reckoned as the fourth class in the new society'. Sharma claims that during Rig Vedic times there was no caste system, and the fourth varna, the Shudras, was not yet developed. He maintains that 'the Rg Vedic society had no recognizable sudra order'.[3] He further claims that the Shudras were a tribe. Sharma produces an account of the caste/varna system with agriculture as the mode of production where the Shudras were collectively forced into being the 'servile class' or the 'labouring class'. Once the Rig Vedic pastoral society gave way to a Vedic agricultural and semi-nomadic society, the four varnas and the caste system stabilized. However, there are other theories of caste and varna as well.

Ambedkar on Shudras

In contrast to this view, Ambedkar provides a fresh perspective on the origin of the Shudras in his treatise 'Who Were the Shudras?'[4] According to him:

> The Shudras were one of the Aryan communities of the Solar race . . . There was a continuous feud between the Shudra kings and the Brahmins in which the Brahmins were subjected to many tyrannies and indignities. As a result of the hatred towards the Shudras generated by tyrannies and oppressions, Brahmins refused to perform the upanayana (the sacred thread-wearing ceremony) for the Shudras. Owing to the denial of upanayana, the Shudras who were Kshatriyas became socially degraded, fell below the rank of the Vaishyas and thus came to form the fourth varna.[5]

He states that 'under the system of Chaturvarnya, the Shudra is not only placed at the bottom of the gradation, but he is subjected to innumerable ignominies and disabilities so as to prevent him from rising above the condition fixed for him by law'.[6]

Ambedkar notes that 'the present-day Shudras are a collection of castes drawn from heterogeneous stocks and are racially different from the original Shudras of Indo-Aryan society'.[7] He states that the original Shudras of the Indo-Aryan society were a particular community, which has ceased to be an identifiable, separate community in present times. They were subjected to a 'legal system of pains and penalties' devised by the Brahmins to control the Shudras. According to Ambedkar, the Shudras of the Indo-Aryan times were degraded to a great extent, consequently leading to a change in the connotation of the word 'Shudra'. He claims that 'the word Shudra lost its original meaning of being the name of a particular community and became a general name for low-class people without civilization, without culture, without respect and without a position'.[8]

Shudras are not a homogeneous category, but a conglomeration of various castes. A few of the dominant Shudra castes claim Kshatriya status, while various others are grouped as Other Backward Classes (OBC).[9] The OBC is an administrative and constitutional category that came about as a result of the recommendations of the Mandal Commission, especially for the use of reservations in public services and education. The Bahujan identity is both a political category as well as a social one whereby Shudras could claim a homogeneous identity that is essentially anti-Brahmin and anti-caste, with a larger identity of its own to claim a larger share.

Bahujan Women in the Caste Matrix

In terms of the economic arrangement, the caste system organizes labour transactions not just according to the division of labour but, as Ambedkar argues, on the basis of division of labourers into graded hierarchies of caste. If one looks closely, this graded division of labourers within the caste system also reproduces gender-graded division of labourers. This gender-graded division of labourers sets apart caste-specific duties for women of the Shudra and Ati-Shudra castes in the larger caste economy. In the traditional economy of caste, Shudra women form the large chunk of producers and service providers and are closely connected with the soil. Their labour and products of labour have systemically been usurped by the Dwija castes. The caste system not only transacts labour through a formal arrangement of the graded economy but also intrinsically extracts surplus from Shudra and Ati-Shudra labourers through religious justifications. Traditionally, economic transactions within Indian villages were governed by rules of caste hierarchies that manifested in various economic subsystems such as the *jajmani* in northern India, and the *balutedari* and *aya* in southern India. Barring the Dwija-caste women who also do not have the right to wear the janeu, the caste system lays a claim on the labour of all Shudra and Ati-Shudra women. In villages, the upper-caste women's domestic sphere hinges on the labour of Shudra and Dalit women. The jajmani and balutedari systems allowed for Shudra women's labour to be appropriated within upper-caste domestic realms wherein the Dhobi (washer) women, the Nai (barber) women and the Kahar (water-bearer) women provide their caste-specific labour to upper-caste women and their households. It is important to recognize that there exist deep hierarchical power relations between Shudra and Ati-Shudra women. The Ati-Shudra women's productive and reproductive labour is exploited across caste lines and not exclusively by Dwija castes.[10] Jyotiba Phule's 'Kulambin',[11] a significant poem in anti-caste feminist literature, documents the labouring lives of women of the Kunbi caste (who are equivalent to Kurmi Yadav women in north India) within and outside the domestic realm in Maharashtra. Phule juxtaposes the labouring Kunbi women with the leisurely Bhat-Brahmin women, with men of the latter caste ridiculing the hard-working Kunbi woman. The poem charts out the gendered work routine of the Shudra women as they labour in their own homes and farms as well as in the Bhat-Brahmin homes. Phule brings out the skewed relations of power and labour between the Kulambin/Kunbi women and the Bhat women that are marked by the unequal flow of labour transactions, wherein the Kulambin women only serve but never get served by the Bhat women. The labour of women from the Dwija castes in a traditional village economy was restricted within their own homes, unlike the labour of Shudra and Ati-Shudra women.

The labour of Shudra women contributes not just to the domestic and caste economy but is also significant in maintaining the economy of the whole society. The domestic economy and caste economy rely on multiple exploitations of Shudra women. Within their own households, Shudra women do gendered domestic labour, along with their husbands they do caste-centric labour in the fields and artisanal markets, and then perform the gendered labour of caste within upper-caste households. William Wiser's (1936) analysis tells us that work under the jajmani system in north Indian villages enlists the caste-specific duties of various castes. The jajmani system was an economic arrangement found in villages in which Shudra and Dalit castes performed various duties for Dwija castes and received grain or other goods in return.

Wiser's work also reflects the gendered characteristics of the caste economy, wherein we find data about the duties of various Shudra–Ati-Shudra caste women but none regarding the work done by Dwija-caste women. In his fieldwork in a village, female folk of the barber caste engaged in oiling, shampooing and massaging children and women in various households of the village, except those of the Dalit households. Women of the Kahar caste supplied water to the households in the village and Teli women pressed oils for their *jajmans* (Dwija lords). Shudra women's labour not just serves members of their own households but also the Dwija households in caste-specific gendered duties.[12]

Resistance of Bahujan Women to Caste and Patriarchy

The structures of caste and patriarchy have not gone unchallenged. Bahujan women have expressed their resistance through the Bhakti movement in pre-colonial India and led the later non-Brahmin movements against the caste system. Bahujan women saints of the Bhakti movement of the medieval era questioned the patriarchy and Brahminical superiority that excluded lower castes from spiritual domains. The knowledge of Shudra women saints like Janabai, Rajali, Gonali, Kalavve, Viramma, Nimmavve, Uttiranallür Nañgai and Alagi was rooted in folk traditions as they had no access to scriptural knowledge of written texts and they used non-Sanskrit languages. Their *doha*s and *abhanga*s questioned patriarchal and caste structures which kept lower-caste women from reaching God. The Bhakti movement attempted to purify Hinduism of its 'evils', it appealed for a change in morality and values, and therefore did not lead to structural changes in the caste system. It was the non-Brahmin anti-caste movements during the colonial period that opened up a space for social and legal reforms.

Savitribai Phule and Jyotiba Phule as a couple led the non-Brahmin anti-caste movement that axed at the roots of patriarchy, Brahminism and untouchability in nineteenth-century Maharashtra. Born in 1831 near Pune, Savitribai was a Shudra woman revolutionary from the Mali (gardener) caste. She completed her formal education at home under her husband's guidance and went on to become the first woman teacher in India. Along with her companion Fatima Sheikh, who was one of the first Muslim women teachers, Savitribai Phule taught girls and boys of the Shudra as well the Dalit castes. She broke several social conventions of gender and caste by venturing out to educate women, Shudras and Dalits even though Brahminism imposed severe restrictions scripturally and socially to keep women outside the sphere of education and social interaction. She encountered strong resistance from male Brahmins who resorted to jeering, verbal abuse and throwing cow dung on her to stop her from going to teach in school. Firm in her resolve, Savitribai, along with Jyotiba, Fatima Sheikh and her aunt Sagunabai Kshirsagar, went on to open more schools for Shudra and Dalit children.[13] Her efforts of social reform encompassed even the caste that opposed her the most, the Brahmins.

Enforced widowhood among Brahmins was at the root of the sexual exploitation of Brahmin widows, leading to out-of-wedlock pregnancies. Due to this, there were rising cases of Brahmin widow suicides and abortions or infanticide of children born in these conditions. As a response to this social evil, the Phules built a home for pregnant widows and an orphanage for out-of-wedlock children. Savitribai also organized a barber's strike in solidarity with Brahmin widows who were customarily forced to shave their heads. Her politics of compassion not only extended to the marginalized Shudra and Dalit castes, but also the downtrodden among Brahmins. Savitribai was a rebel not just in the caste-prescribed public sphere but also within the intimate domains of the private sphere. She challenged the normative ideas of mandatory childbearing by adopting an orphaned Brahmin boy.

As Ambedkar notes, in Hinduism, the onus of maintaining caste purity falls on women. Thus, in many Shudra households, even today women continue to wash their homes and children after they come in contact with Dalits. Being a Shudra woman, Savitribai was above the Dalits in caste hierarchy and was supposed to maintain norms of purity and pollution. Rather, we see her brutally breaking these norms by opening her house's water well for the Dalits. For this, the Phule couple faced boycott and had to relocate to another house. In the caste-ridden patriarchal society, Savitribai was a deviant who refused her caste-centric occupation and gendered duties to become an educator, a social reformer and an institution builder. She was the first woman to perform her husband's last rites by carrying the funeral pot, rejecting the hegemony of the Phule family's male member's right to perform the rites. She did not even allow her adopted son, Yashvantha Rao, to do that job. Such a thing was opposed by all women, including the beneficiaries of her social service. In the Brahminical social order, the male's and son's authority is invoked with a vengeance at the time of a father's or any man's death. The myth they created was that without a son or other male member in the family performing the last rites, no dead man would go to *swarga* (heaven). Savitribai had asserted that she was everything to her husband and he was everything to her. This is perhaps the most revolutionary step in the process of liberation of Indian women of all castes.

She was not just against Brahminism, which put Shudras at a disadvantaged position vis-à-vis the Dwija castes, but also against untouchability, which put Shudras in a privileged position vis-à-vis Ati-Shudras. It is this line of politics that sets the foundation for Bahujan feminism, which is very different from Dalit feminism, though both are anti-caste in their premise.

We also have Tarabai Shinde, a Kunbi-Maratha woman and contemporary of Savitribai Phule who published the essay 'Stri-Purush Tulana' (A Comparison between Women and Men) in 1882.[14] This was in response to the controversy regarding a criminal case against Vijayalakshmi, a young Brahmin widow from Surat who had been convicted to death for killing her child, born out of wedlock, to escape social stigma and boycott. The debate that ensued regarding the case resulted in Vijayalakshmi's sentence being reduced from death penalty to life imprisonment. Tarabai Shinde, aghast at the barbarity of the patriarchal caste society, demonstrated how it was only women who had to bear the brunt of it. The 'unwed mother' became a tragic victim for engaging in her passions, but men were free of any such burden. Tarabai's harsh critique of Brahminical patriarchy not just irked Brahmins but also made various men of her own caste anxious. A diatribe of accusations was unleashed on her to silence her critique. Her article never saw another reprint and was lost in the annals of history till scholars came across a reference to her in Jyotiba Phule's work, where he speaks in support of her.

In the south, in Tamil Nadu, there was Periyar's self-respect movement where women from Shudra castes participated in breaking social norms of caste and gender. Before this was the fight of the Nadar women in Kerala against caste dictums forcing them to unclothe their upper torso in the presence of Nair and other Dwija men. These struggles find no mention in popular conceptions of social history and not in the Indian women's movement either.

Bahujan Women's Position in Contemporary India

In independent India, the question of OBC women has largely come up during debates on women's reservation. The dismal presence of OBC women in the faculty across Indian universities is a curious case to begin with. The flouting and scuttling of OBC reservations and the reluctance to promote OBC women at professorial levels are rampant. Appointments happen only when the whipcord over the constitutional mandates looms large. Though there are very few university-educated Shudra/OBC women, those who struggled through higher education and got well qualified get rejected because they are women, and that too Shudra/OBC women.[15]

Indian feminism has largely been the Dwija-caste feminist perspective. This has been critiqued foremost by Dalit feminists, who have questioned upper-caste women's complicity in their exploitation. However, the Dalit feminist standpoint and upper-caste feminist perspective do not explain the position of women of the middle castes, that is, the Shudra/OBC castes. Besides being an anti-caste force, Bahujan women's standpoint is also the acknowledgement of their dominant power dynamics. Shudra/OBC women have to realize that a whole lot of their history remains to be written and is an open field for discourse. Shudra/OBC women must speak from their unique position. Being the largest group of marginalized women, they need to educate, agitate and organize, taking inspiration from the motto that Ambedkar had left for the oppressed gender, while forging deeper, meaningful engagement with other oppressed groups. Only then can we enter a world that women like Savitribai dared to dream for us.

A New Beginning for Shudras Still a Possibility

Urmilesh

In 2014, a few months before the parliamentary elections in India, the BJP announced that Narendra Damodardas Modi would be running as its prime ministerial candidate. Surprisingly, some days later, Modi asserted that he belonged to the OBC community, a claim he had not made during his tenure as the chief minister of Gujarat. With this statement, he created curiosity amongst the Shudra communities in the northern and central regions of the country, initially due to the fact that never before had an OBC candidate run his prime ministerial campaign using the aircraft of a leading business conglomerate.[1] On the other hand, they also had apprehensions about his claims, because the surname 'Modi' had never before been known as part of a backward community. In addition, Modi had not been known for taking affirmative action for the benefit of this community or extending his support to the Mandal Commission. During the Mandal movement, he never came out in support of reservation. In fact, even within his organization, he was not known as belonging to the OBC community.[2]

During his tenure as Gujarat chief minister, the representation of recognized backward communities and emerging backward communities in his cabinet was miniscule. Initially, there was anxiety and apprehension about his candidature for the post of prime minister. However, that anxiety vanished when India's corporate-controlled media painted a rosy picture of Narendra Modi as the man who had built a successful 'Gujarat model of economy', asserting that he deserved to be handed the reins of the nation—as the first OBC prime ministerial candidate.

Soon after coming to power at the Centre, the Modi-led BJP government began keeping Dalit and Shudra leaders from the Hindi belt on a tight leash. As a result, in Bihar, the chief minister and JD(U) leader Nitish Kumar, questioning Modi's leadership, announced his separation from the National Democratic Alliance (NDA). Eventually, Kumar and Lalu Prasad Yadav joined hands, and in the 2015 assembly elections, the RJD and the JD(U) fought together and won against the BJP. Nitish Kumar returned to the post of chief minister, but that did not stop the BJP's tactical game. After a few years, Kumar bowed to Modi's leadership, the same one he had rejected in 2014. 'My decision to disassociate with the BJP is final. I would much rather get destroyed than join hands with the party in the future,' he had said in February 2014.[3]

However, that sentiment disappeared in July 2017, when he not only dismissed the anti-BJP mandate but also joined hands with the party. Known as one of the most prudent and credible OBC leaders in the state, his decision came as a shock and disheartened the OBC community across the nation. The other prominent leader from the state, Lalu Yadav, was blessed with expertise and far greater charisma and sociability skills compared to Kumar. But unlike erstwhile leaders of the state such as B.P. Mandal and Karpoori Thakur, or his contemporary Nitish Kumar, Yadav lacked political integrity and grit.

The irony is that despite his conscientiousness, grit and prudency, Kumar showed no spine when it came to reforms needed for the economic and social advancement of the OBC communities. Not even once did he focus on the pressing topic of Bihar's land reform. This would have led to him losing the support of the landlord classes. Incidentally, the recommendations of the Mandal Commission, often quoted and supported by leaders such as Lalu Yadav, Ram Vilas Paswan and even Nitish Kumar, include land reforms, an agenda considered critical to the enactment of social justice for the Dalit and landless OBC communities. However, despite their words, no actions were taken in support of this imperative issue in their tenure spanning from the 1990s.

In Uttar Pradesh, Shudra politics saw the rise of a new Dalit political leader, Kanshiram. His ideologies and passion matched that of Chaudhary Charan Singh, who was the first major Shudra leader from north India; he became the first Shudra prime minister for a short period with the support of Indira Gandhi. His contemporary Dr Ram Manohar Lohia and his supporters called themselves 'Kujat Gandhians'. Though Chaudhary Charan Singh's ideology matched that of Indira Gandhi with a dash of rural rusticity, it was Lohia who, in his political strategies, projected himself as the leader of the backward communities. He was considered a 'Kujat Congressman' due to his long association with the Congress. He applied the 'AJGAR formula' in his effort to widen the scope of Shudra politics. AJGAR refers to a social alliance of dominant intermediary castes comprising Ahirs, Jats, Gujjars and Rajputs in Uttar Pradesh and Bihar. But even in his effort, neither did he ever attempt to include Dalits in his network nor did he work towards ending crime and discrimination against them. He never campaigned against barbaric human untouchability.

Unlike Lohia, his contemporary and Bihar's Lok Dal leader, Karpoori Thakur, was a visionary in uniting Dalits and Shudras. Unfortunately, his popularity was less than that of Lalu Prasad in Bihar or of Kanshiram in Uttar Pradesh, who also played a pivotal role in uniting Dalits and Shudras to form Bahujan politics. Kanshiram took vital steps to base this union on Ambedkar's vision. He introduced all major Bahujan icons like Mahatma Phule, Ambedkar and Periyar to north India. This was a new political beginning in the Hindi belt. But the tides changed when the need for numbers in the form of political following took over the need for sociopolitical changes. This further weakened the alliance between the SP and the BSP. Around 2001, Kanshiram had a serious lapse of judgement when it came to choosing Mayawati as his successor.[4] Under her leadership, Bahujan politics, which required a national leader for its steady growth, suffered. Due to Kanshiram's untimely death, Mayawati took over, and like Mulayam Singh Yadav of the SP, ran Bahujan politics rather meekly and nonchalantly. Mayawati, with her overemphasis on electoral politics and no national vision, led the party towards becoming a corporate trap. Soon, Mayawati and Mulayam Singh Yadav were drawn into corruption controversies and lost their political edge, due to which their ideologies were also shaken up.

Amidst these developments, the RSS-controlled BJP got the support of the mainstream media, which emphasized the importance of 'Hindutva'.

After nearly two decades of the Mandal–Kamandal currents and countercurrents in north and central India, the BJP established its hold. This was akin to Brahminic forces mobilizing their resources and getting strengthened as a powerful ruling force in that land. Due to their complete domination of the power structure—the economy, bureaucracy, media and other intellectual institutions—there had never been a need for caste-based mobilization of Dwija castes in north Indian society. Taking into consideration the past three to four decades, it has been noted that the only time Dwija caste members gathered was when their share in government services shrunk, or whenever governments took welfare measures in favour of Dalits, Adivasis or OBCs.

In 1990, after the approval of the Mandal Commission recommendations by the V.P. Singh (himself a Kshatriya) government, there was a hue and cry by many Dwija-caste communities in north and central India. Youth and students were mobilized from the Dwija castes against the implementation of the Mandal report. Though there were other reform agendas in the commission's recommendations, it was the reservations provided to SC, ST and OBC persons that were either questioned or asked to be reduced. And while the protest was initially sporadic, it eventually took a turn for the worse due to support from the media and some political parties. But the aggression in the Dwija caste mobilization seen between 2017 and 2018 was different from the ones seen earlier. Demonstrations, conferences, bandhs, protests and fasts were organized openly under the banner of various Brahmin Sabhas or Savarna Samaj. Today, the message is being conveyed to the youth of Dwija middle-income families that Dalit OBCs are not only eating up their employment opportunities but other social benefits too due to the reservation system.

Dissemination of such poisonous propaganda amongst the Dwija youth has led them to not consider the fact that reservation is only for 50 per cent of the posts. Even those reserved seats and posts are never filled, especially in high-end universities and jobs. The remaining 50 per cent seats and posts are for youth in the general category, which consists of people who account for

15 per cent of the population. The Shudras outside the scope of reservation, like the Jats, Gujjars, Patels, Marathas and so on, due to their social and educational backwardness, were not able to compete with the Dwija youth in the open category, and hence open jobs were being taken over by the Dwija community youth. Yet they were made to feel restless.

On 2 April 2018, when a Bharat Bandh was organized by Dalits against the weakening of the SC and ST (Prevention of Atrocities) Act, 1989 (SC and ST [PoA] Act) in a Supreme Court judgment, and several counter-protests were also organized by the Dwija caste communities, the Shudra/OBC community was also seen taking the side of the Dwijas on social media. While no major political party came out to openly support the counter-bandh, it was found that local leaders of Hindutva organizations were working in favour of Dwija organizations. Hindutva workers were found overseeing the networks working against the Act. At the same time, several babas of Mathura–Vrindavan, Benares, Bhopal–Ujjain and Jaipur were also heard speaking against reservation and the SC and ST (PoA) Act. A large number of those vocal voices belonged to the VHP and BJP workers. During this period, many individuals started pasting doctored images of Hanuman and posting their castes—such as 'Brahmin', 'Rajput' or 'Tyagi'—on the front or back windscreens of their vehicles.

Dalits have been going to Bhima Koregaon every year on a pilgrimage to pay peaceful homage. But in 2018, they were attacked while on the pilgrimage. Despite filing a first information report (FIR), no action was taken against the attackers. On the contrary, the Dalit community got criminalized.[5] Further, many lawyers and human rights activists, in Delhi, Hyderabad, Mumbai and Ranchi, were also taken into custody in connection with this case. Meanwhile, the Supreme Court of India gave a judgment in the direction of diluting the SC and ST (PoA) Act.[6]

The Act was then challenged by certain organizations, including the All India Equality Forum. It is ironical that organizations like the All India Equality Forum, which claims to work towards equality for citizens of India, was a party against the protection of caste-oppressed citizens. Many Dwija forces see the SC and ST (PoA) Act as a source of inequality in the society.

In states like Uttar Pradesh, Madhya Pradesh, Rajasthan and Bihar, issues such as the SC and ST (PoA) Act reservation, and the temple vs mosque debate are topics that are easily radicalized. These are the same states where, since Independence, there have neither been any successful land reforms, nor adequate social justice reforms. Even during the fight for Independence, no step towards social justice for SC, ST and OBC groups were taken as power was in the hands of Dwija castes. Any demand for land reform was violently suppressed, such as in the case of Bihar's Triveni Sangh (1933–39). Triveni Sangh was a Bihar-based sociopolitical organization representing three Backward Castes: Yadav, Koeri (also called Kushwaha) and Kurmi. This organization was formed on 30 May 1933 to resist the repressive acts of the dominant feudal classes in Bihar's rural areas, and also to challenge the political dominance of the Congress in state politics.

Even after Independence, while citizens got political freedom—that is, 'one person, one vote' and 'one vote, one value'—widespread socio-economic inequality remained. This continued to derail our democracy. Ambedkar, in his historic speech on 25 November 1949 in the Constituent Assembly, described this as the most pressing issue of the future of Indian democracy. He said:

On 26th of January 1950, we are going to enter into a life of contradictions. In politics we will have equality and in social and economic life inequality. In politics we will be recognizing the principle of one man one vote and one vote one value. In our social and economic life, we shall, by reason of our social and economic structure, continue to deny the principle of one man one value. How long shall we continue to live this life of contradictions? How long shall we continue to deny equality in our social and economic life? If we continue to deny it for long, we will do so only by putting our political democracy in peril. We must remove this contradiction at the earliest possible moment or else those who suffer from inequality will blow up the structure of political democracy which this assembly has so laboriously built up.[7]

While some states were better than others, at a national level, our elected leaders failed in taking steps to eradicate or at least reduce the existing socio-economic inequalities. States such as Jammu and Kashmir, Tamil Nadu, Kerala and, to a certain extent, Karnataka made significant efforts in the fields of land reform, administrative reform and education. But the government's policies in the northern and central Indian belt did not work in any meaningful way. In the Hindi-speaking states of the north, the structure of democracy is in operation at the political level, but at the socio-spiritual level, the same old system of inequality, oppression and injustice persists. The chief minister's position in these states were occupied by Dwija-caste individuals for a very long time, and they did not show initiatives towards any kind of radical land reform, expansion of education to the masses, and representation of Dalits and OBCs in all spheres. These would have been not only economically effective but rather imperative steps for reducing social inequality, increasing productivity and improving administration.

While certain important steps were taken at the central level in the field of education and health, the same could not be said about the states due to lack of the required resources and will. The north Indian state governments did not bother about disparity due to different mediums of instruction like Hindi in government schools and English in private schools, where the rich study. Similarly, there should have been a decision to run the public health sector purely on government expenditure. Inequality in the fields of farming, education and employment did not allow our society to move towards being an inclusive one at a social level. In such volatile states, any affirmative action taken by the government is viewed as a threat to the Dwija-caste oppressors. The strongest opposition to reservation came from the states of north India. In some parts of Madhya Pradesh, Rajasthan and Uttar Pradesh, even wedding processions by Dalits led to a backlash. Hindutva politics projected the SC and ST (PoA) Act as an enemy to the general public, rather than a social justice safeguard. In the past, these anti-Dalit stances have been used for political gain. The Dwija castes have never come together unless it was to target Dalits, OBCs and the reservation system.

Take, for instance, the time when a leader of the Karni Sena was on live television protesting the release of the film *Padmaavat*; he somehow managed to express his displeasure with the reservation system.[8] Similarly, in 2015, right before the Bihar elections, RSS chief Mohan Bhagwat created a toxic environment by wanting to have a 'debate' on reservation.[9] Despite the efforts of Prime Minister Modi and Amit Shah, the BJP suffered a terrible defeat in that election. Since then, senior BJP–RSS leaders have changed their stance and reiterated their commitment to implementing reservation. The National Crime Records Bureau (NCRB) statistics released by the Union home ministry shows that crimes against Dalits have rapidly risen in north and central India since 2014. The rate of crimes in states which then had a BJP government are at an all-time high, with Uttar Pradesh having the highest numbers, Rajasthan with the worst atrocities and Madhya Pradesh with a growing crime rate after the BJP took over following a fifteen-year Congress rule. In fact, 12.1 per cent of the total crimes against SCs, STs and OBCs occurred in Madhya Pradesh alone.[10]

Even the 2018 Bharat Bandh on the SC and ST (PoA) Act took a violent turn in Madhya Pradesh. All this after the BJP made a surprising announcement that the government had passed an amendment bill to repeal the court verdict, following heavy opposition from the Dalits over the controversial decision of the Supreme Court undermining the Act.[11] Even after the notification by President Ram Nath Kovind, Chief Minister Shivraj Singh Chouhan announced that the stringent provisions of the Act would not be implemented in Madhya Pradesh.[12] There were no comments on this announcement from the OBC prime minister or the Dalit president. The question remains: Why did leaders such as Chouhan, who belongs to the Shudra community, make a comment against the interests of Shudras or OBCs? Naturally, doing so would reassure the groups that govern the BJP. This is a simple route to maintain their powerful position, and a formula employed by Chouhan to sideline the political ascendency of the fiery Uma Bharti.

Chouhan has always been considered a 'balanced' leader in comparison to the other top leaders of the BJP–RSS, which is also why he has been considered more credible than the other Dalit OBC leaders in the party. In recent years, in its experiment with 'social engineering', the BJP brought in many Dalit and OBC leaders into the party fold, however weak they may be in their passion for social reform. The BJP–RSS got more out of the social identities of leaders like Gopinath Munde, Kalyan Singh, Hukumdev Narayan Yadav and Uma Bharti than these leaders got for themselves and their communities.

During 2017–18, the Dwija caste mobilization in north and central India was led by the Brahmin community, which today is known to be the most vocal supporter of the BJP. As per Cobrapost, in a state like Bihar, and especially in central Bihar, many of the private armies which oppress Dalits are supported—directly or indirectly—by a handful of leaders of the BJP, JD(U) or Congress. Cobrapost made a complete documentary on these armies, where the alleged Dwija commanders were seen openly naming their patron leaders. But even after such an open declaration, no action was taken by the appropriate bodies.[13] On the contrary, some of these leaders are now a part of the current central government. However, it is seen that the terror and bloodshed by these armies have now reduced, primarily because their class and caste interests cannot be furthered any more only through their naked display of violent power. In such turbulent times, the direction of the Opposition parties also benefits the Hindutva–Dwija caste agenda. And while the attitude of the Congress has been a positive change in comparison to the previous four decades, its sociological ideologies are still far from clear. As far as the RSS and the BJP are concerned, their strategy and political agenda are quite evident. They are convinced that the savarna Hindu society is going to be associated with them due to their 'social engineering' and the fact that Hindutva is their core ideology.

In alignment with the RSS ideology, right before the 2019 election, the Modi government resolved to give 10 per cent employment and seat reservation to the 'economically weaker sections of the upper caste', a move which was immediately passed by Parliament. This 'unique' provision has been considered a contradiction to the basic principles of the Constitution and the globally recognized standard of affirmative action. This has also been referred to as a part of the Modi government's social engineering agenda, which is undoubtedly more an election strategy rather than a policy for social inclusion.

An example of the nonchalant attitude of the current government's concern towards social reforms is its reservation policy in colleges and universities of the Hindi belt. Somehow, the appointment of Dalit OBC lecturers and professors has come to an abrupt halt because of the appointments under the new roster.[14] This happened despite the government's assurance that discrimination would not be tolerated. Upon the issue being raised in Parliament, the minister for human resource development gave a passionate statement about condemning such behaviour and preventing injustice.[15] After the statement, appointments started getting scheduled under the new roster in universities and colleges located in Benares, Allahabad, Gorakhpur and Bhopal. The roster, nevertheless, considered departments/centres as a unit rather than the university, leading to an automatic reduction in the number of reserved seats. Being relatively more educated, these steps in favour of the Dwija-caste communities instilled a stronger faith in the BJP and the belief that the BJP-led government was doing a lot more for them than promised. The trust of savarnas in the BJP does not just stem from the Mandal–Kamandal and temple campaigning, but also due to similar core socio-economic aspects. In turn, the BJP has emerged as the most trusted and preferred party of the Dwija castes in the Hindi belt.

The RSS-led BJP has worked hard for its political expansion in the Hindi belt. It has also received a lot of support from the bureaucracy and the media, an important section of which is led by Dwija Hindus. Apart from this, the BJP has also taken advantage of Bahujan politics in Uttar Pradesh and Bihar for its own benefit. This began with the Dr Lohia–Deendayal Upadhyaya dialogue. Socialist leader Dr Ram Manohar Lohia and Bharatiya Jana Sangh leader Deendayal Upadhyaya met at Chitrakoot on the initiative of another Jana Sangh and RSS leader, Nanaji Deshmukh, much before the 1967 election. Many political observers considered this meeting as the beginning of the process of formation of a broader anti-Congress alliance between Lohiaite socialists and the RSS-backed Jana Sangh.

Both leaders met again in 1967, and Samyukta Vidhayak Dal (SVD) governments were formed in Uttar Pradesh and Bihar, overthrowing the Congress for the first time. In Uttar Pradesh, socialists and the Bharatiya Jana Sangh joined hands with Charan Singh's newly formed Bharatiya Kranti Dal (BKD). In Bihar, a new SVD government under the leadership of former Congress leader Mahamaya Prasad Sinha was formed. Shudra politics lost its way in the Lohia model of non-Congress politics. The socialists were not choice-less in their anti-Congress politics. They could have established an alliance with the left parties in Uttar Pradesh and Bihar, but they joined hands with the right wing instead. From Lohia to George Fernandes and Jayaprakash Narayan to Nitish Kumar, to even more vigilant and intelligent Dalit leaders such as Kanshiram, all have formed alliances with the BJP in the past as a short cut to power. Such partnerships have always helped the BJP to hide its Hindutva narrative from the Shudra community.

After the Mandal–Kamandal politics, the BJP stole the Congress's Dwija-Hindu base. Through Kamandal, the BJP was able to connect to undereducated and non-political communities of the Shudras. Meanwhile, in the last decade and a half, five prominent leaders of north and central India were imprisoned for corruption. These include Lalu Prasad Yadav, Om Prakash Chautala, Chhagan Bhujbal, Rashid Masood and Madhu Koda. There was no strong reaction within the Shudra communities about the five arrests, even at the political level. It is believed that the biggest reason for this was that these leaders did not undertake any significant reforms to advance Dalit, OBC, SC and ST communities during their administration. If Lalu Prasad had diligently worked towards land reform, education and health during his tenure of almost fifteen years, it would have been impossible for anyone to eclipse him in Bihar politics. Additionally, if Lalu Yadav had had administrative vision, he would have taken concrete steps in the field of land reform—like Sheikh Abdullah of Kashmir, Devaraj Urs of Karnataka or E.M.S. Namboodiripad in Kerala. As far as Nitish Kumar is concerned, he always ruled under the shadow of 'Manuwadi Hindutva'.

Mulayam Singh Yadav, a prominent OBC leader of Uttar Pradesh, is widely believed to have been the frontman for the BJP for several years. There have also been several corruption complaints lodged against him and his family members with various investigating agencies. Mulayam, very dramatically, annihilated his own party's election campaign during the 2017 Uttar Pradesh assembly elections. As a result, the BJP had unprecedented success in the elections. It also led Mulayam's brother, Shivpal, to split from the Samajwadi Party and form a new party. At one time, the Hindutva politics of the BJP in Uttar Pradesh and Bihar was contested by Dalit and OBC parties. Following Lalu Yadav's conviction and Mulayam Singh's soft stance towards the BJP, the sons of both leaders, Tejashwi and Akhilesh, respectively, have been making a desperate bid to save their supporter base from Hindutva aggression.

In a state like Uttar Pradesh, for a long time, instead of developing an inclusive civil society, the ruling parties created a community based on caste enmity. For instance, under Mayawati, a large section of Dwija castes ignored her as they felt that she only worked for the development of Dalits. She immediately addressed this resentment through her adviser Satish Chandra Mishra, who started organizing Brahmin conferences across the state. Furthermore, to strengthen their hold on electoral seats, the BSP started shouting 'Sarvajan' instead of 'Bahujan', a move replicated by the administration under Mulayam Singh Yadav and Akhilesh Yadav.

The SP not only abolished the three-tier reservation formula to address the displeasure of the Dwija castes, but also removed the then chairman of the Uttar Pradesh Public Service Commission, Anil Yadav, in April 2015. One of the allegations against him was that he had ordered execution of the reservation policy in all layers of competitive examinations, which apparently led to huge pressure from Dwija-caste leaders and officials. Allegations of corruption were also raised against him, which led to a huge controversy, and after the court ruled against his appointment, Yadav was removed by the then chief minister, Akhilesh Yadav. Mulayam and Mayawati even moved towards 'appeasement' of the Dwija castes, especially Brahmins, so much so that they repeatedly promised to give the Dwija castes reservation. It was no coincidence that both the SP and the BSP supported the 10 per cent 'economically weaker section' reservation formula of the Modi government.

In order to understand the reasoning behind this, one must understand the sociopolitical scenario of Uttar Pradesh. According to a non-governmental assessment, it is Uttar Pradesh, after Himachal Pradesh and Uttarakhand, which has the third highest population of Dwija castes, especially Brahmins. The Dwija-caste domination in the administrative, judicial, intellectual, cultural and economic fields in the state is still intact. The fact remains that the OBCs are still heavily scattered and have no single political platform. The BJP, through its social engineering, succeeded in connecting OBCs with castes like Kushwaha–Maurya and Rajbhar. Dalits, on the other hand, had a transactional relationship with the BSP and the BJP to expand their community supporters, a move supported by the BJP as the scenario is still suitable for Dwija-caste Hindutva politics. The reality today is that there is no coherent and solid political platform at an ideological level to counter the corporate–communal agenda of the BJP. The Bahujan movement today is headless and battered. Paradoxically, this is unfolding at a time when Dalit and Shudra society has educated—though in Hindi-medium schools—and active members. Their activism is visible at the grassroots level as well as on social media, but there are no English-speaking-and-writing intellectuals among them.

A small portion of the Dalit and Shudra OBCs have become empowered, putting them in a position to pick leaders of their choice and make donations to their organizations. But despite these possibilities, the influence and quality of the Dalit–Bahujan movement and its leadership does not appear to be progressing.

Decades ago, the socialists started a meaningful slogan: 'Make groups, not castes!' But a large section of the socialists later forgot the way themselves, and instead of groups, got caught in the chaos of caste interdictions. In a nation like India, it is almost impossible to challenge the caste system because of its inherent inequality and exploitative nature. Only in light of the broader sociopolitical perspective can the right path for the elimination of the caste system be found. If we look at the sociopolitical history of the last three decades, especially in the Hindi belt, most leaders of this era do not have a strong intellectual and political consciousness in dealing with Hindutva ideologies. One of the biggest crises faced in the Hindi belt in the modern era is that Dalit, Bahujan and OBC communities did not experience any relevant social reform movements. There were no great ideological leaders such as Phule, Shahu Maharaj, Babasaheb Ambedkar, Periyar, Ayankali or Narayana Guru.

After the reformers of the medieval era, such as Kabir, Raidas, Nanak and Dadu, the ideological stream of social reform dried up in modern north India. The British government fully supported Dwija-caste powers in not allowing any anti-caste and anti-racist streams to flourish in the Hindi belt. And today, a large part of the problems that lie in the path of India becoming a strong society and democracy are associated with the same Hindi belt.

Even seventy-three years after Independence, there has been no significant direction towards building an inclusive society here. A big reason behind it is the varna system and the resulting casteism. Corporate India can also easily be compromised by xenophobic narrow-mindedness. This is the reason why, like the capitalists of Europe, India did not have the good fortune of a truly capitalist–democratic revolution. Ambedkar, the greatest political thinker of modern India, had concluded long ago that one of the biggest issues in our society is the caste system and it will not allow India to become a nation and democracy in a real sense.[16] And, that is the reason why Ambedkar had called for the abolition of the caste system. However, it could not become a part of the national agenda at that time. No political party ever considered it seriously.

Not only do Dalit and Shudra leaders need to comprehend it but the whole nation needs to understand that no great political reforms needed for nation-building can emerge based on caste or religion. Our country has become a modern nation state with great difficulties, and to save it and our democracy, there needs to be a serious churning of non-Hindutva powers operating in politics. The caste system is the foundation of the philosophy and structure of Hindutva. Dalits, Shudras, Adivasis and minorities are the prime target of Hindutva as they have continuously been challenging it for the last three to four decades. Therefore, the forces of Hindutva moderated their leaders and organizations in order to capture the support of the entire society. Only the numerous and marginalized communities like Dalits, Adivasis and Shudras can stop India from being enslaved to a 'fascist Hindu raj'.

But then again, that is only possible if all communities unite on concrete socio-economic issues and a new viewpoint is developed in the current political scenario. In a large and diverse country like India, such a change is not possible with a single political party. A major shift in mindset with honest intentions is required, something not visible on the horizon now. But I would not like to end this essay on a pessimistic note. A vibrant Indian society based on diversity can never thrive on Hindutva ideologies. After centuries of Shudra and Dalit slavery, this society started breathing with authority only seven decades ago. And this society will not lose its rights. Shudras are the lowest just above Dalits, but the largest productive class of Indian society. Hence, a new beginning for Shudras is still a possibility for India. This class can liberate the Indian nation state from the caste system and its toxicity if it has the will to re-educate, guide and reform itself.

Production and Protection as Spirituality among Shudras

A New Discourse on Indus Deities and Vedic Gods

Ram Shepherd Bheenaveni

Although the majority of India's population belongs to the Shudra category, hardly any modern scholar is aware of the term 'Shudra', its historical role and identity. The category was constructed by Rig Vedic writers as the fourth varna with a negative connotation, but Shudras as a social force have always remained and continue to be the predominant food producers for this nation. They are the real nation-builders, but have no ownership or control, even at the turn of the twenty-first century. They were actually made to be slaves and workers as they built India's agrarian economy. Till today, their status has not fundamentally changed. This essay attempts to examine the historical process of evolution of this social mass which even today remains subservient to Brahminism.

Origins and Markers

In fact, the Rig Veda describes varna as 'colour, outward appearance, exterior form, figure or shape',[1] and contextually, it stands for the 'colour, race, tribe, species, kind, sort, nature, character, quality, property'[2] of people in almost all Indological texts. It was also referred to as type, order, colour or class[3] to denote the social classes mentioned in the *Manusmriti*, namely Brahmins, or priests; Kshatriyas, or warriors; Vaishyas, or merchants and tax collectors; and Shudras, or servants. The communities which belong to the first three varnas or classes are called Dwijas, which means 'twice-born'.[4] As per this belief, the first birth is natural and physical, and the second birth spiritual and performance-based. The second birth occurs when one takes up a so-called spiritual role from the time of the upanayana ceremony wherein the so-called sacred thread (janeu or *yajnopavita*) is received by a boy (the girl has no such right) aged eight to twelve years. The boy continues wearing it across his chest till death.

The upanayana rite of passage can be seen even today among the Dwija communities, with a relaxation of the age at which it is performed; most of these rituals take place a day before one's own marriage ceremony. The change is now being permitted because of the modern way of life. As per customs and traditions, Dwijas are entitled to the rite of upanayana, but Shudras are barred from partaking in it. Therefore, almost all Shudra castes—except recently Sanskritized Shudra communities—are not entitled to wear the janeu. The janeu is one of the foremost indicators of the segregation between Dwijas and non-Dwijas—who are usually referred to as Shudras, socially, culturally and spiritually. In Bihar, for example, there was an unsuccessful fight for the right to wear a janeu by a Yadav person, in which a few people died during 1910–20.[5]

The genesis and genealogy of Dwijas and non-Dwijas are different. Dwija is itself a varna and also a caste, viz., the Brahmin varna is a Brahmin caste too. Similarly, Kshatriya is both a varna and a caste, as is Vaishya. But Shudra, the varna for masses belonging to the fourth category, has a lot of castes that exist within it, namely Patels, Yadavs, Reddys, Jats, Gujjars, Marathas, Nairs, Lingayats, Vokkaligas and so on, who are known as upper Shudras, and all the OBCs of contemporary times. It is quite important to note that the Dwija varnas became both varnas and castes, but the fourth varna got splintered into countless sub-castes. What made Shudra the fourth varna and mandated that it be divided into many caste groups, instead of only one like the Dwijas? The answer can be traced back to the history of the Indus Valley civilization, and the theories of Aryan invasion and racial segregation.

There is no dispute when it comes to excavating the sites of the Harappan (Indus Valley) civilization in an archaeo-historical sense, but with sociological accounts, particularly with regard to the theory of Aryan invasion and racial descriptions, loads of ambiguities exist. However, recent studies related to the genetics of Harappan–Indus inhabitants have confirmed that indigenous Indian hunting and food-gathering communities gradually evolved into agricultural communities and constructed the Harappan civilization.[6] Almost all the sites situated in the Indus Valley were towns or cites that had a well-developed economy in which day-to-day economic transactions were carried out. The bronze and copper coinage of this era dating back to between 2500 BC and 1750 BC[7] affirms its stable and advanced economic system. Sophisticated infrastructure like sewage and drainage systems, granaries and so forth illustrates the use of advanced science and technology. It is quite easy to analyse and interpret materialistic history based on sites, artefacts, seals, coinage and other physical substances. But explaining the sociocultural and spiritual practices of an ancient civilization is a more complex and strategic job. Hence, descriptions and interpretations of archaeological artefacts such as gods, rituals, customs and other cultural practices in Harappan religion is not only contradictory but also controversial in many ways. However, many scholars have a definite opinion on its religion:

> There are many seals to support the evidence of the Indus Valley deities. Some seals show animals which resemble the two gods, Shiva and Rudra. Other seals depict a tree which the Harappans believed to be the tree of life. The tree was guarded by a spirit to keep the evil forces away from the tree. The guardian was portrayed by many animals such as bull, snake, goat, or any other mythical creature or animal. The evil force is represented by a tiger. One seal shows a figure sitting in a position that may be similar to a yoga pose and is thought to be an early representation of a Hindu God.[8]

Contrary to this account, it is possible that most indigenous Indians had no exposure to the concept of God during the Indus Valley period. For that matter, even today, almost none of the Shudra castes follow the concept of God; instead, they imitate the idea of the deity and treat the deity as God. The notion of God is merely a concept that evolved on the basis of structural functionalism. These structures were designed by the Aryan–Brahminic ruling class in order to establish their hegemony over the groups involved in production and protection. Even today in the village economy, we never see Brahmin–Banias involved in agrarian production and in the protection of village borders, which actually involves a lot of mental and physical labour.

The idea of the deity has emerged out of collective phenomena such as animism, animatism, naturism, totemism and shamanism. And, of course, martyrdom is a more suitable phenomenon to understand and explain the emergence of the deity and its evolution with regard to Shudra religion and worship. Animism and shamanism believe in the natural qualities of living creatures, including human beings, to imbibe the spirit of the indomitable and to receive solace in sorrowful situations. No doubt, nature is very powerful and no human can control its force, so humans, out of fear, started respecting it through animatism and naturism. Also, the fear of dangerous attacks by animals made humans worship them in the form of animism. There are certain plants and animals which are very helpful to humankind in disastrous situations, and offer food, shelter, protection and so on. Those plants and animals were worshipped in the practice of totemism. Meanwhile, shamanism is a kind of belief in imaginary efforts to boost a person who is in a state of acute depression.

By their origin and principle, these worship systems made humans solve everyday problems, but some sort of superstitious practices intruded into their minds to misrepresent the very concept of religion and tribal forms of worship. The structural functionalism of religion believes in extra qualities granted by the supernatural being. In other words, to rely on a force of nature with reasonable human effort is the practice of animism, naturism or shamanism, and resting blindly on the supernatural power of the so-called Almighty is the practice of a structural functionalistic form of religion. Usually, the spirituality of tribal groups evolves on the basis of animism and moves on to become shamanism. But the spirituality of religiously well-organized societies emerges from structural functionalism.

Religions like the Vedic religion (as differentiated from Hinduism), Zoroastrianism, Judaism, Christianity, Islam, Buddhism and Jainism emerged out of the postulates of a structural functionalistic form of religion, theoretically and theologically. That is why all these religions have a founder, foundational texts and formless gods. Religions evolved around animism, shamanism and the like do not have founders or texts but deities which take the form of a specific idol. Thus, it can be inferred that religions in which the God is formless or abstract are merely created out of the speculative ideas of human thinking, but religions wherein the God has absolute form or an idol are evolved in consonance with historical accounts.

It can be seen across all world religions, for instance, that before the emergence of Islam, there were enumerable idols worshipped by the people who lived in the Arabian Gulf. When Islam became powerful, it swallowed the conglomeration of these idols, and also wiped out religions like Zoroastrianism, Vedism and Buddhism in the Middle East. Similarly, when Aryan Vedism entered India, regional and productive Shudra-specific deities were marginalized and treated as inferior. Consequently, no place was found for these deities in any mainstream scripts written by Vedic rishis. But surprisingly, the productive deities were grandly adored in oral histories and folklore by their Shudra followers. The productive Shudra food culture and divine culture were also consciously neglected and marginalized by mainstream spiritual forces. Many of the Hindutva forces have started a campaign to declare India a vegetarian nation. This is anti-Shudra and goes against India's food culture. India, built by Shudra labour with multi-cuisine food culture from the days of the Harappan civilization, would be turned into a Brahmin–Bania anti-production vegetarian nation if this trend is unchecked.

The religions which evolved around animism, naturism and shamanism did not believe in subordinating another's spirituality and never intended to spread their pantheism geographically. But those religions that emerged out of structural functionalism were deeply inclined to contrast and contradict theologies of other religions. This is why Judaism, Christianity, Islam, Vedism, Buddhism and Jainism still clash with Shudra productive theism.

Shudra Sinduism versus Dwija Vedism

Contemporary Hinduism, on the basis of its forms of worship and philosophical postulates, can be classified into two parts, viz., (1) Indus Hinduism and (2) Aryan Vedism. Indus Hinduism is nothing but 'Sinduism', that is, a way of life of Indus inhabitants. Vedism is the religion of Aryans who actually migrated from Ariyana, present-day Iran and Afghanistan. It is strange that Hinduism appropriated the Shudra Harappan civilization and rendered Shudras identity-less. Aryan Vedism deliberately hijacked Indus Sinduism and morphed into Hinduism to keep Shudras as slaves and semi-slaves in a disguised form. Over a period of time, Aryan Vedism gained supremacy over Indus Sinduism and established spiritual fascism by holding all temple posts on the basis of birth and inheritance. Thus, Brahminism has established its modern legitimacy and the RSS–BJP are its political forms.

Shudra Sinduism and Brahminic Hinduism are two distinct spiritual systems. Milton Singer[9,10] and McKim Marriott[11] described them as 'great tradition and little tradition' by adopting the model of Robert Redfield's orthogeneity to heterogeneity.[12] Yogendra Singh also endorsed the cultural change in India from orthogeneity to heterogeneity by commenting on McKim Marriott's concept of 'parochialization' and 'universalization'.[13] I think what is constructed as Dwija Hinduism with Brahminic hegemony is parochialism whereas Shudra Sinduism was universalism by its nature of production and multi-cuisine food culture. Brahminic Hinduism, also known as Hindutva now, is anti-labour and rooted in pure vegetarian parochialism.

The process of Sanskritization elucidated by M.N. Srinivas is nothing but a sociocultural change from heterogeneity to homogeneity. In other words, it means adopting the values of the parochial norm instead of following universalist productive customs and traditions, thus negating Shudra cultural identity. However, parallel cultures have existed throughout history. Though cultural assimilation is quite a natural process, what Brahminism has done to Shudraism is cultural destruction. The theories propounded by Srinivas are the modern intellectual destroyers of the Shudra cultural autonomy. If processes like enculturization, assimilation and other cultural diffusions happen naturally, the question of dominance or superiority does not arise. If the Brahminic vested interest becomes the motto of cultural imperialism, the invaders must manipulate certain things that would swallow the traits of the native culture. Brahminic forces did many things to realize their objective in this way. The first and foremost act was to deny education to Shudras in ancient and medieval times, and bar them from English education through government schools in post-Independence India. Even post-Independence Brahminic scholarship supported the policies of anti-Shudra cultural and educational hegemony.

Since Shudras were traditionally deprived of education for many generations altogether, Brahminic tradition gained an advantage over Shudra tradition and eventually established its hegemony in all its elements and ethos. Historically, Shudras were deliberately denied access to education, and so they lost command over literature, episteme, political economy and so forth, and were enslaved easily by the manipulative tactics of so-called cultural values of the Aryan Vedic system. Despite the serious attack of Aryan Vedic culture on Shudraism, though, it has survived with its unique features.

Indus Deities and Vedic Gods

All deities of the Indus Valley civilization evolved from the heroic endeavours of great people. These endeavours may be an innovation or discovery of a new technology or product. Sometimes martyrdom might have occurred in protecting science and technology or territory. In memory of these legends, their hero stones, known by various regional and linguistic terms such as *paliya, khambhiy khatri, chara, viragal, virakkal, virasilalu, natukal chayasthambha*, etc., commemorated many forms of noble behaviour in ancient India. This could include death in battle, fights with wild animals, or death while protecting other people or cattle,[14] and were not confined to one geographical area. They are particularly numerous in south and west India, and in Telangana, Maharashtra, Andhra Pradesh, Gujarat and other parts of central India,[15] such stone deity images are in plenty. There are many references of the memorial stones of legends in Sanskrit and Kannada literature.[16]

For example, the Maharashtrian Vitthal, originally called Vithoba of Pandharpur, provides an exemplary model for understanding history in an alternative perspective in connection with pastoralist hero cults.[17] Similarly, the Sammakka Saralamma Jatara, a festival honouring the martyr heroines of the Koya tribe, is celebrated in the state of Telangana. Although they emerged as deities from the battlefield, unlike Vedanta gods, they are martyrs, not victors or seducers. It is common for martyrs to be transformed into deities in native Indian and Shudra cultures.[18] There are many martyr deities who exist across India, namely, Khandoba, Masoba, Beerappa, Yellamma, Maisamma, Pochamma, Nukalamma, Gangamma, Reddamma and so on.

Mammayi is the *kuladevi* (caste deity) of the Lohar community and is considered the inventor of *wootz*. Wootz is a word derived from the Telugu and Kannada word *wokku*, which means steel. She is worshipped by members of the bronze-making and blacksmith communities as a testimony to her creation of wootz.[19] Telugu dhobis, who are part of the Shudra community in the region, worship Madelu and consider him their community deity for inventing the technology of washing clothes. Markandeya became the family deity of Padmashali, a weaving community, as he was the inventor of cloth from cotton. Beerappa/ Biroba, a caste God of shepherds in Maharashtra, Karnataka, Telangana and Andhra Pradesh, is known for shepherding and weaving woollen blankets. Katamaiah is known for toddy-tapping technology and considered the inventor of *neera*, toddy, toddy jaggery and toddy fructose crystals, and thereby, he is worshipped as the community deity by toddy tappers in south India. Yellamma is a female deity, her name derived from the Telugu word *yella*, meaning border or boundary. Since she is familiar with martial arts, she used to act as a guard at borders, and her martyrdom transformed her status into a deity in central and south India. All these examples signify that the philosophical notion and cultural root of Shudra deities are different from the so-called Vedic gods who emerged from the discourse of atma (soul) and paramatma (God). Most Vedic god images are of war heroes and have no relationship with production, as Brahmins have had no relationship with production in known history.

The discourse of Vedism is primarily an inquiry into the ontological existence of soul and God, and purely an argumentation of a metaphysical pursuit of the doctrine of the Upanishads, especially in its monistic form; and thus, it resembles idealism. But Vedic Brahminic idealism, while self-centred, is not oriented towards the larger universe. Whereas Shudra deism quests for the logical and physical existence of a being, and thus, it is close to materialism with the spiritual notion of egalitarianism. Materialism was a predominant doctrine in India before the arrival of Vedic discourse. The philosophies of Charvaka, Lokayata, Ajivaka and Sankhya are classic examples to substantiate the very existence and practice of materialism in ancient India, and the same can be seen among Shudra productive masses even today. One does not find such productive spiritual discourse among present-day Brahmin–Bania forces.

Vedism portrays the trinity of Brahma, Vishnu and Maheshwara, and their incarnations are fundamentally derived from imaginary texts: Vedas, Puranas, Ithihasas, the Ramayana, the Mahabharata and so on. Most of the gods in Vedism are merely metaphysical constructions so that locating them in the chronology of Indian history is hazy and perhaps impossible. In fact, gods like Shiva, Vishnu and Brahma are manipulated constructions propagated through various texts. Take, for example, Lord Indra, who is the king of the suras, who are also called devas. He is also known as Devraj (king of kings). Etymologically, the term deva does not imply equality with the idea of God in English, but we are habituated to use it to denote God. However, devas are suras who used to work under the leadership of Lord Indra. In fact, 'Indra' was the title of Aryan chieftains. As Indra was a position, it could be competed for and captured by others also.[20] Hence, there were quarrels between Indra (leader) and other devas who aspired to be leaders. It was a power struggle. We do not find among Shudra divine figures such a power struggle. For example, there was a fight between Beerappa and his maternal uncle but it was about the control of sheep and the love marriage of Beerappa and his uncle's daughter. However, quarrels among many other Shudra divine figures were about their perceptions of production and distribution of food resources.

In Brahminic tradition, Lord Indra was a historical person, but ascribed extraordinary powers through fabulous stories of war and victory. The Rig Veda is a classic example of the glorification of Indra for his killing of asuras. In Shudra tradition, killing was never glorified.

If the idea of God is constructed based on historical realities, the philosophy of the human understanding of generosity, mercy, work ethics, talents and so on plays a pivotal role in rationalizing human life in order to achieve egalitarian socio-spiritualism for building a better human society. If the idea of God is constructed in a mythical mode around war and caste-based superiority, the God will certainly be biased towards the class which constructed him and inculcate a value of superiority that will culminate in ethnocentrism in due course of time. This is the reason why this value of ethnocentrism did not allow the Indus deities into mainstream Aryan Vedic texts.

The deities who are culturally rooted in production, protection and procreation never created a priestly caste. If one wants to offer them something that is relished in real life, the places of worship are open and substances allowed to be offered by anyone irrespective of gender, age and status without the presence of middlemen 'priests' and also without considering the time of offering as good or bad, or the substances offered as pure or impure. Even today, this kind of practice can be seen for Indus deities across regions and castes. It can also be seen that oral histories and folklore around particular deities are sung by members of the community to which the deity belongs. The ballads that bring to life the lived experiences of people spread across generations are more important than the simple chanting of mantras and, of course, the gist orated through ballads is centric to the Shudra consciousness of Indus spirituality.

The Vedic discourse of philosophy is unrealistic as it takes metaphysical and ontological inquiry into consideration to prove the very existence of the atma (soul) and paramatma (God) without supplying a cogent historical analysis of human productive consciousness. The Vedic concept of the Almighty with an abstract form as a super being does not relate to any form of productive human labour. The Shudra spiritual philosophy, as it came down to us from the Harappan civilization, is centred around production and distribution, and this spiritual philosophy was undermined in India and remains so even now.

In Vedic tradition, the super-being will communicate only with the priest who knows the divine language, which is Sanskrit in the Brahminic tradition. The Shudra masses which go to such temples do not have any right to become a priest. But the Shudra spiritual tradition did allow a person from any caste to be a priest, and anybody to talk to the deity in any language. It is this democratic relationship between the divine deity and people that helped Indian democracy sustain after we adopted our democratic Constitution. The secular character remained and operated outside any spiritual discourse, but the BJP is a religious party working with a belief in the Vedic tradition of religion, not the Shudra tradition of what I call 'Sindhutva'.

In Vedic tradition, the priest was entitled to act as a middleman in between the super-being and human being. The productive masses do not matter in this system. No doubt, Vedism allows a priest to use his discretionary powers to control followers by the chanting of metaphysical fables developed to divert the original consciousness, inculcated through the process of socialization as a general member of society and also its productive engagement with nature and soil. Eventually, this kind of religious value system and tradition culminates into spiritual fascism for those who do not believe in priests, idealism, metaphysics and plurality.

The spirituality evolved around production, protection and procreation relies on logic and materialism. It allows historical consciousness with the propositions of realism; thereby, it actualizes human beings as final and ultimate. It treats all humans as equal and inculcates egalitarian values which eventually lead towards spiritual democracy. Therefore, Indus deities of Shudra spirituality can only speak of production as human labour, protection as national duty and procreation as human dignity. This project of democratic enlightenment spirituality was supposed to take place in the aftermath of Indian independence or at least after the adoption of the Constitution, but it could not materialize despite the advent of modernity and democracy. Of course, political democracy and materialistic modernity have reached each and every corner of Indian society for the reason that the idea of democracy and process of modernity originated in Western societies and reached India through the onslaught of European colonialism.

The sociopolitical life of Shudras is very open, and therefore, they welcomed democracy and modernity into their lives. But their spiritual and religious life has been designed and governed by Brahminic priests. Consequentially, Shudras do not have any consciousness of introspection or retrospection to break the shackles of spiritual fascism. Even they are hardly aware of spiritual fascism, wherein they are being manipulated by virtue of the so-called theory of karma. Unlike democracy and modernization, Vedism was coined and developed within the Indian subcontinent; it became rigid with pseudo-egalitarian spiritual practice and has not permitted any sort of change. While the sociopolitical life of Shudras has been changing from time to time to enable them to enjoy their rights and entitlements, their religio-spiritual life still maintains the status quo and is becoming more rigid daily because of the manipulative tactics of Hindutva. Becoming a priest, chanting mantras, learning the Vedas and entering temples are still under the discretionary power of Brahmins, and even the Supreme Court of India may not dictate priests to act in the spirit of spiritual democracy. Surprisingly, priests and their fellow clergy have every right to oppose verdicts of this kind by the traditional power and authority granted by Vedic shrutis and smritis.

When philosophical resistance against the hegemony of Vedic spirituality takes place, the doctrine of the other side is easily appropriated by Vedic tradition through co-optation in a disguised form. The resistance of Sri Krishna and Buddha are classic examples of Vedic co-optation by disallowing the autonomous Shudra discourse of enlightenment. If the resistance was pragmatic, the shrines or idols were also co-opted, like giving the name 'Pashupati' to a deity of the Harappan civilization to attune with Lord Shiva, although Shiva did not exist in that period of time. Shirdi Sai Baba is another example as he was born Muslim but appropriated by Vedic pandits in due course of time. There is an attempt to co-opt Ambedkar's Navayana Buddhism into Hindutva in our times.

It is needless to say that the Buddha's challenge of Brahminic philosophy and Vedic practices changed the course of Brahminism in India. It is in this process that Brahminism brought forth Lord Krishna, a Shudra, and the Bhagavad Gita into its own Vedic tradition. Krishna and Rama represent two opposite cultural values. As a reflection of that, the RSS–BJP own Rama more than Krishna, giving birth to two opposite slogans: 'Jai Sri Krishna' by Lalu Prasad Yadav and 'Jai Sri Ram' by RSS–BJP forces. It was this Shudra–Brahminic conflict that led to Kanshiram's slogan 'Mile Mulayam Kanshiram hawa mein ud gaye Jai Sri Ram' (When Mulayam and Kanshiram come together, the slogan of Jai Sri Ram will be gone with the wind). Krishna even mythologically represents the cattle economy and universal philosophy.

Indus Krishna and Vedic Rama

According to spiritual leader Sathya Sai Baba, Ram's childhood was frequently pathetic despite him being one amongst four siblings. Ram used to weep all the time, confining himself to his bedroom,[21] and his sorrows were curtailed through the lessons taught by Vashishtha, the family priest. Later, Vashishtha elevated Ram to a warrior by performing the Kshatriya dharma. At the age of seventeen, Ram killed Tataki, the destroyer of yagnas. Thus began the legacy of Rama killing the asuras.

Krishna, on the whole, led a blissful childhood even though his biological parents were not with him. He was joyful, playing the flute and rearing cattle on the banks of rivulets and in the forest. During his infancy, Krishna killed Putana, the sister of Kamsa, who was sent to Vrindavan by Kamsa to kill baby Krishna. Putana, disguised as a gopi, tried to lull Krishna and fed him poison but Krishna sucked the life out of Putana and killed her. It is astonishing how a small baby could kill a big lady like Putana. To have a logical retrospection on it, Krishna as a small baby might not have killed Putana but somebody might have killed her and ascribed that murder to him.[22] The killings of Shatakasura, Trunasura, Vatschasura, Bakasura, Kakasura and so forth might have happened on the same lines.

At the age of twelve, Krishna and his brother Balarama visited Kamsa's city and killed his unbeatable uncle without deploying any armed force. This is also an unbelievable story in the historical sense. Ram did not kill his own people, but Krishna was said to have killed Kamsa, who was also a Yadav. However, the stories of killings in the texts try to project Ram as a historic, legendary personality more than Krishna.

Vashishtha strictly counselled Ram to uphold the Manu dharma and made him a warrior to protect the yagnas. Though Krishna was trained under Sandipani, he never followed the conventional culture of Manu. Ram followed Vashishtha's advice but Krishna never accepted any Brahmin guruship. He took his own decisions. Ram was dependent and loyal to the Manu dharma whereas Krishna was independent and possessed the courage to disturb orthodox structures. This is why the Sangh Parivar took Ram as their icon and made Krishna out to be a playboy and love-hero. This image of Krishna has been deliberately constructed but his Shudra cattle-rearing character could not be erased. He represented Sindu agrarian culture throughout his life.

Kuchela was Krishna's intimate childhood friend from Mathura, belonging to a poor Brahmin family, but the difference in social status did not come in the way of their friendship. However, Ram did not cherish any similar and equal friendship during his life.

Ram ordered his brother Lakshman to mutilate Surpanakha's nose, nipples and ears. In a state of shock, she left the place humiliated. But Krishna married Jambavati, who is considered a Dalit in the modern sense. Even though Krishna had no claim upon Draupadi and technically no responsibility towards her, it was he who protected her dignity with the unending supply of her sari.

Krishna rejected outright Indra's mystical powers and authority, and stopped rituals being performed to appease him. This act annoyed Indra and led to a battle between them. Indra is considered a representative of the Aryan gods (kings also usually claim this). In fact, this was a strategic trick of the Aryans to defeat their enemies. Krishna found the hidden strategy of enslavement in the name of God and exquisitely countered them by claiming that he was God Almighty himself. When Krishna used this tactic, all Shudras became confident, proud and self-assured. It was a real paradigm shift in the life worlds of indigenous Indians, and Krishna boosted their indomitable spirit.

Being a learned king, Ram did not contribute much to the philosophical discourse of India whereas Krishna contributed the Gita, which is not merely a song but an advice or rather a serious philosophical discourse. It is a philosophical document that has influence across all religions. The Gita is the text of rejection of the Manu dharma as it declares '*chaturvarnyam maya srishtam gunakarmavibhagashah*'[23] ('the fourfold Varna system is created by me on the basis of individual qualities and deeds'). 'The fourfold order was created by Me according to the divisions of quality and deeds of human beings. I am the Creator, know me to be capable of action or change.'[24] He did not leave anything to a Brahmin guru. The birth-based varna system was rejected by Krishna, which negates Manu's caste ideology entirely. Manu says that the varnas are ascribed status on human birth, and those cannot be changed. Ram was not entitled to choice-based selection as he embodied the varnadharma value system preached by his ancestors and Brahmin gurus. But Krishna had an open mind. Thus, his role can be seen from a cattle-herder to a lovable man to a warrior to a kingmaker to a king to a philosopher to God. This is possible only for a Harappan Shudra, not for a person following the Aryan Vedic ethos.

Indus Linga and Vedic Shiva

Most scholars and traditions believe that Shiva is a god of the Dravidians, but this may not be true as Shiva is entirely different from Linga. In fact, the idol of Linga is the combination of both male and female genitals, that is, the phallus and vagina. The worshipping of Linga might have evolved from the animist/animatic belief system of ancient societies as a marker of respect for pregnancy and childbirth. In other words, indigenous Indians had seen the human body as sacred and procreation as human dignity. This is a perfect symbolism of a productive, protective and procreative worshipping system and spirituality of the Harappan civilization.

   Lord Shiva, who was referred to as Rudra in the Rig Veda, is no doubt a position among suras designed to attack enemies, that is why he was called *layakara,* meaning the destroyer.

He used to live in a burial ground, using skulls as a garland, decorating himself with a poisonous snake around the neck and travelling on a bull—all extreme qualities of ruthlessness. Shiva was thus the destroyer.

Shockingly, Saivite Brahminism projected him as one of the prime gods and further constructed several mythological stories that reveal that Shiva must be worshipped in the form of Linga instead of his original form to conceal the reality; therefore, they had changed the form of Shiva from his idol to Linga.

When a steatite seal named 'Pashupati' was discovered at the Mohenjo-Daro archaeological site, scholars treated it as one of the earliest depictions of Lord Shiva, or a 'proto-Shiva' deity. Finally, the name given to the seal is 'Pashupati', meaning 'lord of animals', and is ascribed to one of Shiva's epithets. The website of the National Museum in New Delhi describes the narrative as 'this seal with [the] anthropomorphic form of ithyphallic Shiva is one of the most significant Indus finds, attesting [to] the prevalence of [the] Shiva-cult, his personalized Mahayogi or Pashupati form as also his iconic "linga" form, as early as Indus days and much before the emergence of [the] Vedic cult'.[25] In fact, the seal is not ithyphallic and an interpretation around its ithyphallic description is now mostly discarded. The seal does not even depict the image that resembles Lord Shiva and there is no scope to correlate the image in the seal with Lord Shiva as Shiva does not exist in Vedic literature itself.

The ithyphallic explanation of the seal might have been derived from the Vatsyayana Kamasutra's point of view. Presenting the seal as one of Shiva's epithets is merely a Brahminic manipulation, and naming the seal as 'Pashupati' is itself a great diversion to marginalize the Harappan civilization. Although Sanskrit did not exist at that time, the so-called scholars named the seal with the words *pashu* and *pati*, which are merely Sanskrit words. Shiva was a warrior and not a protector of animals, but that is the meaning the term 'Pashupati' conveys.

One can imagine the seal depicting a brave bull-man who was a trainer or expert in taming wild animals to augment a flock of domesticated cattle, to create a meat and milk economy, and convert animal power to supplement human labour. This kind of analogy was supposed to take place by the scholars' organic intellectual interpretation. But the majority of scholars who engaged in Indic studies hailed from elitist backgrounds, without production and protection being part of their lives, so they had to invariably depend on textual analysis. A text may not supply the concrete context to ancient history, and moreover not to prehistory.

By deconstructing the arguments surrounding the seal, I name 'Pashupati' here as 'Adi Harappa'. Adi Harappa was a champion in domesticating wild animals and converting that animal force into production in order to build houses, streets, wells, ploughs, settlements, towns, cities and so on. That was how the Harappan civilization was built and developed. Since then, his legacy of production and protection has been continuing among all Shudras in Indian villages in the form of caste occupations, but what is missing is the egalitarian spirit that was boosted by the Harappans due to the conspiracy of so-called unproductive Vedic tradition.

What happens when a party that consists mainly of Brahminical ideology with Bania capital mobilizes the unconscious support of Shudra sanyasis, and the peethas that negate production and protection run the nation? Agrarian economy, mass job creation and the building of the economy and educational institutions for all get destroyed.

In the process, Shudras are suffering the most, and their civilization, built from the days of Harappan agriculture, is slowly but surely being destroyed. To circumvent the Hindutva jeopardy, Shudras must learn the productive ethics of the Harappan Shudra civilization, grasp the political tactics preached by the Shudra Krishna and imbibe the spirit of the indomitable through the lives of Shudra martyrs. It is only then that the glory of the productive and protective Shudra socio-spiritual culture will save multiculturalism, since other religions in India took shape because of caste and untouchability. The anti-Hindutva solidarity comes from these Shudra/Dalit/Adivasi productive and cultural roots.

Sociocultural Identity Formation among Shudras

Bindu N. Doddahatti

Caste has very interesting dimensions and realities in India. We have a prime minister who has very tactically claimed an OBC identity,[1] when in reality he has suffered no ignominy of being a Shudra individual. He was born in the Modh Ganchi caste, which was not in the reservation category then, but was added to the OBC category through a government circular in the 1990s. This allowed him to reach out to the OBC vote bank. On the other hand, we have a vast majority of OBCs who detest being called Shudras, while unwisely clinging on to the historically untenable notions of neo-Kshatriya and neo-Brahmin identities. Dr B.R. Ambedkar has rightly pointed out in his 1946 text, 'Who Were the Shudras?': '. . . the book is written for the ignorant and the uninformed Shudras, who do not know how they came to be what they are. They do not care how artistically the theme is handled. All they desire is a full harvest of material—the bigger the better'.[2] Strangely enough, this statement holds true even to this day.

What was started by Ambedkar in his phenomenal work 'Who Were the Shudras?' is now being taken forward by prominent OBC scholars like Professor Kancha Ilaiah Shepherd. These scholars are igniting the flames of rational inquiry into the minds of other Shudras, urging an exploration of the truth about their material existence and societal identities. Coming back to Ambedkar's text, the phrase 'who do not know how they came to be what they are' is crucial to understand whether Shudras as a community have a collective identity at all. Marc Galanter is of the opinion that it is just too elusive to find any concrete information about who constitutes Backward Classes (BC) in India as these communities are different from one region to another. In the early twentieth century, one could find the term 'Backward Classes' and sometimes 'Depressed Classes' being used to describe all Shudra castes.[3] But in the later period of the twentieth century, Dalits were categorized as Depressed Classes and Shudras as Backward Classes, because Shudra groups did not want to be in the same category as Untouchables.[4] Hence, it is safe to say that OBC as a political category gained importance during the Mandal era, and before that, Shudras remained as disparate sociocultural communities with no specific ideology or identity.

Widespread untouchability united Dalits, but Shudras, despite being ostracized by Dwija castes for being impure, did not feel the need to fight the caste system because they had the opportunity to oppress Dalits while continuing to remain in the Hindu varna system. It would be interesting to explore if this lack of collective identity contributed to Shudras not coming together as a radical sociocultural force to dismantle caste, and remaining as a mere politico-bureaucratic entity called OBCs. On this note, I will examine the dominant OBC castes of Karnataka to show how these communities have been trying to eliminate their Shudra identities with their upward economic mobility, without any significant upward intellectual or spiritual mobility.

One could question the position of dominant OBC castes in Karnataka which control non-upper-caste spaces where they get to exploit caste minorities. Hence, the purpose of this essay may appear unclear as it seems to suggest that upward mobility of Shudras within the traditional varna framework can happen when they start aspiring for positions that have been historically held by Dwija communities. Refuting this proposition, I argue that the main purpose of this essay is to do the following: (1) To understand the scattered Shudra identity through the group's historical and current marginalization as well as privileges; (2) To locate the status of Shudras in modern India, as the country ceased to be an agriculture-based economy decades ago; (3) To politicize the identity of Shudras by instilling anti-caste ideology; (4) To demonstrate how Dwija communities have complete control over Shudra ways of thinking and existing, which results in atrocities against caste minorities; (5) To reflect on Shudra absence in the intellectual and spiritual domains of India.

In order to dismantle the traditional caste structure that thrives on the labour of working-caste communities, it is important to disrupt the caste hierarchy by aspiring for what was once a taboo. This does not in any way suggest integrating into Brahminical power structures or wanting to be accepted by the same.

Origin of Shudras and Absence of an Alternative Consciousness

The word 'Shudra' means a low-caste person without civilization, without culture, without respect and without position.[5] The term 'dominant' indicates their numbers in terms of population, and also political and economic power.[6] Although it is said that the Shudras were a part of the Kshatriya varna in Indo-Aryan society, they were degraded socially and placed as the last varna of the Chaturvarna system.[7]

In order to understand how members of an impure varna, that is, Shudras, came to own land because of which they are now considered a 'dominant caste', one should read historians R.S. Sharma[8] and Suvira Jaiswal,[9] who have explored the transition of Shudras from a semi-pure to an impure varna, which also indicates that they were probably never a fully pure varna. These shifts in their status meant that they could own property at different periods of history. Both these historians have argued that the varna system was not the same in north and south India. While it was to a certain degree rigid in the north, with all four varnas practicing endogamy and functioning on the notion of impurity dictated by Brahminical hegemony, it was not exactly the same in south India because of the absence of the Kshatriya and Vaishya varnas. Shudras were mostly responsible for tasks which would have been typically done by Kshatriyas. However, the Kshatriya and Vaishya varnas did emerge eventually in south India, because of which Shudras came to be treated as members of an impure varna. Since then, they have historically been restricted to productive jobs and to serve the other three varnas: the Brahmins, Kshatriyas and Vaishyas.

Sociologist M.N. Srinivas, in his popular book *The Remembered Village*,[10] has shown that until the 1930s, Brahmins were big landowners in the village of Ramapura in Karnataka, but as they migrated to cities for better prospects, they had to leave behind their lands to peasant-caste members (the current dominant Shudras) for looking after. In the 1950s, the peasant-caste members started demanding that tillers be the owners of the land, which resulted in most of the absentee owners losing their land during land reforms in India. This is a crucial piece of information as land reforms across India post-Independence resulted in similar outcomes as in Ramapura, benefitting dominant Shudra castes, OBCs and also Dalits.

As established before, Shudras such as Vokkaligas and Lingayats have traditionally been the 'tillers of the land, cattle grazers, and harvesters of crops. They were also the soldiers in the service of different rulers through various periods of history'.[11] They did not have the opportunity to learn and get educated until the British took control of India, which meant that they remained completely out of the cultural and intellectual consciousness of the country due to the hegemonic nature of the Dwija castes' social and cultural practices. This process barely left any space for an alternative consciousness of the deprived Shudra and Dalit masses in the sociocultural environment of the country for several centuries together. As social scientist K.N. Panikkar has noted in 'Culture and Consciousness in Modern India: A Historical Perspective',[12] 'Culture is a description of a particular way of life, which expresses certain meanings and values not in art and learning, but also in institutions and ordinary behavior.'[13] This extension of hegemony can be seen even in the freedom struggle, where most of the leading political figures were upper caste and rooted for political revolution over cultural or social revolution, which meant that their caste privilege remained unchallenged.

Despite the consciousness-raising efforts of social reformers like Basavanna and his followers who fought against caste-based discrimination in Karnataka in the twelfth century AD, they were not able to fully annihilate the caste system. The reasons for this are discussed in the upcoming sections.

Does Numerical Strength Signify Social Capital?

The Mandal Commission (1980) pegs the total share of Shudras/OBCs in the population at about 52 per cent.[14] We do not know the current total population of all OBCs, including upper OBCs, as no caste census has happened yet. Yet, as Professor Ilaiah has stated, 'The Shudras remain vastly underrepresented in positions of power across all aspects of political, social and economic life, be it in government or business, religion or education. Particularly at the national level, they remain subordinate to Brahmins and Vaishyas—particularly Banias.'[15]

Social capital is a very useful tool to understand how intangible wealth guarded by communities such as social networks, social relations and informal norms result in a newer kind of social stratification. Social capital, for that matter, is a highly relevant concept to understand caste relations and caste networks that contribute in solidifying the existing hierarchy of the caste system. Upper-caste, right-wing social commentators like R. Vaidyanathan[16] have argued that one should not morally judge the caste system and the social capital it yields because the accumulation of social capital by Dwija castes like Banias leads to an advantage in the global economy. However, as M. Vijaybhaskar and A. Kalaiyarasan[17] have argued, social capital emanating from caste is highly homogeneous in nature, and it reinforces the socio-economic exclusion of communities that do not have the same kind of social capital. This leads to the further reinforcement of caste-based hierarchy in society. This kind of exclusion has always been present in India, leading to generations of structural and systemic inequalities.[18] In this context, it is easy to understand how Dwija-caste members who have historically had access to the upper echelons of various institutions of the state, as well as control over the economy— which is a result of the solidification of the caste structure and prevention of mobility of lower-caste members—continue to guard social capital for their own caste members' benefit.

This accumulation of caste capital by Dwija communities has resulted in OBCs forming just 12 per cent of the lower court judges,[19] and less than 12 per cent in central government jobs.[20] A right to information (RTI) petition was filed in the Supreme Court of India seeking information with regard to the caste of the honourable judges, and the additional registrar and central public information officer of the Supreme Court responded stating that such information is not maintained.[21]

Similarly, even in Karnataka, where upper OBCs like the Vokkaligas and Lingayats have a strong political hold, they are poorly represented in places such as the Karnataka High Court,[22] and elite educational institutions[23] such as the Indian Institute of Management, Bengaluru; Indian Institute of Science, Bengaluru; and National Law School of India University, Bengaluru.[24] This is no surprise as the Shudras, including the upper Shudras in Karnataka, have remained backward when it comes to occupying these power positions because of the lack of access to social capital and English education in these spaces. As shown in this section, Shudras may constitute about 54 per cent of India's population, but it does not mean that they have access to power positions like the numerically smaller Dwija communities, which have cemented their powerful social networks through historical accumulation of wealth, English education and subjugation of Shudras and Dalits.

One way to understand this phenomenon is by recognizing the role played by 'social capital', which has been explained in this section, and another way is through understanding the operation of 'caste pride' amongst Shudras in Karnataka, which has led to their widespread marginalization in the intellectual, spiritual, and sociocultural spheres of India. Further research has to be undertaken to understand if a similar analysis of Shudra castes in different states would bring out similar results. In the face of this historical and contemporary status of Shudras, why are they still proud of their caste lineage?

Understanding Caste Pride and Violence against Dalits

On the question of caste pride and social marginalization, firstly, Shudra castes have fallen prey to the process of 'Sanskritization' and upward caste mobility by brutalizing those below them, such as Dalits and Adivasis. Secondly, they have latched on to the very process of hegemonic erasure that they were subjected to by the Dwija castes. As Dr B.R. Ambedkar has stated repeatedly, the caste system thrives on the practice of graded inequality. Shudras too were oppressed by the Dwija castes, but now they are the greatest oppressors of Dalits and other minority communities.[25] Having no proper understanding of their own oppressed identities and backwardness has made upper Shudras believe that they are the neo-Kshatriyas and neo-Brahmins.

In Karnataka, the Vokkaligas strongly believe that they are the neo-Kshatriyas and take pride in their surname, 'Gowda'. They use it as a weapon to terrorize caste and religious minorities,[26] just like the Jats and Reddys. One can find stickers stating 'Gowdas' behind cars, autos and trucks all over Karnataka. This false caste pride plays out gruesomely when young people from the community try to marry outside of their caste. It's not just the Vokkaligas, even other Shudra castes like the Kurubas indulge in similar branding of the caste name, parading and terrorizing Dalits.

Similar yet distinct, the Lingayats tread a slightly different trajectory, but it does not mean that they have not committed atrocities time and again against Dalits in Karnataka.[27] Although the Lingayats are categorized as OBC by the Government of India, there is a growing demand to recognize them as a separate religion divorced from the roots of Hinduism. It is important to note that the Lingayats are followers of the social reformer Basavanna, who in the twelfth century rose up against the discriminatory Hindu caste system, mainly Brahminism, and built a new dharma which rejected the Vedas, caste and gender discrimination.[28] The majority of Lingayats today have Shudra roots, which could be the reason they have not escaped the viciousness of caste. Even within this fold, there is an ongoing fight with the Veerashaivas, who are also followers of Basavanna and claim that they are Hindus, and that Basavanna never envisioned a separate religion. It will be interesting to see what happens to their OBC status if they are accorded the tag of a separate religion.

On the question of caste pride and marginalization of Shudras in Karnataka, the rise of Hindutva politics and right-wing organizations[29] has made sure that Shudras remain under the control of their upper-caste compatriots who have successfully fed them the false narrative of superiority for decades now. This means they would not challenge their historical relegation or their current absence from the power structures.

To test this argument, when I asked a few members of the Shudra community (Vokkaligas, to be specific) in coastal Karnataka if they were Shudras, they laughingly said that they were not because the Vokkaligas are leaders like the Kshatriyas. And when I revealed that they in fact have Shudra lineage, their reactions ranged from surprise to complete denial. I believe this is the case because of the following three reasons: (1) They know Shudra means 'impure', but they have always treated Dalits as impure, and have not considered themselves having impure caste roots; (2) The absence of a rigid four-varna hierarchy in south India, unlike north India, which meant that Shudras did take the place of Kshatriyas, until they were downgraded to the 'impure' Shudra varna;[30] (3) The control of Shudra OBCs over successive political regimes in Karnataka.

I would not be surprised to see similar reactions from Shudra castes in other regions of Karnataka, as well as the practice of 'limited forms of untouchability'[31] within Shudra castes. I believe this exercise will definitely lead to fascinating information and newer insights into Shudra lives and the understanding of their muddled history.

The practice of untouchability differs between upper- and dominant-caste Hindus against Dalits, and Dwija Hindus against Shudras, besides the limited forms of untouchability within different Shudra castes. Shudra practices of untouchability against Dalits are well documented,[32] but the same is not done for practices within Shudra castes, and by Dwija members against Shudras. However, sociologists have recorded practices of untouchability by Dwija members against Shudras, which has continued till date in various forms.[33] As a Shudra individual, I have experienced untouchability in Dwija households. My ancestors too have experienced untouchability by Dwija communities as well as other Shudra castes. But I need to emphasize that untouchability practised within Shudra castes is not as pervasive and evil as untouchability practised against Dalits,[34] and it has to be enumerated through extensive documentation. Regrettably, my ancestors did practise untouchability against Dalits. This is the travesty of the caste system. The hegemony among Shudras in terms of Sanskritization, caste purity and fight for political and economic mobility needs to be studied meticulously.

Adding to the cacophony of caste politics, some news reports[35] exposed the results of a recently conducted socio-economic survey in Karnataka, according to which there are 18 per cent Scheduled Castes, 12.5 per cent Muslims, 9.8 per cent Lingayats and 8.16 per cent Vokkaligas. The result of this survey has sent shockwaves across political parties in Karnataka, and protests from different dominant caste groups too. Sensing the danger, the Government of Karnataka has not yet officially released the results.

Declining Status of OBC Women

It is important to evaluate the current status of OBC women and the impact of Sanskritization on the growing gender gap between OBC men and women, and women's participation in the workforce. There has been a significant drop in the percentage of women entering the workforce (5.8 per cent for OBCs), according to data from the National Sample Survey Organization (NSSO) from rounds post 2004–05. Analysis of this data shows that there are multiple factors affecting women's employment: globalization and deregulation of the country's economy, as well as the structural inequalities of gender and caste. The former, instead of diminishing the effects of the latter, as is often claimed it does, seems to in fact further perpetuate them. Participation rates of women have declined across all social divisions, and SC, ST and OBC women show the highest decline, which highlights the role of the caste system. At the same time, the gender gap within each of these social categories is itself widening, demonstrating the effects of structural gender inequality.[36]

S. Klasen has argued that the stigma attached to women working outside their homes, and increase in their husbands' income are among the reasons behind decreased female labour participation.[37] There are strong gender biases and harassment which influence the participation of women in the workforce. These often operate within the caste system so that women belonging to different castes are differently affected, with SC and ST women showing the highest increase in this gap, and OBC women not far behind.[38] This is also a reflection of the social pressures that force women to perform all domestic care work, leaving no time for work outside the home.[39] One factor that exacerbates this process is Sanskritization, where OBC castes have been confining women to domestic labour only by not allowing them to pursue work outside their homes even if they had the ability to work, which is essentially mimicking the Brahminical practice of controlling women's lives.[40]

It is precisely for this reason that Dalit women have greater freedom in terms of divorce and remarriage, whereas OBC castes are busy controlling their women's sexuality.

The data[41] on the willingness of women who are currently not working outside their homes to take a job shows that OBC women, despite being educated, are less willing to take a job, whereas SC and ST women are more willing. This is because of the total income of their respective households. Almost 92 per cent of these women reported that taking care of domestic tasks were their primary duty, and about 60 per cent said they had no help or assistance to carry them out.

In terms of the data on primary residence and landownership in rural areas of Karnataka, the gender gap between OBC men and women is wider than the gender gap between SC or ST men and women. The relatively better position of SC and ST women could be explained through the Karnataka government's land distribution programmes, and housing programmes for SC and ST households,[42] which encouraged joint registration of these assets, and safeguarded women's right over property.

The data on instances of domestic violence against OBC women isn't easy to find, and this could be for two reasons: 1. As some studies have shown, dominant and upper-caste women do not talk publicly about the violence they go through in the house as they fear it might malign their family honour. This leads to under-reporting of crimes. India has one of the highest rates of underreporting when it comes to crimes faced by women;[43] 2. Data collected in FIRs does not usually reflect the caste of the victims, unless they are SC or ST, so that appropriate laws could be invoked for crimes committed against SC and ST people.

Further, India has the lowest divorce rates in the world.[44] While conservative caste Hindus claim that this is because of the 'culture' and 'tradition' of Hindu India which keeps families together, the reality is that women have no other option but to stay in abusive marriages and families. This is because of all the above-mentioned reasons, and also because of the corrupt and patriarchal legal and police institutions. The feminization of poverty, and oppressive Hindu traditions have trapped women in abusive situations, where they have no agency to manage their own lives.

The Path Ahead for Shudras

This essay establishes how Shudra castes in India are clearly lagging behind on various societal parameters of growth, while there is a conspicuous absence of any sort of rebellion against established caste hierarchy, and an inquiry into their own roots.

Moving forward, Shudras have so much to learn from the Ambedkarite and Dalit–Buddhist movements. Shudras have played a vital role in many anti-caste struggles before, for instance, the Mahar movement.[45] In fact, the pioneering anti-caste struggle was led by Mahatma Jyotiba Phule, a Shudra individual. The transition of Shudras from rebelling against the caste system to becoming the biggest perpetrators of caste-based atrocities is nothing but a product of Hindutva ideology. Karnataka has had several prominent Shudra poets like Kuvempu who vehemently opposed the caste system and founded a new school of thought called 'Universal Humanism', which called for a rejection of Brahminical rituals and embraced non-hierarchical and secular ways of living. He asked Shudras and Dalits to not enter temples that humiliated them. Unfortunately, the Hindu right wing is busy appropriating even Kuvempu for its Hindutva agenda and upper-caste domination, something the Shudras have failed to notice.[46]

Moving away from their Shudra identities in search of an elusive caste pride by aligning themselves with upper-caste communities has rendered them faceless in the country's cultural consciousness. Shudras need to work towards the annihilation of caste, being fully aware of their privileges as well as their subjugation by upper-caste communities.

Shudra Consciousness and the Future of the Nation

Pallikonda Manikanta

'. . . it is the Shudras who have largely been instrumental in sustaining the infamous system of Chaturvarnya, though it has been the primary cause of their degradation and that only the Shudras can destroy the Chaturvarnya . . .'

—Dr B.R. Ambedkar[1]

The Context

'Most Nobel Prize winners from India, including recent recipient Abhijit Banerjee, are Brahmins, and also, it was B.N. Rau, a Brahmin, who made the draft Constitution and handed it over to Dr Babasaheb Ambedkar,' Gujarat assembly Speaker Rajendra Trivedi said at the inauguration of the Brahmin Business Summit on 3 January 2020.[2] Sometime back, while talking about Banias, Amit Shah, the current minister of home affairs and a well-known Bania BJP leader, had said that Gandhi was a *chatur* (intelligent) Bania.[3] Rajendra Trivedi is an RSS–BJP Brahmin leader and a close confidant of Mohan Bhagwat, a Saraswat Brahmin Sarsanghchalak of the RSS. It is an open secret that Bhagwat runs the BJP from behind the saffron curtain. Amit Shah is also a very powerful national leader of the RSS–BJP, a former party president who is the go-between man of the RSS and the BJP. Brahmins and Banias are not only well-educated and wealthy communities but also the ones that rule the country, with control over important institutions and organizations. They have been making laws and framing rules to control Indian communities even after Independence.

Though Trivedi sounds casteist, there is truth in what he says. Why is there not a single Patel, Jat, Gujjar, Maratha, Kamma, Reddy, Lingayat, Vokkaliga, Nair, Naickers, Yadav or any other Shudra caste among the Nobel Prize winners so far? They are all regional ruling castes and form the upper layer of the Shudras, who were and continue to be the main food producers of the nation. The same Brahmin pandits characterized them as 'dominant castes', and many foreign scholars also followed that theory. But not a single Shudra has an impressive intellectual record that is known globally. They are all treated as Hindu or Hindutva-allied by the same Brahmin spiritual and social pandits. The relatively well-off Shudras accepted that spiritual and social characterization without raising any philosophical questions, and thus remained outside the purview of spiritual citizenship and the Hindu/Hindutva philosophical position.

Trivedi said that out of nine Nobel Prize winners, eight are Brahmins.[4] What is the population of Brahmins in India? It could be roughly around 4 per cent. The Shudra population, including the non-reserved Shudras, in contrast, is roughly about 52 per cent. Leave alone Nobel Prize winners, there is no visible intellectual from the Shudra community who commands a national stature. The Congress claims Sardar Vallabhbhai Patel and Krishna Menon (on whom Jairam Ramesh recently wrote a book), but nobody treats them intellectually on par with Mohandas Gandhi or Jawaharlal Nehru. The moot question, therefore, is why such a vast Shudra agrarian mass did not produce a single internationally renowned intellectual. Why did they not produce a single leader of the stature of Mahatma Gandhi or Jawaharlal Nehru in the Congress party's history, or of the stature of Atal Bihari Vajpayee or even Narendra Modi in the BJP? Why could that social mass, while working as the RSS's mass base, not produce a leader like K.B. Hedgewar or Mohan Bhagwat?

The pre-Independence Muslim society produced Allama Iqbal and Muhammad Ali Jinnah, both of whom acquired not only pan-Indian but global intellectual and leadership stature. Jinnah's intellectuality created rifts even in rival structures like the RSS–BJP.

The most oppressed Dalit society has produced two great national leaders, thinkers and philosophers: Dr B.R. Ambedkar and Kanshiram. Ambedkar is a globally recognized philosopher, thinker, legal luminary, sociologist and economist. Kanshiram was a brilliant political strategist, political thinker and organizer of unmatchable stature at the national level. He proved to be a better mobilizer of the poorest of the poor than Mahatma Gandhi was during the freedom struggle. Kanshiram started his political battle with the support of the most oppressed and exploited Dalit masses. By no means do Shudras suffer such human barbarity; rather they are amongst the perpetrators, next to Brahmins, Banias and Kshatriyas. What did the nation lose in not producing Shudra philosophers and thinkers and great national leaders of intellectual and ideological stature? Did it not cause a lack of intellectual competition in India? Did it not cause harm to the nation's aspirations and ambitions of intellectual achievement in the modern world? Perhaps the communist stream should have produced one from its fold. But it didn't. Did the nation not lose a possible vision that could have emerged from its productive base? This is not a question of caste calculations but an important national aspirational question that could show India a new direction.

Brahmins and Banias have a national identity as a caste. Kshatriyas too have a national identity despite having a relatively small geographical distribution and presence. Where is the Shudra national identity, though they are everywhere in the country? Shudras are the mainstay of many political parties, especially in the RSS–BJP. Brahminism, under the rubric of Hinduism, erased their historical identity as Shudras. In one of his seminal works, *Who Were the Shudras?,* Dr B.R. Ambedkar noted:

> Chaturvarnya would have been a very innocent principle if it meant no more than mere division of society into four classes. Unfortunately, more than this is involved in the theory of Chaturvarnya. Besides dividing society into four orders, the theory goes further and makes the principle of graded inequality the basis for determining the terms of associated life as between the four Varnas. Again, the system of graded inequality is not merely notional. It is legal and penal. Under the system of Chaturvarnya, the Shudra is not only placed at the bottom of the gradation but he is subjected to innumerable ignominies and disabilities so as to prevent him from rising above the condition fixed for him by law.[5]

Thus, through social and religious sanctions, in ancient times, Shudras were denied Sanskrit education, forcing them to be confined to agrarian production and cattle-rearing. Now, even English education is designed in such a manner that Shudras are denied it at the village level; it is available only to children of rich and educated parents.

It is this situation that forces one to examine the consciousness and cultural location of Shudras. In this exercise of examining their lost identity, a fact has to be made clear. Whatever is taking place in India in the name of the Hindu religion and Hindutva ideology, both sociopolitical power operators and the muscle power for these structures come from Shudras, but all its benefits go to three communities—Brahmins, Banias and Kshatriyas. The brain power of all these structures at the national level comes from Brahmins and Banias.

Shudra physical labour is the source of national wealth, but the main national wealth—in the form of industrial and service sectors—is in the hands of the three Dwija communities. Most of the top educational institutions are in the hands of Brahmins and Banias, all forms of Hindu/Hindutva spiritual and manipulative knowledge are in the hands of Brahmins, and industrial and business wealth is in the hands of Banias and Brahmins. Though Brahmins did not have much industrial wealth before the software industry came into being, now they own most information technology (IT) companies as they were the English-educated social force with international exposure. The policymaking power of national political parties, whether it is the BJP, Congress, Hindutva organizations or even communist parties and organizations, rests with Brahmins and Banias, who work in those structures as leaders. Shudras, on the other hand, are still in the agrarian sector and control some amount of regional political power, which, however, hardly influence *national policies*.

Shudras and Philosophy

Philosophy and spiritual authority are interlinked. Though philosophy's roots are in agrarian production, its base has slowly shifted into spiritual discourse. Oral philosophy survives even today among illiterate food producers, but text-based discourse has become the dominant mode of philosophizing. Since Brahmins controlled book-based philosophy, they denied Shudras the right to engage with that philosophy. Consequentially, Shudra mental growth around book-based philosophical discourse is stunted and remains so even today. It can be strengthened only with mass English education in rural India, as English is both a national and international language.

Shudras have a strong base in agrarian philosophy and they have never felt the need for textualizing that philosophy. Since agrarian production continued to operate among illiterate and semi-literate regional-language-educated Shudra/Ati-Shudra masses, high-end philosophical education shifted into religion, and thereby into the houses of Brahmins first and Banias later. It is from such Bania spiritual discourse that Mahatma Gandhi and Ram Manohar Lohia emerged. Venkaiah Naidu, though he comes from the rich Shudra Kamma community, could not acquire any philosophically independent leadership status because he did not have the vision and courage to challenge RSS–BJP Brahminism. If only he were to initiate a Shudra assertion movement from within, asking for spiritual and philosophical equality within the Hindu/Hindutva system, perhaps he would have left a lasting impact on the nation itself.

It is well known that Sardar Patel did not leave any philosophical legacy. The Congress's V.K. Krishna Menon, a rich Nair from Kerala, too suffered from a lack of such philosophical background, though he was educated at the London School of Economics. He was a brilliant scholar, but he did not write anything substantial to uplift the poor and disadvantaged. He never mobilized Shudras to be an equal force with Brahmin–Bania nationalists. He never exhibited any awareness about the role of caste in India.

It is difficult to operate from New Delhi without a philosophical support base in temples, media, bureaucracy and top operational networks of Hindu/Hindutva systems. Shudras didn't have a firm grounding in any of the nationally dominant languages such as Sanskrit, Persian, Urdu and, most importantly, English. As a class, they are still unable to find significant footing in premier universities, where the Brahmin–Bania monopoly prevails. Also, the condition of OBCs (especially women) is much worse in all fields, and by not releasing the caste census, the RSS–BJP leadership has denied OBCs knowledge both about the strength of their population and their socio-economic situation.

The development of the Shudra self is uneven, because the numerous castes remained ideologically disconnected across states and even regions. They never developed a social mass that could communicate in one national language. Language plays a key role in formulating ideas and translating them into philosophical discourse. Since they are stuck with regional languages, masked in the discourse of safeguarding their mother tongue, they could not acquire a national communication network. Acquiring a fertile intellectual imagination in a developed language is more useful than a language that is understood only in a small region. No Shudra owns an English-language national paper; no Shudra owns an English-language news channel that is known nationally. It's true that they own regional-language newspapers such as *Eenadu*, *Sakshi* and *Andhra Jyothi*, Telugu newspapers with the largest circulation. In states like Kerala, Tamil Nadu, Karnataka, Maharashtra and so on, Shudras own regional media houses. But the intellectual input to those papers comes largely from Brahmin writers and journalists. The major English newspapers are owned by Brahmin–Banias. Regional capital or regional political powers do not play a nationally influencing role—though they play a nationalist role.[6]

Brahmin–Banias have become a national (intellectual and ruling) mass, leaving aside their regional identities, because of their common goal, name and socio-spiritual unity. They control spiritual institutions and organize business summits in their caste name—Brahmin Business Summit, Bania Business Summit and so on.

The Brahmin–Bania presence in superstructural, power-based institutions is as visible as their absence in base agrarian tasks such as tilling land, sowing seeds, weeding crops and harvesting. They are also absent in cattle-grazing, protecting village borders from thieves, and encroachment by other villagers. Their absence is also felt in house and temple construction work, in brick making, woodcutting, pottery and so on. Perhaps the absence of Brahmins–Banias from productive work for millennia united them against Shudras to ensure that they remained under their control. Their self-constructed definition of the self as sacred generated the conditions for their dominance.

Their intellectuality did not stop there. They also constructed the Shudra self as polluted and inferior. This is where the Shudras of India lost their national self as human beings created by the same God who created Brahmins–Banias. Brahmins, especially, remained alchemists, transforming all that is social to the biological–natural or metaphysical. While the material relations of the oppressed and the oppressor presuppose revolt against oppression, the metaphysical relation invented in the mind of a Brahmin and implanted on to the minds of the toiling masses forbids any such attempt.

The appropriation of the oppressed is not through physical coercion, but through something much more violent—the violence of religious rituals sanctioned by the divine being, which exists only in the minds of the people who control them and demand their devotion through fear and superstition. The Brahmin rules the realm of materials through the sanction of the non-existing realm, the realm of the divine. At every instance of non-compliance, at every instance of resistance against the unjust social order, at every instance of insubordination, at every instance of social unrest, the Brahmin invented a new incarnation of the divine to scuttle resistance and stagnate the process of social transformation.

For example, making Gautama Buddha one of the incarnations of the god Vishnu goes against the very radical principle that Dr Ambedkar advocated during his conversion to Buddhism (for emancipation). These divine inventions, or co-opting anti-caste thinkers and revolutionaries into the larger Hindu caste harmonious fold, would allow the Brahminical body politic to legitimize every kind of oppression, humiliation and exploitation.

In this unjust social order, Shudras are positioned oddly. They do not ask for equality from above and do not want to grant equality to those below. The life that does not aspire for equality and does not want others to be equal is a sinful one. Shudras have paid the price for their ignorance of the idea of equality.

The classical Brahminical definition of the production and food culture of Shudras is that they are ritually impure. The worst is that Brahminism does not allow spiritual knowledge and authority to be handled by Shudras. They are made out to be people with no aspiration for spiritual equality in this life, and their attainment of moksha after death is not possible. Shudras don't have the right to be equal with Brahmins on earth or in heaven.

Shudras have not acquired the philosophical ability to grasp this spiritual ideology. Many generations are made to follow the Brahmin pandit without acquiring the mental ability to question that pandit's authority to preach and practise spiritual inequality. Their spiritual and social status has remained stagnant for millennia. Shudras are seen as physical and material beings but not as philosophical and social beings. They never realized that their material is subject to a Brahmin's philosophical management. Consequentially, Shudra society was not able to produce a philosophical being who could challenge the Brahmin mind at the national level.

Shudra Consciousness and Self-negation

Shudra consciousness has not yet been liberated due to the continuous negation of Shudra existence. A Shudra is conceptualized as all things that a Brahmin is not. The Shudra was seen as a labouring body right from the days of the Rig Veda. It was the knowledge bank of Shudras that built the Harappan civilization, but once Brahminism established its hegemony with written texts, the Shudra mind was effaced and they were seen as mere bodies. Their consciousness is conditioned, and now needs to be reconditioned towards liberation.

In domains such as text-based spiritual discourse, occupational culture, historical memory and food habits, we can witness the process of self-negation and alienation of the Shudra selfhood. From closely following these processes, we can understand the multiple dimensions of oppression the Shudra community suffers in socio-psychological terms.

Shudras are a huge social community in between Dalits at the bottom of society and Brahmins/Banias/Kshatriyas at the apex. They are like the massive stock and branches of a huge tree, of which Dalits are the roots, and Brahmins/Banias/Kshatriyas the flourishing leaves. As we know, without the roots, neither the stock, branches nor leaves will survive. But the whole visible tree is working against its roots. That is its self-destructive nature. If Shudras do not become conscious spiritual and philosophical beings, they will not be able to fight Brahminism and will not allow Dalits to be equal to them.

Philosophical churnings in the Shudra community are much less developed than that of average Africans who were underdeveloped tribes in Africa and slaves in Euro-America just a few decades back. Look at the philosophical and spiritual writings of Africans and African-Americans. There are Nobel laureates and globally influential politicians, thinkers, writers and singers among them. Where are the globally known Shudras from India?

During British rule, in 1817, Christian English educational institutions came into being in India. But that language fell into the hands of either Brahmin Christian converts or non-Christian Brahmins–Banias. The doors to English-language education were closed to Shudras. Mahatma Jyotirao Phule was the first known English-educated Shudra in the 1840s. He wrote at least one philosophical text, though in Marathi—*Gulamgiri*[7]—with an English introduction. But after that, the first ever Shudra English text was written by Kancha Ilaiah Shepherd—*Why I Am Not a Hindu: A Sudra Critique of Hindutva, Philosophy, Culture and Political Economy*—as late as 1996.[8]

Shudras and Their Mother Culture

A few Brahmin–Banias at the university level entered courses that deal with agriculture and found government and private sector employment as agricultural specialists. Historically, agriculture has been a Shudra occupation. But once modern jobs in urban centres came in, Brahmin–Banias started treating Shudras as non-experts in their own historical work. Though agriculture is their mother culture, once it started being disseminated through modern education, Shudras got eliminated from it.

It was the Shudras who developed regional languages in the process of their productive work on soil, in water and in forests—agriculture and its language. But they do not represent their mother culture in any international fora on agriculture. For Shudra farmers, the field is an everyday laboratory. But they were never allowed to learn from, read and write books on their experiments. Even when their children got some education, their confidence level was so low that they didn't consider writing about their mother culture. Now, texts in English have gained prominence, and the skill to write those texts is not available to Shudras.

This is because the Shudra mass remained outside the modern education system introduced by the British, just as they remained outside Sanskritic ancient and medieval education. Brahmin–Banias, though, learned the language and left Shudras with a deep inferiority complex about speaking and writing in English. Now the fear of English is so deep that it would take a serious cultural effort to remove it. They can neither enter Sanskrit-based spiritual philosophical positions—whether of priesthood or interpretative philosophical positions—nor can they write world-class books in English.

Shudra Memory

It appears that Shudras have no memory of history. Normally, human memory has three characteristics—long memory, short memory and no memory. Brahmins have, perhaps, acquired the longest memory. They wrote Vedas to suit their leisure-oriented life by dividing Indian society into Brahmin, Kshatriya, Vaishya and Shudra. Shudras were said to have been created by the Brahmin God from his feet. All through their living history, they never forgot that creation theory. They remained at the top of Indian society and kept Shudras at the bottom of the fourfold varna system, which is still in operation. The RSS–BJP maintains that system with a new name, Hindutva, given to the very same Brahminism. Shudras, without invoking the historic memory of their own slavery, or of their culture being treated as unworthy of equal spiritual and social respect, accept Brahmins as their priests and leaders. At no point of time have Brahmins accepted any Shudra as their guru or priest.

The theory that Shudras are 'feet-born' is the greatest humiliation heaped on any human being since the idea of creationism—that is, God creating human beings—came into human consciousness. Only Shudras suffered that humiliation. There are no other human beings condemned for millennia to live as unequals. Brahminism made slaves of those doing physical work without allowing for their mental development.

Shudras have become people of no memory; therefore, the history of humiliation does not appear to them as human history. Indian Dalits lived a life of short memory. But they are now slowly overcoming that short memory because of a great doctor who nurtured their intellectual progress, Dr Babasaheb Ambedkar. But no such doctor was born among the Shudras of contemporary India.

Shudras and Brahminic Vegetarianism

Ever since Shudras domesticated animals and birds, the food resources of India increased. Before ancient indigenous people discovered agriculture, forest food and animal food were their mainstays. Shudra food culture has always been multi-cuisine. It was this food culture that developed into Shudra spiritual food culture. Jainism and Brahminism introduced pure vegetarianism both into daily food culture and also spiritual food culture, only in India. The world over, food culture remained multi-cuisine. Now the Brahminic RSS–BJP leadership (though there could be meat-eating Shudras and Dalits in those structures) is pushing the nation towards being vegetarian.[9] The BJP government in Madhya Pradesh, for instance, stopped serving even an egg in mid-day meals to school children of all castes and communities in the name of Hindu sentiment. This is akin to making vegetarianism a state policy. That would have a massive implication on the food resources of the poor masses who survive by eating food items available in their economic environment and production systems.

If all Shudras become pure vegetarians, the national economy and environment will collapse, because Shudras are the main food producers of meat, milk, vegetables and fruit. It is a logical corollary that without any use of domesticated animals and birds, people would not feed such creatures and sustain the animal economy. Once Shudras give up animal husbandry, the whole rural environment will collapse. But there is little Shudra opposition to this kind of disastrous pure vegetarianism which has never been part of their food culture. Shudra thinkers and philosophers have barely studied the evolution of human food philosophy. Food is not just a material issue but a very serious philosophical issue.

Shudras and the Enemy Image of Others

Shudras constantly get instigated by the Hindutva *parivar* to endorse the othering of Muslims and Christians. Shudras respond and participate in physical violence against these communities since structures under the control of Muslim and Christian elites too never aided in providing them with education and employment. There is a systemic disconnect between the institutional arrangements of these two communities and Shudras. Either because of existential fear or convenience, the Muslim and Christian ruling elite, during Muslim rule and British rule, respectively, helped Brahmin–Banias in education, employment and cultural engagement.

Though the economy that the British exploited was built by Shudras, they gave better positions to Brahmins–Banias during their rule. The colleges and universities that the British built were populated by Brahmins and Banias, and Shudras were forced to remain illiterate.

Brahmins–Banias benefited the most during British rule as they became better educated in English-medium schools. Some of them got education in the Persian language also. That education helped them become leaders in pre- and post-Independence India. At least Dalits became aware of this fact because of Babasaheb Ambedkar. But no such thinker-philosopher emerged even from feudal Shudra families.

Also, since Islam is projected as a Middle Eastern foreign religion and Christianity as a British colonial religion, Shudras bought into the Muslim other image very easily. They treated whatever the pandit told them as true, including their subordinate status.

CAA and NRC Controversy

By the end of 2019 and the beginning of 2020, India witnessed massive civil resistance. The Citizenship Amendment Act (CAA) passed by the BJP-led government in 2019 engendered nationwide protests cutting across religion, caste, gender and political parties. Police firings, lathi charges, Internet bans, imposition of Section 144 of the Criminal Procedure Code (CrPC) and arrests of innocent people became a systemic normal. More than twenty persons were shot dead by the police in BJP-ruled states.[10]

The Hindutva parivar has created an image of the Muslim other and used the muscle power and self-consciousness of Shudras against Muslims in India.[11] Shudras, more so the OBCs, are likely to be lured towards such thinking because they are not aware of the international opinion on minority cleansing and its dire consequences. During these mass movements, the RSS–BJP stood on one side and the other sociopolitical forces on the other side. The BJP took several radical steps which fuelled tension along communal lines after they came to power in 2014, and continued to take further aggravating steps after winning the elections in 2019. The RSS–BJP operates under the Hindu/Hindutva spiritual rubric, both of which are Brahmin–Bania-controlled structures. Though Kshatriyas have some place in these structures, the main driving forces are Brahmins and Banias.

Shudras in general and OBCs in particular, without understanding the long-term design of Brahmins–Banias, lend their muscle power and also vote power to the RSS–BJP with a view that the anti-Muslim position is to their advantage. But the ninety-five-year existence of the RSS and its functioning did not prove that. It did not alter the Brahmin–Bania monopoly and control of Indian institutions in any form. Shudra liberation in spiritual and social fields remains a distant goal. Unfortunately, Shudras are not aiming for socio-spiritual liberation from the grip of Brahmins–Banias as they have not yet imagined that their liberation is possible.

Shudra communities of all regions are not allowed to occupy the main Hindu theological structures, including priesthood. No Shudra can head a Hindu mutt, including the Krishna temple of Mathura, even though Lord Krishna himself has a Shudra background. Though Mahatma Jyotirao Phule initiated a philosophical discourse for their empowerment and emancipation, they did not understand the main message of the English-language education both Phule and his wife Savitribai Phule—who was the first woman teacher—gave in their lifetime.

Hence, using this situation of mental slavery of the OBCs and non-OBC Shudras, the Hindutva parivar is aggressively manufacturing a monolithic Hindu identity which is against minorities, especially Muslims, by systematically claiming the cultural injustice stance—that is, by showing Muslims and

Christians as the other/invaders/enemies who suppressed or were trying to suppress the Hindu cultural and historical fabric of the nation.

Shudras and the RSS–BJP

Though the RSS–BJP stance is anti-Muslim, it adversely affects many other sections such as Shudras, Dalits, Adivasis and other minority religious groups like Christians, Sikhs and others. They first started the right-wing radical agenda of a beef ban with an idea called *gau raksha* (cow protection). This immediately affected the Dalit and Muslim food source and had a massive impact on the Shudra agrarian economy across the country. Cows, bulls and bullocks went out of market, which led to a huge loss for farming Shudras, Dalits and Adivasis. Their savings in the form of cattle were taken away by the *goshala* networks nurtured by RSS–BJP forces. They prospered with the freely accessed cattle wealth of farming communities. Many Muslims and Dalits were lynched, and often, it was Shudra muscle power deployed for the purpose.

Brahminism is more powerful today than ever before, with national power at its command and Shudra muscle power under their control. As long as Shudras have no intellectual power and don't challenge Brahminism in its spiritual and sociocultural realm, it will not stop its exploitation of labour power. Right now, only a new Shudra consciousness can save India. A reformed Shudra consciousness should be able to offer equality to Dalits on the one hand and demand the same from Dwija castes. The RSS–BJP finds the self-negating consciousness of Shudras as very fertile ground to thrive in. Should Shudras remain in that condition and consciousness even in the twenty-first century?

The India of My Dreams

Dr P. Vinay Kumar

The India of my dreams is Bhimrao Ramji Ambedkar's India: A nation characterized by equality, inclusive growth, and development of the country through the development of all sections of society, especially the Scheduled Castes and Backward Classes. The last of these points is what I will reflect on in this essay.

More than 80 per cent of the country's population is vulnerable and lives largely below the poverty line. Undoubtedly, inclusive growth that reaches this vulnerable section is a necessary precondition to the attainment of our national dream. The wide gap between the extremely privileged classes—which constitute around 10 per cent of the population—and the utterly deprived sections must be eliminated for the balance to shift in favour of the latter, both socially and economically.[1]

At the same time, it is also important to critically examine the distribution of the benefits of reservation and affirmative action within the Shudra and OBC community. To what extent have upwardly mobile members of Dalit, Bahujan and minority classes been willing to let go of their hold over benefits in favour of other sections of their respective communities which have not benefited as much from affirmative action? To what extent have they monopolized benefits within their immediate families?

Merits and Demerits of the 'Creamy Layer' Argument

The Indian Constitution describes the OBC community as 'socially and educationally backward classes', and the Government of India is enjoined to ensure their social and educational development. Among other privileges, the Constitution entitles OBCs to 27 per cent reservations in higher education and public sector employment. The term 'creamy layer' was coined in 1971 by the Sattanathan Commission to refer to the relatively forward and better-educated members among OBCs who should not be eligible for government-sponsored affirmative action, especially in education and public employment. The commission recommended that the 'creamy layer' should be excluded from reservations in civil posts. The creamy layer criterion was defined by annual family income from all sources. In 1993, eligibility for reservation depended on an annual family income of up to Rs 1 lakh. The range was progressively raised to Rs 2.5 lakh per annum in 2004, Rs 4.5 lakh per annum in 2008 and Rs 6 lakh per annum in 2013, and finally to Rs 8 lakh in 2017.

In October 2015, the National Commission for Backward Classes (NCBC) had proposed that an annual family income of up to Rs 15 lakh be considered as the minimum ceiling for OBCs. The NCBC also recommended the subdivision of OBCs into 'backward', 'more backward' and 'extremely backward' blocks and recommended division of the 27 per cent quota amongst them in proportion to their population, to ensure that stronger OBCs did not corner the quota benefits.

The 'creamy layer' categorization applies only to OBCs and not Scheduled Castes and Scheduled Tribes, as in the latter case, reservations are aimed at removal of social disabilities, and not only economic marginalization.

Argument for and against 'Creamy Layer' Criteria

The following arguments were put forward against the application of the criteria in the implementation of OBC reservation. First, OBCs are so delineated primarily because of social backwardness, similar to the Scheduled Castes, and therefore must enjoy the same privileges of affirmative action. Second, the quantum of reservations designated for OBCs, 27 per cent, is grossly insufficient, considering that they form the single largest population category—above 50 per cent collectively across the country, and quite likely individually in most states if the caste-wise census is conducted.[2] Third, even without applying the 'creamy layer' bar, the quantum of 27 per cent reservations had never been fulfilled because of the low literacy rate among its people. If the 'creamy layer' is implemented, the quota utilized may not even cross 9–10 per cent, leaving the rest to be transferred to the general quota, thus defeating the foundational basis of reservation.

There are a few contested arguments about the propriety of the 'creamy layer' criteria or even the whole idea of OBC reservation. First, a few people think that all such measures are a means to vote-bank politics, while the real development for which certain measures were included in the Constitution have either never happened or have not been helpful because of the very large population of OBCs. Second, as an extension of vote-bank politics, Backward Classes are being divided into OBCs and MBCs.

Lessons from My Personal Experience

I belong to a backward caste. I am a surgical gastroenterologist, trained in the United Kingdom with a medical practice that ensured me a personal income way above the 'creamy layer' bar. I have two sons. My wife is a professor of dance, a renowned Kuchipudi exponent and presently the first woman registrar of a public university. My father was a judge of the Andhra Pradesh High Court and a very important Union minister. My mother, eighty-eight years old, has in the last decade accomplished a DLitt, as well as two PhDs, with a gold medal and a university rank. My children were born and grew up in an atmosphere that instilled the aspiration of academic achievement in them. They went to the best educational institutions and had the privilege of their parents monitoring, on a day-to-day basis, their performance and extra- and co-curricular activities to ensure all-round development.

In stark contrast, children born in poor families in rural areas see both their parents struggling—doing menial work as either labourers or farm helps and the like—depriving them of basic exposure to a different future for themselves. School means little to most of these children, and often they are enrolled in school for the midday meals provided there. The teaching standards at school as well as the studying atmosphere at home are abysmal. In addition, the children are compelled to do a lot of household work to help their parents. Most of them are school dropouts, either because of no interest in academics due to these circumstances, lack of encouragement, or in order to work to supplement the family income.

It is creditable when children manage to survive through all this, burn the midnight oil and reach a certain standard in academics. But when they finally reach the competitive arena, completely self-made, with their own grit and determination, whom do they compete with in the race for further academic growth? With people like my son, who had the best facilities, atmosphere and immense support in every academic step to reach the same stage! Isn't such discrepancy a gross injustice? And an insult to the founding fathers of the nation, who envisaged erasure of inequalities through support and certain privileges to the underprivileged? To this effect, the 'creamy layer' criteria may appear justified. But what about the argument that it does not take into consideration the socially backward angle?

Formulating a Tentative Proposal

There could be an alternative solution which does not involve the 'creamy layer' criteria. This would involve filling seats according to economic criteria from among the candidates who have crossed the cut-off point in terms of marks. The student from a lower-income category of Backward Classes would get precedence over his higher-income counterpart, irrespective of his marks, as long as he has crossed the general cut-off point. This way, economically underprivileged students would get priority, all the 27 per cent seats are bound to be filled and the 'creamy layer' would not and cannot be used for vote-bank purposes. Otherwise, successive governments will increase the economic cut-off limit to bring that many OBCs into their vote zone. Although the Supreme Court of India in 1992 set out a requirement that 27 per cent of civil service positions be reserved for members of OBCs, in August 2010, the *Times of India* reported that only around 7 per cent of eligible positions in government jobs had been filled by OBCs.[3]

In higher educational institutions, the difference in the proportion of different communities is mainly because of the difference in primary school enrolment. The obvious reason for the low eligibility is that educational as well as economic levels of OBCs are very low. Most join their community and parental artisan professions midway through school or after basic education, mostly because of economic needs and the low socio-economic status of their families. In addition, low standards in rural schools fail to create an academic interest in them. Another important reason why there has been very little economic and educational progress in these sections is that political parties in India attempt to use these communities as vote banks.

The architect of the Indian Constitution, B.R. Ambedkar, had envisaged time-bound development and had hoped that the underprivileged sections would not need reservations a decade or so after the Constitution was put in place. But even the shrewd lawyer in him did not foresee the propensities of the shrewd Indian politician who saw this as a means for extending his political life. To this political class, the vulnerable sections became a vote bank, and fostering development among them would lead to the destruction of their vote bank. So, rather than changing the lives of the vulnerable and marginalized sections to such an extent that they did not need support systems, they let them remain in the same state. Further, they brought in more and more sections into the underprivileged category. Essentially, if Ambedkar's dream were fulfilled, those sections which had developed should not have needed support systems any more, passing on the privilege to the lesser developed. But even cursory estimates will reveal that the OBC numbers have nearly doubled since the time the category was created in the 1950s.

It is not that there has been development in the lives of the ones earmarked earlier—they're nearly in the same state as previous generations—but newer communities have been added by political groups. In addition, within the OBCs themselves, the politician periodically juggles the sub-castes in the categories available, from a lesser level of privilege to the category having higher privilege in a pretence of concern. Courts invariably strike down these changes as unconstitutional, but the politician's purpose is served by his well-advertised action. Those opposing affirmative action entirely should understand that there are very genuine reasons behind them. It is only when these sections develop that the country will make all-round progress.

But India's history has proven that development and vote-bank politics seldom go hand in hand. Literate people might make an effort to acquaint themselves with party policies and ideologies and read the list of contestants before casting their vote. A non-literate or uneducated voter mostly goes by the party symbol and things he or she has heard about the party. This might be one reason why in India we attribute so much importance to a party symbol.

Ambedkar had opined that the reservations he was proposing should have a time frame. He had envisaged that during this period, with the help of reservations, there would be significant social as well as economic development in the lives of the underprivileged, who would thereafter not need support. But rather than working towards Ambedkar's dreams in their true spirit, reservations have been used towards building up vote banks. For instance, there were around seventy-odd Backward Class communities in the 1970s, all classified as socially backward. Ambedkar would have wanted successive governments to make clinical assessments of the development made by these communities over the decades. The number of OBCs in united Andhra Pradesh increased as new castes demanded to be included in the list year after year. Even after the division of the state in 2014, some agrarian castes like the Kapus in Andhra Pradesh demanded inclusion in the OBC list. What progress did the previous communities make over six decades, either with governmental or political help? Not much, seems to be the sad answer. So, in what way are we guaranteeing that the freshly added communities would make any progress other than having a 'BC' label?

In my alma mater, the Hyderabad Public School, there are seats earmarked for Scheduled Castes and Scheduled Tribes, with rooms being provided to them in the school hostel. A common complaint heard is that the school's standard gets affected by these allotments, since these students fare poorly in studies. A responsible, socially oriented school or government should oversee that the true benefits of admitting such students accrue to them. The seed of academic interest should be implanted in their mind through counselling. Teachers should be given the responsibility, in turn, to ensure that children are able to study by themselves. Special classes should be organized for all of them. If they are keen on sports, every attempt ought to be made to propel them in the right direction.

But the policy has been significantly harmed by the fact that political groups have usurped it to enhance their vote banks. A similar motive can be seen in the three acres of land being promised to Scheduled Castes in Telangana by the Telangana Rashtra Samithi government. Over a period of time, if a person who benefited from the scheme sells that land, loud murmurs will be heard: 'Why should land be allotted for these people if it is going to be sold?'

There is a huge difference between Ambedkar's thought process and that of the present-day politician. If governments were to lend their wholehearted support to affirmative action for at least one generation, there would be no future generations of backward communities, just as Ambedkar had envisioned.

In fact, it is seen that all the sections which have until now enjoyed political power have progressed to such an extent that they not only enjoy a high status in society but are economically well-off. The lower echelons of society which have never come anywhere close to power continue to depend on doles given out by the ones in power, like free housing schemes and free land schemes, thereby submitting themselves as vote banks to the forward sections. The latter prefers to keep them underdeveloped so that their vote banks remain intact, and they propel themselves towards higher economic development. Until this is overcome, India cannot achieve high levels of development, and this nation cannot be the 'India of our dreams'.

To achieve such a dream, Shudras who have tasted development through social, educational as well as economic benefits earmarked for OBCs should allow for their redistribution to generate an inclusive, all-round development of the community.

Caste and Political Economy

A Shudra Team

Shudras and Feudalism

In economic terms, Shudras are historically known as agriculturists, artisans and cattle-rearers. Broadly, they are known as a farming community. All interconnected production-related work was done by Shudras in the fields, and Dwijas (Brahmins, Banias and Kshatriyas) *never had a role in labour-related work in the production process.*[1] We characterize all Dwijas, including Khatris and Kayasthas, along with Brahmins, Banias and Kshatriyas as bhadralok. They hardly have a role in national agrarian wealth production, whether feudal or pre-feudal. The intellectual legitimacy for such non-participation was achieved through Brahminic texts which characterized any field-based manual labour work in a negative sense. Hence, production was treated as pollution in the Brahminic economic world view.

The upper Shudras owned large amounts of cultivable land. A small section of them were/are known as landlords or, in the recent past, kulaks. Communist and left liberal activists, thinkers and writers have done a lot of analytical and critical writing on labourers, landlords and even artisans, but there is no Hindutva literature on agrarian production and distribution-related tasks. The BJP intellectuals hardly produced any literature on the agrarian economy, its problems, social relations and their stand on those questions. Their theory of nationalism, particularly cultural nationalism, is totally silent about caste-based economic, cultural and social relations within India.

The left[2] designated the Indian economy as feudal and focused their attack on feudal landlordism, which in physical terms targeted the Shudra upper layer for a long time. The radical left defined the Indian economy as semi-feudal and semi-colonial and attacked for almost three decades the Shudra upper layer landed forces. Of course, the conflict in the vast agrarian system was between Shudra/Dalit labour and Shudra landlords. In this context, it is not only legitimate to study agrarian relations but indeed necessary to conceptualize and carry out an in-depth study of how agrarian relations operate within the caste matrix and why there are frequent violent attacks by upper Shudra landlords against Dalits and Shudra labourers and tenants. At the same time, it is important to study how caste capitalism got institutionalized in India within the broad global capitalist mode of production.

The issue we are pointing out is the almost exclusive 'scholarly' attention given to the discourse of Shudra dominance and violence while discussing caste in relation to the political economy. For instance, at no stage has the left or radical left not characterized the Indian economy as primarily feudal even after the liberalization process began in the 1990s. Since Indian capitalism is caste capitalism, they never wanted to examine it from that point of view and problematize it. How much of bhadralok intellectuality—right, left and liberal, in which there were no Shudra intellectuals—and the bhadralok capital outside the agrarian process colluded in hiding the facts must be examined elsewhere, but suffice it to say here that the Shudra feudals have no place at the top of the massively accumulated industrial economy of India in the 1990s and 2000s. This collective work of the Shudra intellectual team will present arguments and evidence in this regard, which, though, is preliminary.

The RSS[3] and BJP combination is in collusion with the brutally exploitative monopoly capital of India, which made the Shudra agrarian sector a marginal appendage, particularly after the 1990s process of globalization and liberalization. How much of this happened because of cheap sale of government industries, landed properties and institutions to bhadralok monopoly capitalists should be left for a separate study. But the present caste-wise studies of capital control indicate—even though they are few in number—that Brahmins/Banias/Khatris hold hegemonic control over the Indian capitalist economy. The mainstream political economy discourse is silent on this aspect. It is this silence that led to the massive rise of RSS–BJP networks in the country and is leading the nation to a self-destructive stage.

Brahminical Capitalism and Its Link with RSS–BJP

The political control of the Indian monopoly capital that plays a critical role in the election process at the national level shifted largely into the hands of the RSS–BJP in the recent past.[4] The Congress got weakened in the regional agrarian and real estate economies as Shudra regional parties have a significant say in this sector, but the RSS–BJP have major control even there. However, we must see whether old Shudra feudals who were much abused as kulaks transformed themselves into capitalists. Or whether they still remained within the agrarian economy where their grip on the vote bank was lost with the deployment of what could be called Gujarat–Mumbai Bania capital to serve the RSS–BJP's 'nationalism' and dislocate Shudras/OBCs from all power positions. There is also an attempt to destroy the Muslim survival economy with capitalist money, and the deployment of Shudra/OBC muscle power during riots such as in Gujarat in 2002.

Where do the Shudras/OBCs stand in this new game on the RSS–BJP capitalist chess board? With the use of big monopoly capital, massive resource mobilization is done for spending on elections and nationwide organizational strength. Shudras across the country do not find any significant space in that big economy or in the so-called nationalist economic patronage. There are not many studies on caste and capital control, but sporadic studies that have come out since 2010 show a definite move in this direction.

As per 'Corporate Boards in India: Blocked by Caste?', a study published in 2012, Banias comprise 46 per cent (of corporate boards), Brahmins 44.6 per cent, Kshatriyas 0.5 per cent, OBCs—that includes all Shudras—3.8 per cent, SC/ST 3.5 per cent, and others 1.5 per cent. This shows the absolute control that two castes (Brahmins and Banias) possess on industrial and financial capital.[5]

In this situation, a national political party cannot win elections without the patronage and blessings of Bania–Brahmin industrial power, and a national leader cannot attract the imagination of masses across the country without the support of media houses controlled and run by these two communities. The space in propaganda and financial availability for such a massive public mobilization is a constant process. We have seen how Narendra Modi achieved that both in the 2014 and 2019 elections. The presence of business in elections, Modi's vibrant business-friendly governance during his chief ministership, and most importantly, his relationship with the businessmen throughout allowed the BJP to realign many strategies that projected him as the messiah of development and saviour of the nation (essentially a Hindutva nation).[6] Massive media support allowed him to overcome the negative image of the 2002 Gujarat riots. However, Shudras do not have much space in media either in terms of ownership or even as employees.

Let us not forget that even Mahatma Gandhi, though for a different national cause during the freedom struggle, got the financial and propaganda support of industrialists such as the Birlas and Goenkas. Pandit Jawaharlal Nehru also got Brahmin–Bania intellectual and capital support within the framework of secularism. But now, the support of Brahmin–Bania capital has shifted to the right-wing. The Bombay and Gujarat Bania capital was already a leading force in media networks and Gandhi–Nehru got that support in building their image, though they could never be compared to Narendra Modi–Amit Shah in ethical and historical location.

However, so far, no Shudra leader has got the promotional acceptance of big capital to be a national leader, and the Shudras themselves have not yet become a conscious industrial and political force at the national level. At best, they are rich regionally and are regional political leaders. Unless they evolve a Bahujan consciousness of their own outside the fold of the RSS–BJP, they cannot reach the national leadership stature and become the prime minister of India in their own capacity. The Congress also did not promote anyone with that identity at the national level.

Who Are the Richest? Bania–Brahman–Khatri Monopoly

The Forbes list of Indian billionaires would give us a clear picture of the caste composition and to what extent capital has been monopolized in recent years. The 2018 Forbes list shows that, out of 119 billionaires, sixty-five are from the traditional mainstream mercantile castes. Harish Damodaran breaks them down caste-wise as follows: thirty-eight non-Gujarati Bania/Marwari, ten Gujarati Bania/Jain, eight Parsi, six Sindhi, two Kutchi Bhatia and one Lohana. The remaining fifty-four represent a mixed bag: fifteen Brahmins (including three Bhumihars, a caste that claims Brahmin status), twelve Khatris/Aroras, five Muslims, four Patidars, three Christians, two Jats, two Nadars and one Nair,

Kayastha, Bunt, Konkanastha Vaishya Vani, Lingayat, Kamma, Reddy, Saini, Ezhava, Ramgarhia and Isai Vellalar each.[7]

Who Are the Poorest? STs, SCs and OBCs

A study[8] shows that 50 per cent of Brahmins, 31 per cent of Rajputs, 44 per cent of Banias and 57 per cent of Kayasthas fall in the richest category. For other caste groups, only 5 per cent STs, 10 per cent SCs, 16 per cent OBCs and 17 per cent Muslims fall in the richest category. The percentage of caste groups falling in the 'poorest category' is lowest for Kayasthas (2.2 per cent), followed by Brahmins (4.6 per cent), Rajputs (7.3 per cent), Banias (5.8 per cent) and other forward castes (9.7 per cent).

Whereas, among STs, SCs and OBC, the combined poorest and poorer percentages are as high as 74 per cent, 53 per cent and 41 per cent, respectively. These wide disparities are never taken into account even as ceaseless discussions take place on the growth or dip in the Gross Domestic Product.

Table1. Wealth and Poverty across Caste Clusters[9]

	Wealth Index				
	Poorest	Poorer	Middle	Richer	Richest
Overall	20.63	19.82	19.86	19.6	20.09
ST	51	23.09	12.87	7.78	5.26
SC	28.47	24.8	21.19	16.08	9.46
OBC	18.87	21.66	22.94	20.7	15.83
FC(Brahman)	4.62	9.7	13.86	21.9	49.91
FC(Rajput)	7.27	13.78	21.9	25.89	31.15
FC(Bania)	5.8	11.86	16.52	22.17	43.66
FC(Kayasth)	2.17	5.25	10.89	24.67	57.02
FC(Other)	9.75	13.42	17.13	24.45	35.26
Muslim	20.91	21.19	19.11	21.8	16.99
Other	2.45	4.08	9.45	22.2	61.81

Source: Nitin Kumar Bharti, 'Wealth Inequality, Class and Caste in India, 1951–2012', master's thesis, Paris School of Economics, 2009, Table 22: Wealth Index, NFHS 2005.
Note: FC stands for Forward Caste.

The Bania–Brahmin Sensex

Aakar Patel, who comes from the Shudra (Patel) community of Gujarat and is a well-known journalist who was also harassed for his association with Amnesty International, compiled data on the caste control of wealth in share markets and banks. His article in *Mint* titled 'When Will the Brahmin–Bania Hegemony End' was first published in 2009.[10] Though there may have been some changes in the names of heads of organizations, the basic trend remains the same even now. We are reproducing his list here:

The Sensex comprises the 30 largest traded companies of India.

ACC is run by a Brahmin (Sumit Banerjee)
BHEL is run by a Brahmin (Ravi Kumar Krishna Swamy)
Bharti Airtel is run by a Bania (Sunil Mittal)
Grasim and Hindalco are run by a Bania (Kumar Mangalam Birla)
HDFC is run by a Bania (Deepak Parekh)
Hindustan Unilever is run by a Brahmin (Nitin Paranjpe)
ICICI Bank is headed by a Brahmin (K.V. Kamath)
Jaiprakash Associates is run by a Brahmin (Yogesh Gaur)
L&T is run by a Brahmin (A.M. Naik)
NTPC is run by a Brahmin (R.S. Sharma)
ONGC is run by a Brahmin (also called R.S. Sharma)
Reliance group firms are run by Banias (Mukesh and Anil Ambani)
State Bank of India is run by a Brahmin (O.P. Bhatt)
Sterlite Industries is run by a Bania (Anil Agarwal)
Sun Pharma is run by a Bania (Dilip Shanghvi)
Tata Steel is run by a Brahmin (B. Muthuraman)

Punjab National Bank is run by a Brahmin (K.C. Chakrabarty)
Bank of Baroda is run by a Brahmin (M.D. Mallya)
Canara Bank is run by a Bania (A.C. Mahajan).

Of India's software companies,
Infosys is run by a Brahmin (Kris Gopalakrishnan now and
Narayana Murthy and Nandan Nilekani before him)
TCS is run by a Brahmin (Subramanian Ramadorai)
Wipro is owned by a Khoja (Azim Premji). Khojas are Shias
of the Sevener sect, converted from the Luhana trading
community (same caste as L.K. Advani and M.A. Jinnah)

India's two largest airlines are:
Kingfisher, owned by a Brahmin (Vijay Mallya)
Jet, owned by a Bania (Naresh Goyal)

Of India's mobile phone firms:
Reliance Communications (Ambani)
Airtel (Mittal)
Vodafone Essar (Ruia)
Idea (Birla), Spice (Modi) are owned by Banias
BSNL is run by a Bania (Kuldeep Goyal)
Tata's TTML is run by a Brahmin (K.A. Chaukar).

Cricket in India is run by a Bania (Lalit Modi, now he is
in London), and before him it was run by another Bania
(Jagmohan Dalmiya).
Media in India is almost entirely controlled by Banias and
Jains.

Of the two largest English newspapers:
The *Times of India* is owned by Jains and
The *Hindustan Times* is owned by Banias (Birla)

The Hindu is owned by Brahmins (Kasturi Iyengar family)
The *Indian Express* is owned by Banias (Goenka)
Zee TV is owned by a Bania (Subhash Chandra Goel)

Of the two largest Hindi newspapers:
Dainik Jagran is owned by Banias (Gupta), and
Dainik Bhaskar is owned by Banias (Agarwal)
The Agarwals also own Gujarati daily *Divya Bhaskar*
The largest Gujarati newspaper, *Gujarat Samachar*, is owned
by Jains (Shah)
The largest Marathi paper, *Lokmat*, is owned by Jains (Darda)
Rajasthan Patrika is owned by Jains (Kothari)
Navbharat Times is owned by Jains and
Hindustan owned by Banias (Birla)
Amar Ujala is owned by Banias (Maheshwari)

Of India's steel companies:
Essar is owned by Banias (Ruia)
ArcelorMittal is owned by a Bania (Lakshmi Mittal)
Ispat is owned by Banias (Mittals)
Jindal Steel is owned by Banias
Bhushan Steel is owned by Banias (Singhal)
VISA Steel is owned by Banias (Agarwal)
State-owned SAIL is run by a Bania (S.K. Roongta) and
Lloyd Steel is owned by Banias (Gupta)

Of India's cement companies:
Ambuja is owned by Banias (Neotia and Sekhsaria)
Dalmia Cements is owned by Banias
Ultratech and Vikram Cement are owned by Banias (Birla)
and JK Cement is owned by Banias (Singhania)
Hindustan Motors is owned by Banias (Birla)
Bajaj Auto is owned by Banias.

Old economy, new economy: All economy in India is owned
and run by two castes.
The Brahmin used his monopoly on knowledge and the Bania
used his high-trust culture of trade to become dominant.
Their skills are world-class. Given the realities of capital
formation, it is difficult for other castes to catch up soon.

This unbridled Bania–Brahmin hegemony in the ownership and
executive functioning of capitalist corporate structures works
through insidious channels of nepotism and casteism.

Rereading the Political Economy as the Caste Economy

Aakar Patel's list and Forbes's data tells us where the studies on
India's political economy went wrong. The European Marxist
methodology or liberal methodology from the days of Adam
Smith completely misled the Indian nation. For instance, a
fact that is not known much is that the Khatri community—a
Punjabi Patwari (land record maintenance) community, which
is also largely a migrant community from West Punjab—is now
one of the richest in the country. They are well educated and
live around Delhi and Punjab without engaging in any social
discourse or agrarian production. Two communities in north
India, the Khatris and Kayasthas, though small in number,
have emerged as very powerful castes who work hand in hand
with Brahmins, Banias and Jains. They are part of the newly
formulated bhadralok of India. The Bengal formula of bhadralok
with a combination of Brahmins, Kayasthas and Baidyas has
come to be formed as the economic analytical category for a
study of India in the new globalized capitalist economy. These
caste groups were historically against reservation in education
and employment.

Among them, a small section is secular or liberal democratic in the ideological framework. But the vast majority is deeply Brahminic Hindu and now supports the RSS–BJP, knowing well that their comments against Muslim and Christian communities may isolate India in the international domain. Though the Hindutva Parivar relies on the Muslim terrorism issue for expanding its space globally, the Hindutva communal capital poses a threat to the nation in the long run as any religious communal agenda would destabilize the civil societal markets that would gradually become self-destructive. They prefer to stay with the RSS–BJP since the idea of socialism and distributive welfare in Indian democracy don't hold much appeal for them. Now, the Congress, with its secularism agenda, does not appeal to them either.

Bhadralok intellectuals educated in foreign universities or in the country's best institutions take up the cause of secularism and pluralism but they largely didn't oppose the caste–capital nexus and never upheld the theory of Shudra/OBC/Dalit/Adivasi forces being the national wealth producers. For a long time, they spoke a class language and remained silent about caste exploitation and oppression. They now voice their sympathy for Dalits but not Shudras/OBCs. On the contrary, there's plenty of written discourse around kulak exploitation. Communist thinkers, having come from the same bhadralok social forces, never understood that India is not China; in India, class is not real class and is actually caste with a class within it. There is no Shudra/OBC intellectual force in any political formation to reformulate the debate on the Indian caste-centred economy. Such a debate will save India from entering a vortex of communal carnage and constant disruptions of the capitalist market where the very same rich are sellers and most Shudras/OBCs/Dalits/Adivasis and minorities are only buyers. The Indian monopoly capital has grown in the secular, democratic atmosphere created by the state. Communal carnage will halt the growth of capital as well as lead it to lose its global acceptability. In no theocratic state in the world has the capitalist free market grown. Theocracy is anti-welfare capitalism and political democracy by nature. When Brahmin–Bania casteism is coupled with spiritual theocracy, the destructive process gains more strength and vigour.

It is well known that Banias and Brahmins own the highest amount of wealth.[11] Apart from being national rulers, Brahmins are also regional rulers. For example, West Bengal and Odisha have been under perpetual Brahmin-controlled regional parties. West Bengal chief ministers have been Brahmins or Kayasthas, whether under Congress, CPI(M) or Trinamool Congress rule. This is also because the economy of the state is in the hands of those two communities.

The Brahmins of Bengal and Maharashtra controlled the intellectual discourse of the nation for centuries with a profitable collaboration with the colonial machinery. And they continue to do so. Even if we look at the poorest people among different castes, the Kayasthas have the least number in this category, followed by Brahmins and Banias. The number of the poorest among any Shudra upper caste will be more than a combination of Brahmins, Banias and Kayasthas. As per the table, the poorest in the country are Muslims. What is strange is that this new bhadralok section became economically powerful during the Congress rule of P.V. Narasimha Rao and Manmohan Singh. In the present regime, they continue to prosper. Even though some Indian capitalists acquired their monopoly capitalist status during Congress regimes, there is little support for the Congress and its discourse on secularism now from the monopoly capital. Communism's egalitarian ideology too has no space in the political economy forged from the caste monopoly capital.

Monopoly capitalists, constituted mainly of Banias and Brahmins, became what they are mainly when the Congress and non-RSS–BJP secular alliance parties were in power. Yet, they moved on to support the BJP's bid for power. If constant disturbances with an open communal discourse against Muslims and Christians become part of governance, the urban markets of monopoly companies will face a crisis. How and why did the Indian monopoly capital move from showing a preference for communalism over a secular democracy? No bhadralok economist has examined this troublesome question.

As the methodology of the Euro-American political economy is premised on class formation without the mediation of any other non-class agency in the process of wealth concentration and labour exploitation, it is grossly inadequate for the Indian situation. In India, it is actually the caste economy that grips every field of production and accumulation. Caste relations shape the economy with their own logic.

In the wealth index cited earlier, there is only a meagre Shudra presence. Yet, Shudras as a class have been at the receiving end of political and ideological wrath—for being feudal kulak exploiters from the days of the anti-colonial freedom movement to being equated now with the big capitalist who runs the share market. They are only regional capitalists, landholders and regional political power managers, who were the targets of the left movement and now the right movement. The hold of Shudras is somewhat consistent in south Indian states because of a strong anti-Brahmin movement. North India never had such a movement. There is an attempt by some bhadralok writers to state that the regional Shudra capital accumulation by Kammas, Reddys, Marathas, Nadars and so on is comparable to the monopoly capital of Banias and Brahmins. Such regional Shudra entrepreneurs and their regional parties are no match for the Mumbai, Ahmedabad and Delhi Dwija monopoly capital and the combined strength and reach of the RSS–BJP. An abundant presence of Banias, especially in the monopoly capital, and their symbiotic relationship with Brahmins in the software capital and other Dwija entrepreneurs, indicates that the theory of 'field to factory' movement of Shudras is more of an imaginary one.[12] The entry of a few Shudras into agribusinesses has not undermined the control of Banias in all business and industrial sectors.

Our study clearly indicates that Indian feudal Shudras did not transform into capitalists, and other lower working castes in the larger feudal economy could not emerge from what is known as early mercantile capital to monopoly capital. The whole wealth was, generation after generation, controlled by Brahmins and Banias who escaped any critical economic analysis. In fact, Shudra landlords, who are nowhere in the present globalized monopoly capital, faced the brunt of Western-educated bhadralok economists, whether of liberal or communist hue. Hindutva economists targeted the Muslim or minority economy, which barely has a presence in the list, except for Azim Premji. RSS–BJP economists also attack the Christian conversion capital, but not a single Christian is in the monopoly industrialist list.[13] Actually, this Muslim–Christian control myth misled the Shudra communities, as if the RSS's Hindutva ideology works for them, which it does not.

An important economical aspect is the financial circuit that, from untraceable sources, flows continuously to Hindu temples/mutts/peethas. This economy is not listed anywhere. Shudras/OBCs have no hold on this temple-based economy. Only a Ramdev (a Shudra Yadav)-like institution has some wealth, but it also serves the RSS–BJP interest.[14] The Muslim economy has a distributive character through Zakat, and the Christian economy is vastly distributed among the poorest of the poor non-Muslim castes and communities through education and small employment. The RSS–BJP constantly shows this act of redistribution as dangerous, and Shudras/OBCs also believe it to be to their own detriment. Hindutva economists and politicians criticize Christian distributiveness in the name of conversion because they are trying to spread education, which is seen as disruptive. Unfortunately, a large number among the Shudra agrarian rich also believe in this propaganda, without examining their own education status.

Shudra Ignorance

Shudras and OBCs form the main muscle power squads for Hindutva networks. Shudras/OBCs/Dalits have no communal history, but are being mobilized to serve a communal cause. The fundamentalist Hindutva Shudra mobilization is based on propaganda that Muslims and Christians are the main threat to the nation, which is an abstract idea. The entire economic analysis above shows that the Shudra/OBC/Dalit labour power is being plundered by the bhadralok economic exploiters without them being co-workers anywhere in the production fields. The Dalit, Muslim and Christian masses are co-workers in the agrarian and industrial sectors. But the RSS–BJP combination wants to hide this fact under the broad rubric of Hindu nationalism and mobilize money from bhadralok capitalists and muscle power and votes from Shudras/OBCs.

The solution to the present Shudra/OBC/Dalit/Adivasi crisis lies in the Shudra upper layer realizing that as long as they do not come on to the centre stage of national polity in a broad coalition format with an imaginative intellectual force behind them, they will be more and more marginalized. Communalized politics will only lead Shudra/OBC youth into jails while the Muslim and Christian question will become an international diplomatic issue. An exposé by Raju Solanki, a Gujarat-based Dalit poet and activist, revealed that in the 2002 Godhra riots, there were 2945 arrests in Ahmedabad. Of these, 1577 were Hindus and 1368 Muslims. Among the Hindus arrested, 797 were OBCs, 747 Dalits, nineteen Patels, two Banias and two Brahmins. The upper castes became members of the Legislative Assembly, while the rest were jailed.[15]

At least what happens to Muslims and Christians is debated globally as they are global religious communities. The backwardness or exploitation of Shudras/OBCs/Dalits/ Adivasis does not become an issue in any international forum or intellectual wing. The outside world sees them all as Hindu. This is tragic. The RSS–BJP might show some small-time benefits to a section of Shudras/OBCs but the real wealth of the nation is neither with them nor will it be allowed to come into their hands, as history clearly shows us. Even the land power that the Shudra upper layer controlled in rural areas has now shifted to monopoly industrialists.

Though bhadralok forces are not in the agrarian sector as producers, they found a way to control large tract of land through Special Economic Zones (SEZs). They own thousands of acres as private school, college and university campus builders. They have lands for their hardware and software industrial campuses. Hardly any Shudras control the SEZ economy. Around Delhi, Mumbai, Kolkata, Bengaluru, Chennai, Hyderabad and so on, vast tracts of land are in the hands of monopoly capitalists. The RSS–BJP combine is in support of this ownership as long as they supply them resources for their activities and elections. None of their organizational wings protest against the SEZ ownership of monopoly capitalists.

The Question of the Shudra–Dalit Contradiction

A positive sign is the emergence of a small group of Dalit intellectuals, including economists. But their focus is still on the agrarian sector, and contradictions and conflicts between Shudras/OBCs and Dalits. Their studies reveal crucial fault lines between upper Shudra landlords and Dalit landless labourers. While this should be taken for constructive political agenda, this isolated narrative tends to find exceptional resonance in the bhadralok academic engagement because through this they can hide the capital control of Brahmin–Bania forces. Keeping Shudras/OBCs and Dalits as marginal and antagonist in the labour market is of strategic interest to the bhadralok. The Shudra regional power, based on small regional capital and agrarian relations without being backed by critical intellectual resource, should also be a cause for concern for Dalit intellectuals. But after Ambedkar and Kanshiram, Dalit politicians have failed us by not offering a systemic sociopolitical and spiritual vision. Ambedkar wrote 'Who Are the Shudras?' with a long-term vision, though he organized the All-India Scheduled Castes Federation exclusively.[16]

The Shudra social status is not at all part of the present Dalit intellectual discourse. Since Shudras/OBCs and Dalits live in the agrarian economy, the physical conflicts are around untouchability and agrarian labour. Shudras have land, and most Dalits live on labour in villages. They have not even become proletariat in the big capital. Shudras/OBCs and Dalits must work for a share in the monopoly capital both in employment and ownership. Shudras/OBCs must work for social and land reform within the agrarian sector as violent expressions have become more frequent. This situation is constructed by the varnadharma ideology, which is followed by the RSS–BJP. This should be a common concern. The conflict between Shudras/OBCs and Dalits has broken the electoral collaboration among the Shudras/OBCs and Dalits, which is a profitable situation for the bhadralok monopoly capital and the RSS–BJP. This operates as the varnadharma economic and political control system, as it was meant to be in the larger Hindutva framework.

It is unfortunate that after Kanshiram worked out a Dalit/Shudra/OBC alliance in Uttar Pradesh, Mayawati and Mulayam Singh broke that for local power in the state. Due to electoral competition and compulsions, both of them reduced themselves to leaders with some local caste mobilization capacity, instead of leading as a national political force. They are struggling to mount a successful challenge to the RSS–BJP bhadralok monopoly capital and its fundamentalist national vision. Be it Shudras, Dalits or Adivasis, for all of them, the problem is that the support of the bhadralok monopoly capital is with the RSS–BJP. Bhadralok capitalists have to distance themselves from the RSS–BJP in a globally negative atmosphere after a series of anti-Muslim measures taken by the RSS–BJP after the 2019 elections. Otherwise, the entire capitalist market will suffer stagnation. For example, the recent abrogation of Article 370, the passing of the Citizenship Amendment Act, talks of a National Register of Citizens and so on will disturb monopoly capital and the daily movement of markets, which puts national wealth at a loss. The West and the Muslim world, along with China, are looking at RSS–BJP-controlled India as a new problem creator.

Post-COVID-19, India will be mired in major economic and livelihood problems.[17] The lives of labourers have been hit hard with the nationwide lockdown and economic downturn. The national lockdown period and national and international economic downsizing will certainly impact labour and semi-employed millions, which may lead to them unexpectedly slipping into poverty. Those affected would mostly be the Shudra/OBC/Dalit masses as they constitute the bulk of the labour force. The massive problem of survival of migrant labour will be framed in class terms so that their caste background does not come into the discourse. Given the poverty levels among

Dalits/Adivasis/OBCs, as shown earlier, there is hardly any possibility that the bhadralok social mass was among the migrant labourers who walked thousands or hundreds of kilometres in the lockdown economy, and starved or died on the way.

As mentioned earlier, the Muslim question may draw more international attention,[18] in particular that of the Muslim world, but the suffering of Shudras/OBCs/Dalits/Adivasis will continue to be seen as a Hindu problem. Though one cannot predict what social and communal conflicts the post-COVID-19 economic and social situation would create, what seems to be certain is that there will be huge economic and social distress. Indian monopoly capitalists, given their history of indifference to philanthropy, may not spend much on saving these starving and collapsing lives. Though they treat Mahatma Gandhi as 'their Mahatma', monopoly capitalists have never accepted his theory that the 'wealthy must act as trustees of their wealth' for the good of the poor. On the contrary, they treat the starving bodies of labourers as their cheap labour banks. Caste culture has created an unfortunate Indian psyche of the rich treating the poor as not only 'untouchable' but the unthinkable Other. A sense of shame and guilt by the bhadralok rich and the intellectual and political elite who support them for exploitation and oppression of the poor was never a part of the nationalist parampara, because their God created them from his feet as modern slaves.

The only way now is a gradual change. The Shudra upper layer, which is outside Mandal reservation, and the OBCs must move away from the RSS–BJP ranks and realize that their share in capital and power is minimal. All political formations like the Congress and regional parties must come to the conclusion that monopoly capital needs to be owned by plural communities and Shudras/OBCs/Dalits must fight for their share in the monopoly capital.

Conclusion

Politically promoting strong Shudra, Dalit and Adivasi leadership at the national level with a national promise should be the number one priority. The intellectual and bureaucratic leadership should shift into Shudra/OBC/Dalit/Adivasi hands. These are sure-fire ways to checkmate the disastrous RSS–BJP network that is dismantling the democratic and constitutional fabric of India in very subtle ways. As Kancha Ilaiah Shepherd warns in a recent article, the RSS–BJP combination and bhadralok monopoly capital in the name of Hindutva nationalism might bring back varnadharma dictatorship.[19] If that happens, India as a nation will slip back to medieval formations where caste culture ruled the roost, in which even the bhadralok monopoly capital will get weakened and slowly destroyed, resulting in a total economic meltdown.

Notes

Introduction

1. Ram Sharan Sharma, *Sudras in Ancient India, A Social History of the Lower Order Down to Circa A.D. 600* (Delhi: Motilal Banarsidass, 1958), pp. 90–156.
2. M.S.S. Pandian, *Brahmin & Non-Brahmin, Genealogies of the Tamil Political Present* (New Delhi: Permanent Black, 2017), pp. 77–83.
3. G. Aloysius, *Nationalism without a Nation in India* (New Delhi: Oxford University Press, 1997); Parimala V. Rao, *Foundations of Tilak's Nationalism: Discrimination, Education and Hindutva* (New Delhi: Orient BlackSwan, 2011).
4. Satyakam Joshi and K.S. Raman, 'Jotirao Phule: An Incomplete Renaissance', *Economic and Political Weekly* 26.21 (6 March 1991): 1325–27, http://www.jstor.org/stable/4398051.
5. G. Aloysius, *Dalit-Subaltern Self-Identifications: Iyothee Thassar And Tamizhan* (New Delhi: Critical Quest, 2010).
6. Bhimrao Ramji Ambedkar, *Dr Babasaheb Ambedkar: Writings and Speeches,* Vol. 1 (Bombay: Government of Maharashtra, 2016).
7. सिद्धार्थ, 'सच्ची रामायण छापने वाले ललई यादव क्यों बन गये बौद्ध?', Print, 7 February 2019, https://hindi.theprint.in/opinion/why-did-become-a-buddhist-the-sachchi-ramayana-printer-lalai-yadav/44163/. Accessed 10 July 2020.

8. Christophe Jaffrelot, *India's Silent Revolution: The Rise of the Lower Castes in North India* (New Delhi: Orient BlackSwan, 2003).

9. Judgment of *The State of Madras v. Champakam Dorairajan* is available on https://indiankanoon.org/doc/149321. Accessed 10 July 2020.

10. G. Aloysius, *Periyar on Category-Wise Rights* (New Delhi: Critical Quest, 2016), p. 4.

11. Satish Deshpande, 'Caste and Castelessness', *Economic and Political Weekly* (2013), https://www.epw.in/journal/2013/15/perspectives/caste-and-castelessness.html.

12. H.S. Verma and Arun Kumar Singh, 'Debate on Identification, Scheduling and Reservation for the OBCs: Misdirection, Disinformation and Partisanship by the Mainstream Social Scientists', in *The OBCs and the Ruling Classes in India*, ed., H.S. Verma (New Delhi: Rawat Publications, 2005).

13. Vivek Dhareshwar, 'Caste and the Secular Self', *Comparative Studies in Society and History*, 2006, https://doi.org/10.1017/S0010417506000065.

14. Dilip M. Menon, *The Blindness of Insight, Essays on Caste in Modern India* (New Delhi: Navayana, 2011).

15. M.S. Golwalkar quoted in Subhash Gatade, 'Modi: Fascinated by Manu', mainstreamweekly.net, 2019, https://www.mainstreamweekly.net/article9017.html. Accessed 12 July 2020.

16. Gatade, 'Modi: Fascinated by Manu'.

17. Bhanwar Meghwanshi, *I Could Not Be Hindu: The Story of a Dalit in the RSS* (New Delhi: Navayana, 2020), pp. 36–37.

18. The RSS in its ninety-five years of existence has exclusively chosen its sarsanghchalak from Dwija castes, and that too almost exclusively Brahmins.

19. Mohan Bhagwat, quoted in Dinesh Narayan, 'Closed Ranks, The Rashtriya Swayamsevak Sangh's Tribulations over Caste', *Caravan*, April 2020.

20. Meghwanshi, *I Could Not Be Hindu: The Story of a Dalit in the RSS*.

21. Ibid, p. 190.

22. Ramachandra Guha, 'Which Ambedkar?', *Indian Express*, 21 April 2016, https://indianexpress.com/article/opinion/columns/br-ambedkar-2762688. Accessed 12 July 2020.

23. Anish Gupta and Aaleya Giri, 'Violation of Reservation in Top Posts at Universities', *The Hindu*, 2 June 2019, https://www. thehindu.com/opinion/op-ed/violation-of-reservation-in-top-posts-at-universities/article28252966.ece.

24. Kancha Ilaiah Shepherd, *Why I Am Not a Hindu: A Sudra Critique of Hindutva Philosophy, Culture and Political Economy* (New Delhi: Sage India, 2019), pp. 36–53.

25. G. Aloysius, *Contextualising Backward Classes Discourses* (New Delhi: Critical Quest, 2016).

26. Asha Singh and Nidhin Donald, 'Asking Questions to OBC as a Category', 'Has Capitalism Destroyed Caste and Race; Does Capitalism Equalize or Perpetuate Age-Old Inequalities?', *Prabuddha: Journal of Social Equality 3.1 (2019)*, http://prabuddha. us/index.php/pjse/article/view/9.

The Nation and Its Shudras

1. The title of this essay is not inspired, rather provoked, by the title of an important work on the subject of postcolonial studies by Partha Chatterjee, *The Nation and Its Fragments: Colonial and Postcolonial Histories* (Oxford University Press, 1997). The provocation comes primarily from the fact that various excluded and marginalized subaltern groups have been made part of this book as a subject of study vis-à-vis the nation, be it outcastes, women and peasants, but not Shudras. The Shudra subject has suffered pernicious neglect in the epistemology of the making of the modern nation called India. This essay, therefore, is an exploration of the existing intellectual gap. It seeks to highlight the missing Shudras from the imagination of a nation from the vantage of two questions. The first was posed by B.R. Ambedkar in 1946, on the eve of Independence, *Who Were the Shudras? How They Came to Be the Fourth Varna in the Indo-Aryan Society* (see, B.R. Ambedkar, *Who Were the Shudras? How They Came to Be the Fourth Varna in the Indo-Aryan Society* [Delhi: Gautam Book Centre, 2008]), and the second by Kancha Ilaiah Shepherd in 2018, more than seventy years after Independence, *Where Are the Shudras? Why the Shudras Are Lost in Today's India* (see, Kancha Ilaiah, 'Where

Are the Shudras? Why the Shudras Are Lost in Today's India', *Caravan*, 30 September 2018). A special acknowledgement is due to Prof. Ilaiah, who keeps inspiring Shudra scholars to write more and more, for even Dalits, who have been socially much more deprived than Shudras, have been successful in creating a scholarship and substantive corpus of literature under the banner of Dalit Studies.

2. See, Jyotirao Phule, *Shetkaryaca Asud,* 'Introduction', trans. Gail Omvedt and Bharat Patankar (Round Table India, 28 November 2010). *Setkayaca Asud* is one of Phule's original Marathi writing that literally means 'The Whipcord of the Cultivator', published in 1881.

3. *Political Theory*, textbook for Class XI (New Delhi: National Council for Education Research and Training), pp. 100–01. For detailed discussion, see Partha Chatterjee's essay, 'Whose Imagined Community?' in *Partha Chatterjee Omnibus* (New Delhi, Oxford University Press), pp. 4–5. Also see, Benedict Anderson, *Imagined Communities: Reflections on the Origin and Spread of Nationalism* (London: Verso, 2006).

4. Romila Thapar, 'The Past As Seen in Ideologies Claiming to Be Nationalist', in *What the Nation Really Needs to Know: The JNU Nationalism Lectures*, eds Rohit Azad, Janaki Nair, Mohinder Singh and Mallarika Sinha Roy (New Delhi: HarperCollins, 2016), p. 180.

5. Ibid, p. 180.

6. Romila Thapar, 'Renunciation, Dissent and Satyagraha', Twelfth V.M. Tarkunde Memorial Lecture, India International Centre, 6 December 2019, as reported in *The Hindu*, 7 December 2019.

7. Gopal Guru, 'Taking Indian Nationalism Seriously' in *What the Nation Really Needs to Know: The JNU Nationalism Lectures*, eds Azad, Nair, Singh, Sinha Roy, p. 3.

8. Ibid, p. 4.

9. See, Kancha Ilaiah, *Why I Am Not a Hindu: A Shudra Critique of Hindutva Philosophy, Culture and Political Economy* (Kolkata: Samya, 1996); G. Aloysius, *Nationalism Without A Nation in India* (Oxford University Press, 1997); Braj Ranjan Mani, *Debrahmanising History: Dominance and Resistance in India* (New Delhi: Manohar Publishers and Distributors, 2005); Gail Omvedt, *Seeking Begumpura: The*

Social Vision of Anti-Caste Intellectuals (New Delhi: Navayana, 2011).

10. Gail Omvedt, *Dalits and the Democratic Revolution: Dr Ambedkar and the Dalit Movement in Colonial India* (Sage, 1994), p. 97.

11. Ibid, p. 15.

12. Phule, in his deliberate attempt to reverse Aryan race theory, argued that Shudras, Ati-Shudras and Adivasis were the original inhabitants of this nation who were enslaved, exploited by barbaric Aryans who later formulated caste-based Hinduism for deceiving the Bahujan masses and legitimizing their might over them (see, Omvedt, *Dalits and the Democratic Revolution: Dr. Ambedkar and the Dalit Movement in Colonial India*). However, Ambedkar concluded that Shudras did not form a separate varna in the Indo-Aryan society when there were only three varnas and then the Shudras were part of Kshatriyas. Later, due to continuous feuds between Shudra kings and Brahmin priests, the latter refused to perform upanayana for the former and were therefore degraded to the fourth varna, below Vaishyas (see, Ambedkar, *Who Were the Shudras? How They Came to Be the Fourth Varna in the Indo-Aryan Society*).

13. Omvedt, *Dalits and the Democratic Revolution: Dr Ambedkar and the Dalit Movement in Colonial India*, p. 148.

14. Ambedkar, *Who Were the Shudras? How They Came to Be the Fourth Varna in the Indo-Aryan Society*, p. 9.

15. Sharad Patil, *Dasa-Sudra Slavery: Studies in the Origins of Indian Slavery and Feudalism and their Philosophies* (New Delhi: Allied Publishers), p. 3.

16. R.S. Sharma, *Sudras in Ancient India: A Social History of the Lower Order Down to Circa A.D. 600* (Delhi: Motilal Banarsidass, 2016 reprint), p. 34.

17. Ibid, p. 44.

18. *A Code of Gentoo Laws* was a legal document developed by the early colonizers in India. It was translated from the Persian by Brahmin scholars and later into English by Nathaniel Brassey Halhed, a British orientalist and philologist working with the East India Company. The sole purpose of this translation project funded by Warren Hastings was to increase the hold of the colonizers over colonial subjects.

19. Braj Ranjan Mani, *Debrahmanising History: Dominance and Resistance in Indian Society* (New Delhi: Manohar Publishers, 2005), p. 15.

20. M.N. Srinivas coined and popularized the term based on his fieldwork. See, M.N. Srinivas, *The Dominant Caste and Other Essays* (New Delhi: Oxford University Press, 1995).

21. There are numerous instances of upper Shudra castes being involved in atrocities against Dalit castes in changing agrarian relations owing to the ownership of agricultural land.

22. Omvedt has endorsed this point, saying Marathas and other castes may have been dominant castes at the village level but Brahmans were the dominant caste in the system as a whole. See Omvedt, *Dalits and the Democratic Revolution: Dr Ambedkar and the Dalit Movement in Colonial India*, p. 149.

23. Ibid, p. 67.

24. Ibid.

25. This slogan literally meant, 'Karpoori, do your work, get a shaving knife and perform a barber's job.' See, Prem Kumar Mani's interview with Nawal Kishore titled, 'Karpuri Thakur ne Uttar Bharat Ki Rajneeti Ki Disha Badal Di', *Forward Press*, 24 January 2020. Accessed 26 January 2020.

26. 'Sharad Yadav, go back, get a stick and start shepherding buffaloes', as told by an upper-caste informant on the condition of anonymity during a field visit in March 2019.

27. Kancha Ilaiah, 'Where are the Shudras? Why the Shudras Are Lost in Today's India', *Caravan,* 30 September 2018.

28. The idea of 'Unequal Citizens' is borrowed from K.C. Yadav's book *India's Unequal Citizens*, written at the height of the Mandal agitation. K.C. Yadav, *India's Unequal Citizens: Study of Other Backward Classes* (Delhi: Manohar Publishers and Distributors, 1994).

29. Ambedkar, *Who Were the Shudras? How They Came to be the Fourth Varna in the Indo-Aryan Society.*

30. Ambedkar's acknowledgement reads, '. . . inscribed in memory of the greatest shudra of modern India who made the lower classes of Hindus conscious of their slavery to the higher classes and who preached the gospel that for India social democracy was more vital than independence from foreign rule . . .' See, Ambedkar, *Who*

Were the Shudras? How They Came to Be the Fourth Varna in the Indo-Aryan Society.

31. Ibid, p. 18.
32. Constituent Assembly Debates, Volume I. See, 'Proceedings of 13 December 1946', p. 85.
33. G. Aloysius, *Nationalism Without a Nation in India* (Oxford University Press, 1998), p. 64.
34. Ibid, pp. 64–65.
35. See, B.R. Ambedkar, *States and Minorities: What Are their Rights and How to Secure Them in the Constitution of Free India* (New Delhi: Samyak Prakashan, 2014 reprint).
36. Omvedt, *Dalits and the Democratic Revolution: Dr. Ambedkar and the Dalit Movement in Colonial India*, p. 239.
37. This slogan translates to 'We are children of Lord Rama and our life holds meaning only if sacrificed for the sake of motherland'. From the author's field notes from Banka and Bhagalpur districts of south-eastern Bihar from fieldwork conducted during April–May 2019. Bhagalpur was engulfed in major communal riots during late 1989 and early 1990. The clash was primarily between one of the Shudra castes and the Muslim minority.
38. This slogan of the Sanyukta Socialist Party literally meant: 'The Socialist Party has taken a resolve that backwards must get their share at least sixty out of hundred.' See, Raghuniram Shastri, 'Eyewitness Account: When Jagdeo Babu Said, "Ninety Parts of the Hundred Are Ours"', *Forward Press*, 27 September 2018. Accessed 30 May 2019.
39. See, *Indra Sawhney Etc. v. Union of India and Others*, 16 November 1992 (AIR 1993, SC 477, 1992 Supp. 2 SCR 454, author B.J. Reddy).
40. See, Office Memorandum No. 36011/6/2010-Estt.(Res), Government of India, Ministry of Personnel, P.G. and Pensions, Department of Personnel and Training, North Block, New Delhi, 25 June 2010.
41. See, D. Suresh Kumar, '24 Years On, OBC Workforce in Centre Still Short of Mandal Mark', *The Hindu,* 9 December 2017.
42. See, Shyamlal Yadav, 'Reservation Candidates Are Under-represented in Govt's Upper Rungs', *Indian Express*, 17 January 2019.

43. Even subaltern historians did not bring up this subject, considering it trivial owing to its everyday nature. Gyanendra Pandey wrote *A History of Prejudice* as late as 2013, chronicling the prejudices and impact of damage done by social prejudices. He substantiates how historians' crafts have missed out on an important social phenomenon as there were no traces of prejudice available in the archives which make the basis of modern historiography. If one looks objectively, there are numerous proverbs and humiliating jokes which are part and parcel of the everyday life of numerous caste groups belonging to the Shudra category, and have hardly been considered of any worth to be mentioned in academic writings.

44. See, Sidharth Yadav, 'They Are Upset with Our Rise in Society: OBC Groom', *The Hindu*, 5 December 2019.

45. Ibid.

46. See, Christophe Jaffrelot, *India's Silent Revolution: The Rise of the Lower Castes in North India* (London: C. Hurst & Company, 2003).

47. For Michel Foucault, knowledge always acted as an agency for power. He rightly delineates that for human beings, the goals of knowledge and goals of power cannot be separated from each other because in knowing we control and in controlling we know. See, Gary Gutting and Johanna Oksala, 'Michel Foucault', *Stanford Encyclopedia of Philosophy* (Spring 2019 Edition), Edward N. Zalta, ed., https://plato.stanford.edu/archives/spr2019/entries/foucault/>.

The Socio-spiritual Slavery of Shudras: A National Agenda for Their Liberation

1. M.K. Gandhi, *Collected Volumes of Mahatma Gandhi,* Vol. 59 (Ahmedabad: Navajivan Press, 1972), pp. 66–67.

2. Ashwini Deshpande, *The Grammar of Caste: Economic Discrimination in Contemporary India* (New Delhi: Oxford University Press, 2012), p. 68, emphasis in original.

3. Kancha Ilaiah Shepherd, *From a Shepherd Boy to an Intellectual: My Memoirs* (New Delhi: Sage, 2019).

4. Valmiki and Hari Prasad, trans. Hari Prasad Shastri, *The Ramayana of Valmiki* (London: Shanti Sadan, 1957), p. 1585.

5. Avantika Lal, 'Chandragupta Maurya', Ancient History Encyclopedia, 2019, https://www.ancient.eu/Chandragupta_Maurya.
6. Braj Ranjan Mani, *Debrahmanising History* (Delhi: Manohar, 2011), p. 123.
7. Ibid, pp. 124–25.
8. Mahatma Jyotirao Phule, *Slavery* (Bombay: Education Department, Government of Maharashtra, 1991).
9. Rosalind O'Hanlon, *Caste, Conflict and Ideology: Mahatma Jotirao Phule and Low Caste Protest in Nineteenth-century Western India* (Chennai: Cambridge University Press, 2002), pp. 79–80.
10. G.P. Deshpande, *Selected Writings of Jotirao Phule* (Delhi: Left Word Books, 2010), p. 10, emphasis in original.
11. Gail Omvedt, *Cultural Revolt in a Colonial Society: The Non-Brahmin Movement in Western India* (Delhi: Manohar, 2011), p. 117.
12. Deshpande, *Selected Writings of Jotirao Phule*, pp. 73–75.
13. Himanshu Roy and M.P. Singh, *Indian Political Thought, Themes and Thinkers* (Chennai: Pearson, 2017).
14. Bhimrao Ramji Ambedkar, *Dr Babasaheb Ambedkar: Writings and Speeches,* Vol. 11 (Mumbai: Government of Maharashtra, 2016).
15. Kancha Ilaiah Shepherd , *Why I Am Not a Hindu,* second edition (Kolkata: Samya, 2009), p. 135.
16. Ibid, p. 136.
17. Bhimrao Ramji Ambedkar, *Who Were the Shudras?* (New Delhi: Ministry of Social Justice, 2013), https://www.mea.gov.in/Images/attach/amb/Volume_07.pdf.
18. Mahatma Jyotiba Phule, *Gulamgiri* (Mumbai: Milind Prakashan, 2017).
19. Deshpande, *Selected Writings of Jotirao Phule.*
20. Mahatma Jotirao Phule, *Slavery* (Mumbai: Education Department, Government of Maharashtra, 1991), p. 13.
21. *DNA*, 'Narendra Modi Belongs to Modh–Ghanchi Caste, Which Was Added to OBC Categories in 1994, Says Gujarat Government', 9 May 2014, https://www.dnaindia.com/india/report-narendra-modi-belongs-to-modh-ghanchi-caste-which-was-added-to-obcs-categories-in-1994-says-gujarat-government-1986389. Accessed 12 July 2020.

22. Vijay Korra, *Forgotten Communities of Telangana and Andhra Pradesh: A Story of De-Notified Tribes* (Palgrave-MacMillan, 2019), p. 2.

Shudras and Democratic India

1. B.R. Ambedkar, 'Who Were the Shudras?' in *Dr Babasaheb Ambedkar: Writings & Speeches,* Vol. 7 (Mumbai: Government of Maharashtra, 1990), pp. 21–22.
2. Kancha Ilaiah Shepherd, 'Shudras, Not Aryans, Built the Indus Valley Civilisation', DailyO, 19 August 2018, https://www.dailyo.in/variety/harappan-civilisation-indus-valley-civilisation-shudras-mohenjodaro-sanskrit-texts-dholavira-rig-veda/story/1/26155.html. Accessed 20 June 2020.
3. According to the 1931 Census and the 1980 Mandal Commission, the backward classes (Shudra communities) numbered around 54 per cent of the total population. See Rajesh Ramachandran, 'Socio-economic Caste Census: Numbers Not Being Revealed to Hide Upper Caste Dominance in Governance', *Economic Times*, 12 July 2015. The percentage of Shudras automatically went up after Partition because the Muslim population came down.
4. Mallepalli Laxmaiah, 'Caste Rules in Text and Context', *Outlook*, 18 December 2017, https://www.outlookindia.com/magazine/story/caste-rules-in-text-and-context/299610. Accessed 2 July 2020.
5. Nelanshu Shukla, 'Modi Included His Caste in Backward Category for Political Advantage: Mayawati', *India Today*, April 2019, https://www.indiatoday.in/elections/lok-sabha-2019/story/modi-included-his-caste-in-backward-category-for-political-advantage-mayawati-1512342-2019-04-28. Accessed 3 July 2020.
6. Abhishek Srivastava, '53 Years and Counting: CPI(M) Still Has No Space for a Dalit Leader', Youth Ki Awaaz, 15 May 2018, https://www.youthkiawaaz.com/2018/05/no-land-for-dalits-in-cpms-kingdom. Accessed 12 July 2020.
7. *The Hindu*, 'RSS Chief Mohan Bhagwat Calls for Dialogue on Reservation', 19 August 2019, https://www.thehindu.com/news/national/rss-chief-mohan-bhagwat-calls-for-dialogue-on-reservation/article29129128.ece. Accessed 12 July 2020.

8. Swarajya, 'Congress Is Wooing Upper Castes in Rajasthan by Relaxing the Criteria of Modi's EWS Quota, and It Already Seems to Be Working', 11 November 2019, https://swarajyamag.com/news-brief/congress-is-wooing-upper-castes-in-rajasthan-by-relaxing-the-criteria-of-modis-ews-quota-and-it-already-seems-to-be-working. Accessed 13 July 2020.

9. Jawhar Sircar, 'Why the BJP Feels It Has to Appropriate Sardar Patel', Wire, October 2019, https://thewire.in/history/bjp-sardar-vallabhbhai-patel. Accessed 3 July 2020.

The Importance of Shudra Politics in India

1. All personal narratives and reference to pronouns such as 'I' and 'we' are for the first author, Sharad Yadav.

2. Ram Manohar Lohia, 'Seven Revolutions and Five Hidden Imperialisms', in Verinder Grover, ed., *Ram Manohar Lohia: Political Thinkers of Modern India,* Vol. 9 (New Delhi: Deep and Deep Publications, 1996), pp. 270–71.

3. Ram Manohar Lohia, 'A Note on India's Ruling Classes', *Mankind* 4.4 (November 1959); Adi H. Doctor, 'Lohia's Quest for an Autonomous Socialism', *The Indian Journal of Political Science* 49.3 (1988): 312–27.

4. Lohia, 'A Note on India's Ruling Classes', p. 34.

5. Ibid, p. 35.

6. Ibid.

7. Ram Manohar Lohia, *The Caste System* (Navahind, 1964).

8. Dr B.R. Ambedkar's speech in the Constituent Assembly, 25 November 1949.

9. Ibid.

10. Christophe Jaffrelot, *India's Silent Revolution: The Rise of the Lower Castes in North India* (Orient BlackSwan, 2003).

11. Gowd Kiran Kumar, 'Why Are There No OBC Professors in Central Universities?' Wire, 2018, https://livewire.thewire.in/campus/why-are-there-no-obc-professors-in-central-universities. Accessed 22 February 2020.

12. Ibid.

13. Nomita Yadav, 'Other Backward Classes: Then and Now', *Economic and Political Weekly* 37.44-45 (17 July 2002): 4495–4500, http://www.jstor.org/stable/4412801.
14. Government of India, 'Census Report', 1931, https://censusindia.gov.in/Census_And_You/old_report/Census_1931n.aspx.
15. Indra Sekhar Singh, '30 Years On, Mandal Commission Is Still a Mirror for India', Wire, 2020, https://thewire.in/politics/vp-singh-mandal-commission.
16. The first author was privy to this information due to his capacity as a member of Parliament and also someone with an influential role in the internal politics of that time.
17. Kumar, 'Why Are There No OBC Professors in Central Universities?'
18. Press Trust of India, 'OBC Representation in Central Jobs Less Than Actual Quota: Government', Wire, 2018, https://thewire.in/rights/obc-representation-in-central-jobs-less-than-actual-quota-government.
19. Jaffrelot, *India's Silent Revolution: The Rise of the Lower Castes in North India*, p. 185.

The Question of Bahujan Women

1. F.M.P. Dalton, *Transforming Dalit Identity: Ancient Drum Beat, New Song*, master's thesis (New Zealand: Victoria University of Wellington, 2008), p. 48.
2. Bhimrao Ramji Ambedkar, 'Who Were the Shudras?' in *Dr Babasaheb Ambedkar: Writings & Speeches,* Vol. 7 (Bombay: Government of Maharashtra, 1990), p. 23.
3. Ram Sharan Sharma, *Sudras in Ancient India, A Social History of the Lower Order Down to Circa A.D. 600* (Delhi: Motilal Banarsidass, 1958), p. 45.
4. Ambedkar, 'Who Were the Shudras?'
5. Ibid, p. 12.
6. Ibid, p. 9.
7. Ibid, p. 10.
8. Ibid.

9.   Some like the Jats, Patels and Kunbi-Marathas have achieved dominant status due to landownership and political representation, while others like the Telis, Malis, Nais and Dhobis remain marginalized.

10. Shudra women's productive and reproductive labour has from time to time come under state control. During the Peshwa rule in Maharashtra, the Kunbi female slaves of the Shudra caste performed productive labour in domestic and agricultural spheres, and the Bateeks performing sexual labour were drawn from both Shudra and Ati-Shudra castes. The Bateek slaves were purchased by individuals or for state-run dancing houses.

11. Jyotirao Phule, *Collected Works of Jotirao Phule,* Vol. 2 (Bombay: Government of Maharashtra, 1991), pp. 111–14.

12. Harold A. Gould, 'A Jajmani System of North India: Its Structure, Magnitude, and Meaning', *Ethnology* 3.1 (3 May 1964): 12–41, https://doi.org/10.2307/4617554.

13. For more about this, see Braj Ranjan Mani and Pamela Sardar, eds, *A Forgotten Liberator: The Life and Structure of Savitribai Phule* (New Delhi: Mountain Peak, 2008).

14. Tarabai Shinde came from one of the influential Maratha families which claimed its lineage to the royal Rajput families of northern India. The Shindes were originally from an obscure family from within the complex of peasant castes (Rosalind O'Hanlon, *Caste, Conflict and Ideology, Mahatma Jotirao Phule and Low Caste Protest in Nineteenth-Century Western India* [Ranikhet: Permanent Black, 2016]). Many agriculturist families which held powerful positions in Chhatrapati Shivaji's army laid a genealogical claim to Kshatriyahood, calling themselves *assal* (real) Marathas to distance themselves from their Shudra status. In the context of this aspirational varna mobility among the Kunbi castes, O'Hanlon points to an adage in Marathi: '*Kunbi Majhala ani Maratha Jhala*' (When a Kunbi prospers, he becomes Maratha).

15. Prachi Patil, 'Where Are the Women Professors from the SC/ST/OBC Categories?', Round Table India, 2016, https://roundtableindia.co.in/~roundta3/index.php?option=com_content&view=article&id=8842:where-are-the-women-professors-from-the-sc-st-obc-categories&catid=120&Itemid=133.

A New Beginning for Shudras Still a Possibility

1. Piyush Mishra, 'Fleet of 3 Aircraft Ensures Modi Is Home Every Night after Day's Campaigning', *Times of India*, 22 April 2014, https://m.timesofindia.com/news/Fleet-of-3-aircraft-ensures-Modi-is-home-every-night-after-days-campaigning/articleshow/34069525.cms. Accessed 2 February 2020.

2. Sheela Bhatt, 'Is Narendra Modi Really an OBC?', Rediff, 5 June 2014, https://www.rediff.com/news/column/ls-election-sheela-says-is-narendra-modi-really-an-obc/20140510.htm. Accessed 16 February 2020.

3. ANI, 'No One Can Defeat Modi in 2019 Elections: Nitish Kumar', *Outlook*, 30 July 2017, https://www.outlookindia.com/newsscroll/no-one-can-defeat-modi-in-2019-elections-nitish-kumar/1112680.

4. Sharat Pradhan, 'Kanshi Ram Declares Mayawati as His Successor', Rediff, 15 December 2001, https://m.rediff.com/news/2001/dec/15bsp.htm. Accessed 16 February 2020.

5. Debayan Roy, 'Bhima Koregaon: How and Why the January Violence Snowballed into Arrest of Rights Activists', News18, 29 August 2018, https://www.news18.com/news/india/bhima-koregaon-how-and-why-the-january-violence-snowballed-into-arrest-of-rights-activists-1860141.html. Accessed 16 February 2020.

6. Press Trust of India, 'Supreme Court Justifies Its March 20 Verdict on SC/ST Act', *New Indian Express*, 16 May 2018, https://www.newindianexpress.com/nation/2018/may/16/supreme-court-justifies-its-march-20-verdict-on-scst-act-1815516.html. Accessed 20 February 2020.

7. B.R. Ambedkar's speech in the Constituent Assembly, 25 November 1949.

8. Press Trust of India, 'Rajasthan: Karni Sena Demands Review of Reservation System', *Deccan Chronicle*, 9 February 2017, https://www.deccanchronicle.com/nation/politics/090217/rajasthan-karni-sena-demands-review-of-reservation-system.html. Accessed 8 July 2020.

9. Siddhartha Rai, 'RSS Chief Mohan Bhagwat's Comments on Reservation Policy Stirs Controversy', *India Today*, 22 September

2015, https://www.indiatoday.in/mail-today/story/rss-chief-mohan-bhagwats-comments-on-reservation-policy-stirs-controversy-264144-2015-09-22. Accessed 12 July 2020.

10. NCRB report, 2017.

11. Press Trust of India, 'Government Wants to Pass SC/ST Bill in Current Parliament Session, Says Rajnath Singh', *Financial Express*, 2 August 2018, https://www.financialexpress.com/india-news/government-wants-to-pass-sc-st-bill-in-current-parliament-session-says-rajnath-singh/1267084. Accessed 12 July 2020.

12. Milind Ghatwai, 'To Placate Protesting Upper-Castes, MP CM Shivraj Singh Chouhan Announces Move to Dilute SC/ST Atrocities Law', *Indian Express*, 21 September 2018, https://indianexpress.com/article/india/madhya-pradesh-cm-chouhan-announces-move-to-dilute-sc-st-atrocities-law-5367446. Accessed 15 July 2020.

13. Quint, 'Watch: Cobrapost Catches Ranveer Sena Killers Confessing on Camera', 20 August 2015, https://www.thequint.com/news/india/bihar-dalit-massacre-killers-confess-after-courts-let-them-off. Accessed 10 July 2020.

14. V. Ajmal, 'Why Is Academia Opposing New Higher Education Roster?' *Deccan Herald*, 1 February 2019, https://www.deccanherald.com/specials/why-academia-opposing-new-716162.html. Accessed 12 July 2020.

15. Press Trust of India, 'UGC University Teacher Reservation: Ordinance within 2 Days, Assures Prakash Javadekar', Times Now, 7 March 2019, https://www.timesnownews.com/education/article/reservation-roster-prakash-javadekar-assures-action-within-2-days/377461. Accessed 11 July 2020.

16. Bhimrao Ramji Ambedkar, *Dr Babasaheb Ambedkar: Writings and Speeches,* Vol. 1 (Bombay: Government of Maharashtra, 2016), pp. 50–51.

Production and Protection as Spirituality among Shudras

1. Monier Monier-Williams, *A Sanskrit-English Dictionary: Etymologically and Philologically Arranged with Special Reference to*

Cognate Indo-European Languages (New Delhi: Motilal Banarsidass, 1899, 2005 reprint), p. 924.

2. Ibid.
3. Andrea Stanton, *An Encyclopedia of Cultural Sociology of the Middle East, Asia, and Africa* (Thousand Oaks: Sage, 2012), pp. 12–13.
4. Julia Leslie, *Authority and Meaning in Indian Religions: Hinduism and the Case of Valmiki* (Ashgate Publishing, 2003), p. 189.
5. Daine M. Cocarri, 'Protection and Identity: Banaras's Bir Babas as Neighbourhood Guardian Deities', in *Culture and Power in Banaras: Community, Performance, and Environment, 1800–1980*, ed. Sandria B. Freitag (Oxford, UK: University of California Press, 1992), p. 137.
6. *The Hindu*, 'Indus Valley Settlers Had a Distinct Genetic Lineage', 17 September 2019, https://www.thehindu.com/sci-tech/science/indus-valley-settlers-had-a-distinct-genetic-lineage/article29355941.ece.
7. Robin Coningham and Ruth Young, *The Archaeology of South Asia: From the Indus to Asoka, c.6500 BCE–200 CE* (New York: Cambridge University Press, 2015), pp. 339–48.
8. Mahadev Chakravarti, *The Concept of Rudra-Siva Through the Ages* (Delhi: Motilal Banarsidass, 2009), pp. 130–45.
9. Milton Singer, 'The Great Tradition in a Metropolitan Center: Madras', *Journal of American Folklore* 71.281 (1958): 347–88.
10. Milton Singer, *When a Great Tradition Modernizes* (New York: Praeger, 1972).
11. McKim Marriott, 'Little Communities in an Indigenous Civilization', in McKim Marriott, ed., *Village India* (Chicago: University of Chicago Press, 1955).
12. Robert Redfield, 'The Social Organization of Tradition', *Far Eastern Quarterly* 15.1 (November 1955), pp. 13–21.
13. Yogendra Singh, *Modernization of Indian Tradition: A Systemic Study of Social Change* (Faridabad: Thomson Press [India] Publication Division, 1973), pp. 13–15.
14. Mary Storm, 'Unusual Group of Hero Stones', Freer Gallery of Art, Smithsonian Institution and Department of the History of Art, University of Michigan, *Ars Orientalis* 44 (2014): 61–84.

15. S. Settar, Günther D. Sontheimer, 'Memorial Stones: A Study of Their Origin, Significance and Variety', *I.A.H. Series 2, South Asian Studies 11* (1986).

16. Lata Aklujka, 'Variety of the Hero-Stones in Solapur District in Early Medieval Period', *Proceedings of the Indian History Congress* 66 (2005–06): 1450–53.

17. Ramachandra Chintaman Dhere, *The Rise of a Folk God: Vitthal of Pandharpur* (Ranikhet: Permanent Black, 2011).

18. Kancha Ilaiah Shepherd, *Why I Am Not a Hindu: A Shudra Critique of Hindutva Philosophy, Culture and Political Economy* (New Delhi: Sage, 2018).

19. S. Jaikishan, 'Historical Note on Konasamudram: The Famous Wootz Steel Production Centre', *Indian Journal of History of Science* 42.4 (2007): 697–703.

20. C.G. Uragoda, *Traditions of Sri Lanka: A Selection with a Scientific Background* (Vishva Lekha Publishers, 2000).

21. 'Rama stayed mostly indoors. He did not bathe at fixed hours, as he had done before. He disliked wearing royal robes; he desisted from delicacies; he never sat on the golden throne; he appeared as if immersed in contemplation of the Absolute, of something beyond the senses and the mind . . . The guru arrived, and they fell at his feet, showering him with eager questions about the boy's peculiar malady and the change that had come upon them. They were all in tears. Noticing the agitation of the king and the queens, Vasishta turned his attention inward and sought the reason for the sorrow, through inner vision'. Bhagawan Sri Sathya Sai Baba. *Ramakatha Rasavahini, Part I: The Rama Story (Stream of Sacred Sweetness)* (Anantapur: Sri Sathya Sai Books and Publications Trust, 2004), pp. 38–40.

22. Most of the stories in Indian epics were written on the basis of imagination. Of course, the story might be true but explanations in such stories are merely imagined constructions. Therefore, if one critically examines the killings of baby Krishna, the murders are not possible for a small baby to commit at any given point of time. Thus, the logical argument can infer that somebody killed all the asuras and ascribed the murders to baby Krishna.

23. Bhagavad Gita, 4:13.

24. Sarvepalli Radhakrishnan, *The Bhagavadgita* (London: George Allen and Unwin, 1948).

25. National Museum, Government of India, New Delhi, 2020, http://nationalmuseumindia.gov.in/prodCollections.asp? pid=42&id=1&lk=dp1. Accessed 15 March 2020.

Sociocultural Identity Formation among Shudras

1. *Telegraph*, 'Fake OBC Finger at Modi', 9 May 2014, https://www. telegraphindia.com/india/fake-obc-finger-at-modi/cid/182604. Accessed 14 December 2019.

2. Dr B.R. Ambedkar, 'Who Were the Shudras?' Ministry of External Affairs, 1946, https://www.mea.gov.in/Images/attach/ amb/Volume_07.pdf. Accessed 11 December 2019.

3. Marc Galanter, 'Who Are the Other Backward Classes? An Introduction to a Constitutional Puzzle', *Economic and Political Weekly* 13.43/44 (1978): 1812–28.

4. Ibid.

5. Ambedkar, 'Who Were the Shudras?'

6. M.N. Srinivas, *The Dominant Caste and Other Essays,* revised and expanded edition (Oxford University Press, 1994).

7. Ambedkar, 'Who Were the Shudras?'

8. R.S. Sharma, *Sudras in Ancient India*, fifth edition (Delhi: Motilal Banarsidass, 2016).

9. Suvira Jaiswal, 'Changes in the Status and Concept of the Sudra Varna in Early Middle Ages', *Proceedings of the Indian History Congress* 41 (1980): 112–21.

10. M.N. Srinivas, *The Remembered Village* (Oxford Scholarship Online, 2012), https://www.oxfordscholarship.com/view/10.1093/acprof:oso/ 9780198077459.001.0001/acprof-9780198077459-chapter-7.

11. Kancha Ilaiah Shepherd, 'The Shudras Want Empowerment, Not a Giant Statue of Their Iron Man', Wire, 31 October 2018, https://thewire.in/caste/sardar-patel-statue-of-unity-shudra- brahmin-bania. Accessed 11 December 2019.

12. K.N. Panikkar, 'Culture and Consciousness in Modern India: A Historical Perspective', *Social Scientist* 18.4 (April 1990): 3–32. https://www.jstor.org/stable/3517525.

13. Raymond Williams, *The Long Revolution* (Harmondsworth, 1984), p. 57.
14. Kancha Ilaiah Shepherd, 'Where Are the Shudras?' *Caravan*, 1 October 2018, https://caravanmagazine.in/caste/why-the-shudras-are-lost-in-today-india. Accessed 14 December 2019.
15. Ibid.
16. R. Vaidyanathan, 'India Growth: The Untold Story—Caste as Social Capital', 2012, https://rvaidya2000.com/2012/10/18/india-growth-the-untold-story-caste-as-social-capital. Accessed 13 December 2019.
17. M. Vijaybhaskar and A. Kalaiyarasan, 'Caste as Social Capital', *Economic and Political Weekly* 49.10 (2014): 34–38.
18. Akhil Alha, 'The Other Side of Caste as Social Capital', 2018, https://journals.sagepub.com/doi/full/10.1177/0049085718801490. Accessed 13 December 2019.
19. Pradeep Thakur, 'Data: OBCs Just 12% of Lower Court Judges', *Times of India,* 29 January 2018, Times of India, http://timesofindia.indiatimes.com/articleshow/62687268.cms?utm_source=contentofinterest&utm_medium=text&utm_campaign=cppst. Accessed 13 December 2019.
20. Sidharth Prabhakar, '20 Years after Mandal, Less than 12% in Central Government Jobs', *Times of India,* 26 December 2015, https://timesofindia.indiatimes.com/india/20-years-after-Mandal-less-than-12-OBCs-in- central-govt-jobs/articleshow/50328073.cms. Accessed 12 December 2019.
21. Dy. No. 2016/RTI/18-19/SCI.
22. RTI reply from the High Court said, 'Information not maintained.'
23. Siddharth Joshi and Deepak Malghan, 'Why Are There Still Such Few SCs, STs and OBCs at IIMs?' Wire, 18 January 2018, https://thewire.in/caste/iim-sc-st-obc-diversity. Accessed 12 December 2019.
24. Chirayu Jain, Spadika Jayaraj, Sanjana Muraleedharan, Harjas Singh and Marc S. Galanter, 'The Elusive Island of Excellence: A Study on Student Demographics, Accessibility and Inclusivity at National Law School 2015–16', 2016, https://ssrn.com/abstract=2788311 or http://dx.doi.org/10.2139/ssrn.2788311. Accessed 12 December 2019.

25. M. Kalyanaraman, Bosco Dominique, 'Why Caste Battle in Tamil Nadu Never Ends', *Times of India*, 24 August 2015, http://timesofindia.indiatimes.com/articleshow/48646204.cms#?utm_source=contentofinterest&utm_medium=text&utm_campaign=cppst. Accessed 10 December 2019.

26. K. Keshava Raju, 'Atrocities of Scheduled Castes and Scheduled Tribes in Karnataka since 1980: A Case Study of Socio-economic and Political Causes', Department of Political Science, Karnatak University, 31 December 2003, http://shodhganga.inflibnet.ac.in/handle/10603/95396. Accessed 15 January 2019.

27. Ibid.

28. Gauri Lankesh, 'Making Sense of the Lingayat vs Veerashaiva Debate', Wire, 5 September 2017, https://thewire.in/history/karnataka-lingayat-veerashaive-debate. Accessed 10 January 2019.

29. Greeshma Kuthar, 'How Coastal Karnataka Was Saffronised', Firstpost, 7 April 2019, https://www.firstpost.com/tag/how-coastal-karnataka-was-saffronised/page/2.

30. Jaiswal, 'Changes in the Status and Concept of the Sudra Varna in Early Middle Ages'.

31. It's limited because the practice of untouchability against and within Shudras is not as dehumanizing as against Dalits.

32. S. Senthalir, '"We Do Not Touch Them": Shocking Caste Discrimination in Karnataka District, Finds New Study', Scroll, 21 January 2019, https://scroll.in/article/909979/we-do-not-touch-them-shocking-caste-discrimination-in-karnataka-district-finds-new-study. Accessed 11 December 2019.

33. Suvira Jaiswal, 'Some Recent Theories of the Origin of Untouchability: A Historiographical Assessment', *Proceedings of the Indian History Congress* 39.1 (1978): 218–29.

34. Anitha Pailoor, 'Annihilation of Dignity: Untouchability in Karnataka', *Deccan Herald*, 22 September 2019, https://www.deccanherald.com/specials/insight/annihilation-of-dignity-untouchability-in-karnataka-763126.html.

35. News Minute, 'Are Dalits the Biggest Caste Group in Karnataka? Census Result Triggers Debate, Political Panic', 12 April 2016, https://www.thenewsminute.com/article/are-dalits-biggest-

caste-group-karnataka-census-results-trigger-debate-political-panic-41511.

36. N. Neetha, 'Crisis in Female Employment', *Economic and Political Weekly* 49.47 (2014).

37. Stephan Klasen, 'Low, Stagnating Female Labour Force in India', Livemint, 21 March 2017, https://www.livemint.com/Opinion/vgO1ynMV6UMDnF6kW5Z3VJ/Low-stagnating-female-labourforce- participation-in-India.html. Accessed 13 December 2019.

38. S. Senthalir, '"We Do Not Touch Them": Shocking Caste Discrimination in Karnataka District, Finds New Study'.

39. Udayan Rathore, Pramit Bhattacharya, 'Why So Few Women Enter the Job Market in India', Livemint, 21 June 2018, https://www.livemint.com/Companies/Jf6nR0giRAWIeO94zexvdM/Why-so-few-women-work-in- India.html. Accessed 11 December 2019.

40. Shreya Parikh, 'Sanskritization & Gender: Discrimination in Labor Market at the Intersections of Religion and Caste in India', 2015, https://www.aiel.it/cms/cms-files/submission/all20160320214200.pdf. Accessed 13 December 2019.

41. Erin K. Fletcher, Rohini Pande and Charity Troyer Moore, 'Women and Work in India: Descriptive Evidence and a Review of Potential Policies', Centre for International Development at Harvard University, 2017, https://www.hks.harvard.edu/sites/default/files/centers/cid/files/publications/faculty-working-papers/women_work_india_cidwp339.pdf. Accessed 14 December 2019.

42. Hema Swaminathan, Rahul Lahoti, Suchitra J.Y, 'Gender Asset and Wealth Gaps: Evidence from Karnataka', *Economic and Political Weekly* 47.35 (2012): 59–67.

43. Aashish Gupta, 'Reporting and Incidence of Violence against Women in India', Rice Institute, 2014, http://riceinstitute.org/wordpress/wp-content/uploads/downloads/2014/10/Reporting-and-incidence-of-violence-against-women-in-India-working-paper-final.pdf. Accessed 15 December 2019.

44. DailyO, 'India Has the Lowest Divorce Rate in the World: 5 Reasons Why It's Not a Good Thing', 31 January 2019, https://www.dailyo.in/variety/india-has-the-lowest-divorce-rate-in-the-world-5-reasons-why-its-not-a-good-thing/story/1/29213.html.

45. Yashwant Zagade, 'How Dalit-"Lower Caste" Unity Laid the Foundation for the Ambedkarite Movement', Wire, https://thewire.in/caste/lower-caste-ambedkar-anti-caste-struggle. Accessed 12 December 2019.
46. Amrita Dutta, 'In Fact: For Kannadigas, a Breathing, Living Presence', *Indian Express*, 30 March 2018, https://indianexpress.com/article/explained/in-fact-for-kannadigas-a-breathing-living-presence-amit-shah- siddaramaiah-kuvempu-5116622.

Shudra Consciousness and the Future of the Nation

1. B.R. Ambedkar, *Who Were the Shudras?* (New Delhi: Ministry of Social Justice, 2013), p. 18, https://www.mea.gov.in/Images/attach/amb/Volume_07.pdf. Accessed 12 July 2020.
2. *Indian Express*, 'Most Indian Nobel Winners Brahmins: Gujarat Speaker Rajendra Trivedi', 4 January 2020, https://indianexpress.com/article/cities/ahmedabad/most-indian-nobel-winners-brahmins-gujarat-speaker-rajendra-trivedi-6198741. Accessed 12 February 2020.
3. Press Trust of India, 'Mahatma Gandhi Was a "Chatur Baniya": Amit Shah', Livemint, 2017, https://www.livemint.com/Politics/QG7VMLy33uLwe56TfqTnhO/Mahatma-Gandhi-was-chatur-baniya-Amit-Shah.html. Accessed 14 February 2020.
4. Wire, 'Gujarat Assembly Speaker Claims Brahmins Have "Different DNA"', Wire, 4 January 2020, https://thewire.in/caste/gujarat-assembly-speaker-rajendra-trivedi-dna. Accessed 24 February 2020.
5. Ambedkar, *Who Were the Shudras?*, p. 9.
6. Nithya Subramanian, 'In Charts: India's Newsrooms Are Dominated by the Upper Castes—and That Reflects What Media Covers', Scroll, 2019, https://scroll.in/article/932660/in-charts-indias-newsrooms-are-dominated-by-the-upper-castes-and-that-reflects-what-media-covers. Accessed 22 February 2020.
7. Mahatma Jyotirao Phule, *Slavery* (Mumbai: Education Department, Government of Maharashtra, 1991).
8. Kancha Ilaiah Shepherd, *Why I Am Not a Hindu: A Sudra Critique of Hindutva Philosophy, Culture and Political Economy* (New Delhi: Sage Publications India, 2019).

9.   IndiaSpend, 'BJP-Governed States Not Serving Eggs in Mid-Day Meals, Cite "Vegetarian Sentiments"', FirstPost, July 2018, https://www.firstpost.com/india/bjp-governed-states-not-serving-eggs-in-mid-day-meals-cite-vegetarian-sentiments-4862671.html. Accessed 17 July 2020.

10. Wire, 'These Are the 25 People Killed During Anti-Citizenship Amendment Act Protests', 23 December 2019, https://thewire.in/rights/anti-caa-protest-deaths. Accessed 24 February 2020.

11. Raju Solanki, 'Blood under Saffron: The Myth of Dalit–Muslim Confrontation', Round Table India, 23 July 2013. https://roundtableindia.co.in/index.php?option=com_content&view=article&id=6774:blood-under-saffron-the-myth-of-dalit-muslim-confrontation&catid=119:feature&Itemid=132. Accessed 22 February 2020.

The India of My Dreams

1.   Oxfam, 'India: Extreme Inequality in Numbers', Oxfam.org, 2017, https://www.oxfam.org/en/india-extreme-inequality-numbers. Accessed 10 July 2020.

2.   Rahul Tripathi, 'OBC Count to Be Part of Census 2021, 3 Decades after Mandal Commission', *Indian Express*, 1 September 2018, https://indianexpress.com/article/india/obc-count-to-be-part-of-census-2021-3-decades-after-mandal-5334643. Accessed 14 July 2020.

3.   Suresh Kumar D., '17 Yrs after Mandal, 7% OBCs in Govt Jobs', *Times of India*, 31 August 2010, https://timesofindia.indiatimes.com/india/17-yrs-after-Mandal-7-OBCs-in-govt-jobs/articleshow/6465115.cms. Accessed 14 July 2020.

Caste and Political Economy

1.   See, for instance, Jotiba Phule's 'Kulambin' (A Peasant Woman), a poem that exposes the condition of Shudra peasant women who work tirelessly in their homes and at the farms and homes of Bhat–Kshatriya families whereas the Bhat women do nothing and despise working as labourers on Shudra farms, indulging in idle tricks

and finery. His *Cultivator's Whipcord* also gives an account of extortion by Brahmins in religious festivals throughout the year; of the Aryan defeat of indigenous inhabitants; of the exploitation of 'Shudra and Ati-Shudra farmers' by the British and Brahmin bureaucracy; a minute description of the living standards of his farmers; then his own suggestions, along with a condemnation of the Swadeshi movement, which was beginning at that time. Also see his four poems (in English prose) on the craftiness of the Marwaris and Bhats in exploiting Shudras. *Collected Works of Jotirao Phule,* Vols 1 and 2 (Mumbai: Government of Maharashtra, 1991), pp. 76–83, 111–14. *Cultivator's Whipcord* can be accessed at https://drambedkarbooks.files.wordpress.com/2009/03/phule.pdf.

2.   T. Nagi Reddy, *India Mortgaged: A Marxist-Leninist Appraisal* (TNR Memorial Trust, 1978); Bharat Patankar and Gail Omvedt, 'The Dalit Liberation Movement in Colonial Period', *Economic and Political Weekly* 14.7–8 (1979).

3.   As a matter of fact, in the RSS world view, the Banias are seen as the best people in the country (for RSS's accounting too) that can maintain and keep the money safe. See, for instance, Bhanwar Meghwanshi, *I Could Not Be Hindu* (New Delhi: Navayana, 2020), chapter 7.

4.   See two recent works, C. Jaffrelot, A. Kohli and K. Murali, eds, *Business and Politics in India* (Oxford University Press, 2019); Angana P. Chatterji, Thomas Blom Hansen, Christophe Jaffrelot, eds, *Majoritarian State: How Hindu Nationalism Is Changing India* (Oxford University Press, 2019), chapters 9 and 10.

5.   D. Ajit, Han Donker and Ravi Saxena, 'Corporate Boards in India', *Economic and Political Weekly* (2012), https://www.epw.in/journal/2012/32/insight/corporate-boards-india.html. Accessed 23 February 2020.

6.   For instance, James Crabtree in his book *The Billionaire Raj says* on the Modi–Adani relationship, 'The two men enjoyed symbiotic careers. Modi's pro-business policies helped Adani expand. Adani's own companies, meanwhile, built many of the grand projects that came to symbolise Modi's "Gujarat model", with its emphasis on infrastructure investment, attracting foreign capital and export industries . . . The duo were said to get on well.

Adani was loyal too, defending Modi in the aftermath of the
bloody Hindu-Muslim riots that hit Gujarat in 2002, a time
when Modi faced fierce public criticism.' Excerpt taken from
James Crabtree, 'The Symbiotic Careers of Narendra Modi and
Gautam Adani', Wire, 17 July 2018, https://thewire.in/books/
the-symbiotic-careers-of-modi-and-adani. Also refer to Aseema
Sinha and Andrew Wyatt, 'The Spectral Presence of Business
in India's 2019 Election', *Studies in Indian Politics* 7.2 (2019):
247–61; Jaffrelot, Kohli and Murali, eds, *Business and Politics
in India*, especially chapter 8; Prakash Nanda, 'Why Narendra
Modi Supporting an Ambani and Adani Is More Myth Than
Fact', Firstpost, 25 December 2016, https://www.firstpost.
com/politics/why-narendra-modi-supporting-an-ambani-
and-adani-is-more-myth-than-fact-3173142.html; Vivashwan
Singh, 'The "Beneficiaries" of Modi's Globetrotting: Adani and
Ambani', NewsClick, 1 April 2019, https://www.newsclick.in
/%E2%80%98Beneficiaries%E2%80%99-Modi%E2%80%99s-
Globetrotting-Adani-Ambani; Bodapati Srujana, 'The Billionaire
Beneficiaries of BJP's Schemes', NewsClick, 3 May 2019,
https://www.newsclick.in/BJP-Schemes-Modi-Ambani-Adani-
Baba-Ramdev-Indian-Billionaire; Amit Mudgill, 'How Tata,
Ambani, Birla and Adani Stocks Fared during Modi Regime',
Economic Times, 23 May 2019, https://economictimes.indiatimes.
com/markets/stocks/news/how-ambani-adani-birla-tata-stocks-
fared-during-modi-regime/articleshow/69441110.cms; Subodh
Varma, 'Under Modi Rule, Ambani, Adani Have Doubled Their
Wealth', News Click, 13 October 2019, https://www.newsclick.
in/Under-Modi-Rule-Ambani-Adani-Have-Doubled-Their-
Wealth. Accessed 12 January 2020.

7. Harish Damodaran, *India's New Capitalists: Caste, Business, and
Industry in a Modern Nation* (Gurgaon: Hachette, 2018), pp. xvii,
xxiii, xxiv.

8. Nitin Kumar Bharti, *Wealth Inequality, Class and Caste in
India, 1951–2012,* master's thesis report (Paris: Paris School of
Economics), p. 57, http://piketty.pse.ens.fr/files/Bharti2018.pdf.
Accessed 20 January 2020.

9. Ibid.

10. Aakar Patel, 'When Will the Brahmin–Bania Hegemony End', Livemint, 28 August 2009, https://www.livemint.com/Leisure/3u2QUPuXBEFPaBQXU2R8mJ/When-will-the-BrahminBania-hegemony-end.html. Accessed 24 January 2020.

11. See N. Tagade, Ajaya Kumar Naik and Sukhadeo Thorat, 'Wealth Ownership and Inequality in India: A Socio-religious Analysis', *Journal of Social Inclusion Studies* 4.2 (2018): 1–18; also, Bharti, *Wealth Inequality, Class and Caste in India, 1951–2012.*

12. See Sanjaya Baru, 'Economic Policy and the Development of Capitalism in India: The Role of Regional Capitalists and Political Parties' in *Transforming India: Social and Political Dynamics of Democracy*, eds Francine Frankel et al. (Oxford University Press, 2000, 2002), pp. 207–30; Harish Damodaran, *India's New Capitalists: Caste, Business, and Industry in a Modern Nation* (Gurgaon: Hachette, 2018).

13. Rajeev Khanna, 'Call For Economic Boycott of Muslims In the Wake of CAA–NRC–NPR Protests in Kutch', *Citizen*, 2 February 2020, https://www.thecitizen.in/index.php/en/NewsDetail/index/9/18255/Call-For-Economic-Boycott-of-Muslims-In-the-Wake-of-CAA-NRC-NPR-Protests-in-Kutch; Naren Karunakaran, 'Muslims Constitute 14% of India, but Just 3% of India Inc', *Economic Times*, 7 September 2015, https://economictimes.indiatimes.com/news/politics-and-nation/muslims-constitute-14-of-india-but-just-3-of-india-inc/articleshow/48849266.cms; Asim Ali, 'Covid an Excuse to Push Indian Muslims Out of Informal Sector Jobs. Apartheid the Next Step', Print, 9 April 2020, https://theprint.in/opinion/covid-an-excuse-to-push-indian-muslims-out-of-informal-sector-jobs-apartheid-the-next-step/398236. Accessed 12 May 2020.

14. Pralay Kanungo, 'Gurus and the Hindu Nationalist Politics: The Baba Ramdev–BJP Partnership in the 2014 Elections' in *The Algebra of Warfare-Welfare: A Long View of India's 2014 Election*, eds Irfan Ahmad and Pralay Kanungo (Oxford University Press, 2019).

15. Suraj Yengde, 'Delhi Pogrom Is an Attempt to Divert Attention from Government's Failures', *Indian Express*, 8 March 2020, https://indianexpress.com/article/opinion/columns/delhi-violence-

clashes-maujpur-babarpur-shiv-vihar-chand-bagh-6304430. Accessed 12 May 2020.

16. Bhimrao Ramji Ambedkar, 'Who Were the Shudras?' in *Dr Babasaheb Ambedkar Writings & Speeches*, Vol. 7 (Bombay: Government of Maharashtra, 1990).

17. Amnesty International India, 'The Novel Coronavirus and Its Impact on the Most Marginalised Communities', 14 April 2020, https://amnesty.org.in/opinion-the-novel-coronavirus-and-its-impact-on-the-most-marginalised-communities.

18. Bilal Kuchay, 'Why Arabs Are Speaking Out against Islamophobia in India', Al Jazeera, 30 April 2019, https://www.aljazeera.com/news/2020/04/arabs-speaking-islamophobia-india-200423112102197.html. Accessed 14 May 2020.

19. Kancha Ilaiah Shepherd, 'Ambedkar's Warnings about Three Types of Dictatorships', Wire, 29 February 2020, https://thewire.in/politics/ambedkar-three-types-dictatorship. Accessed 14 May 2020.

About the Contributors

Arvind Kumar is an assistant professor at the Centre for the Study of Social Exclusion and Inclusive Policy, Jamia Millia Islamia, New Delhi. He obtained a master's in politics and subsequently an MPhil and PhD from the American Studies Division, Jawaharlal Nehru University. He has been an Independent Fellow at SARAI, Centre for the Study of Developing Societies (CSDS), Delhi, and a recipient of the Independent Doctoral Fellowship and Fellowship for Data Collection from Abroad under the aegis of the Indian Council of Social Science Research (ICSSR). His research interests include comparative politics, history and politics of discrimination and exclusion, and anti-race and anti-caste movements. His academic writings and reviews have appeared in *South Asian History and Culture*, *South Asia: Journal of South Asian Studies*, *History and Sociology of South Asia*, *India Quarterly*, *Mainstream Weekly*, *Economic and Political Weekly*, *Pratiman: Samay Samaj*, *Sanskriti*, *The Book Review*, *Biblio: A Review of Books*, Wire, Print, among others. He is a bilingual author and political commentator who also participates as a panellist on major national television news channels.

Reverend Sunil Sardar is a social activist and pastor who has led the movement for reconciling castes in India since 2001. Throughout his life, Sunil has engaged in direct action and organizing for social justice, socio-spiritual and political reform, and economic empowerment for OBCs and Dalit castes. He founded Truthseekers International in 2001, inspired by the Society of Truthseekers started by Mahatma Phule in 1873. Sunil is deeply critical of the religious scriptures of Hinduism (or what he regards as 'Brahmanism') for their promotion of a caste-based discriminatory system. He launched a Balijan cultural movement in 2004 with prominent activists and writers, focused on reconciliation between the OBC and Dalit caste groups in order to confront the caste system. In 2009, he led a Biblical translation project to contextualize the New Testament into the lower-caste languages of the northern Indian belt. He published it in both Hindi and English in an attempt to offer an empowering spiritual alternative for lower castes.

Sharad Yadav is the founder of the Loktantrik Janata Dal party. He has been elected to the Lok Sabha seven times and to the Rajya Sabha thrice. He was the national president of Janata Dal (United) since its formation till 2016. He was the key young OBC leader in the cabinet who forced V.P. Singh to implement the Mandal Commission report in 1990, and he led the pro-Mandal movement in north India in the face of anti-Mandal Dwija agitations. When P.V. Narsimha Rao was hesitating to implement the Mandal reservation, Yadav organized a movement to force him to implement the 27 per cent OBC quota. He has won the Outstanding Parliamentarian Award for the year 2012. Known for his oratorical skills in both houses of Parliament, Yadav joined politics after being influenced by socialist icons Ram Manohar Lohia and Jayaprakash Narayan. He has made significant contributions to the growth of Bahujan politics in north India.

Omprakash Mahato is a senior research scholar at the Centre for Political Studies, Jawaharlal Nehru University. He is working on his PhD thesis, 'Confrontation and Fragmentation in OBC Politics of Bihar: A Study of Extremely Backward Castes from 1990–2020'. He submitted his MPhil dissertation, titled 'Accommodating Disadvantaged Groups in Higher Education: Lingering Challenges', with the supervision of Prof. Gurpreet Mahajan. He has published several articles on political affairs on the online platform Round Table India.

Prachi Patil teaches sociology at a private university. She has completed her PhD on motherhood among sex workers in Mumbai from the Centre for the Study of Social Systems, Jawaharlal Nehru University. Her research interests are in gender, social reproduction, sex work, motherhood and social stratification. She is one of the young, upcoming Shudra woman scholars in India with a deep understanding of women's issues, caste and feminism.

Urmilesh is a Delhi-based independent journalist and writer, and a former executive editor at Rajya Sabha TV. He presents the weekly shows 'Media Bol' for Wire, and 'Aaj Ki Baat' for NewsClick. He also writes weekly columns for a prominent Hindi news website. He has authored eight books, which have been published by prominent Hindi-language publishers in India. *Kashmir: Virasat Aur Siyasat* and *Christinia Meri Jaan* are his most recent ones.

Ram Shepherd Bheenaveni has been working as assistant professor in the department of sociology at Osmania University, Hyderabad, since 2010. He acquired his MPhil and PhD distinctions from Osmania University. He has been chosen for the Indian Council of Social Science Research's doctoral fellowship for his PhD, as well as for the University Grants Commission Research Award for 2015–17. At present, he is the chairman, Board of Studies in Sociology and Social Work, at Osmania University, Hyderabad. His papers and articles have been published in reputed international magazines, and he has also published papers in national and international journals.

Bindu N. Doddahatti has previously worked as a social justice litigator at the Alternative Law Forum, Bengaluru, and with Indira Jaising, senior advocate, New Delhi. She got her undergraduate law degree from Karnataka State Law University, and joined the University of Pennsylvania Law School's graduate degree programme as a Fulbright and Dean's scholar and graduated in 2020. She was awarded the Penn Law Human Rights Fellowship to work on post-conviction relief projects at the Philadelphia district attorney's office. Bindu has engaged in the reformation of the criminal justice system in different capacities. Her primary interest is to put a check on the policing powers of the state, and to decarcerate prisons. She is also associated with various people's groups working on the issues of caste and gender in India.

Pallikonda Manikanta is an MPhil scholar at the department of political science, University of Hyderabad. As a Phule-Ambedkarite scholar and activist, he researches and publishes on anti-caste thought and politics, Hindu nationalism and political culture in Telangana. His active association with the Bahujan Students' Front at the University of Hyderabad and the Birsa Ambedkar Phule Students' Association at Jawaharlal Nehru University provided many entry points in understanding the politics of the oppressed in its theoretical and practical dimensions.

Dr P. Vinay Kumar is a senior consultant in surgical gastroenterology and laparoscopic surgery at Apollo Hospitals, Hyderabad. He served as the senior registrar in abdominal surgical cancer at Tata Memorial Cancer Hospital, Mumbai, during 1989–90; senior registrar at Royal Liverpool University Hospital, Liverpool, during 1994–95 in colo-rectal surgery; and senior registrar at the world-renowned Ninewells Hospital and Medical School, Dundee, Scotland, from 1995 to 1998, becoming the first Asian to join the prestigious institution.

About Samruddha Bharat Foundation

Samruddha Bharat Foundation is an independent sociopolitical organization established after the Dr B.R. Ambedkar International Conference held in July 2017 to:

1. Further India's constitutional promise
2. Forge an alliance of progressive forces
3. Encourage a transformative spirit in Indian politics and society.

Addressing both the symbolic and the substantive, SBF works to shape the polity, serve as a platform for participatory democracy, shape public discourse and deepen engagement with the diaspora.

In doing so, SBF works closely with India's major secular political parties on normative and policy issues. It has also created a praxis between India's foremost academics, activists and policymakers, as well as people's movements, civil society organizations, think tanks and institutions. Finally, it has established Bridge India as a sister organization in the United Kingdom to do similar work with the diaspora.

For further details, see:

www.samruddhabharat.in

 @SBFIndia

 Samruddha Bharat Foundation

@SBFIndia